THE PORTENT

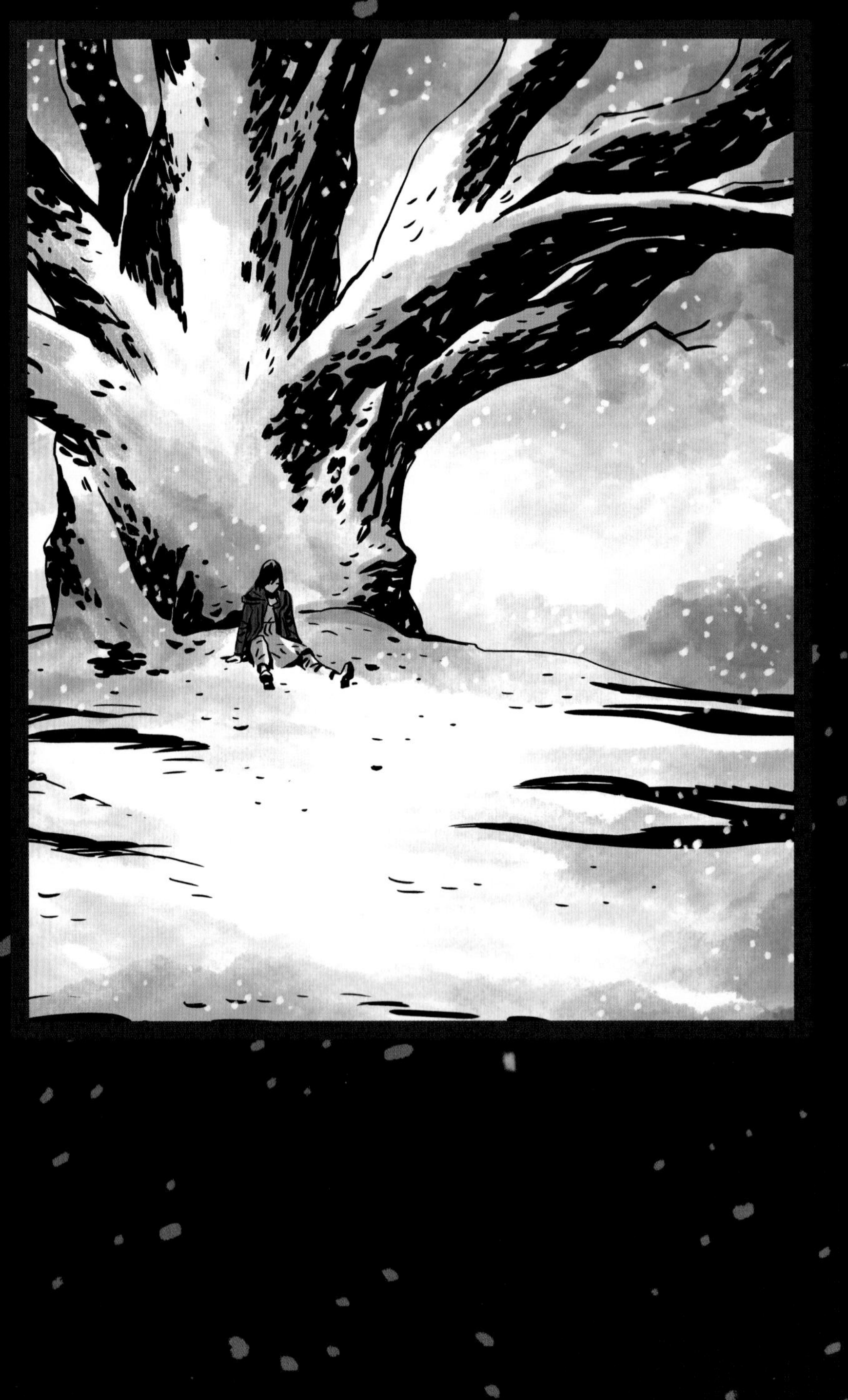

THE PORTENT™
ASHES

PETER BERGTING

DARK HORSE BOOKS

President and Publisher
Mike Richardson

Editor
Daniel Chabon

Assistant Editor
Ian Tucker

Designer
Sandy Tanaka

Special thanks to Christina McKenzie

DarkHorse.com
Bergting.com

International Licensing: (503) 905-2377

Published by Dark Horse Books
A division of Dark Horse Comics, Inc.
10956 SE Main Street
Milwaukie, OR 97222

First Edition: June 2014
ISBN 978-1-61655-355-5

1 3 5 7 9 10 8 6 4 2

Printed in China

Neil Hankerson Executive Vice President Tom Weddle Chief Financial Officer Randy Stradley
Vice President of Publishing Michael Martens Vice President of Book Trade Sales Anita
Nelson Vice President of Business Affairs Scott Allie Editor in Chief Matt Parkinson Vice
President of Marketing David Scroggy Vice President of Product Development Dale
LaFountain Vice President of Information Technology Darlene Vogel Senior Director of Print,
Design, and Production Ken Lizzi General Counsel Davey Estrada Editorial Director Chris
Warner Senior Books Editor Diana Schutz Executive Editor Cary Grazzini Director of Print
and Development Lia Ribacchi Art Director Cara Niece Director of Scheduling Tim Wiesch
Director of International Licensing Mark Bernardi Director of Digital Publishing

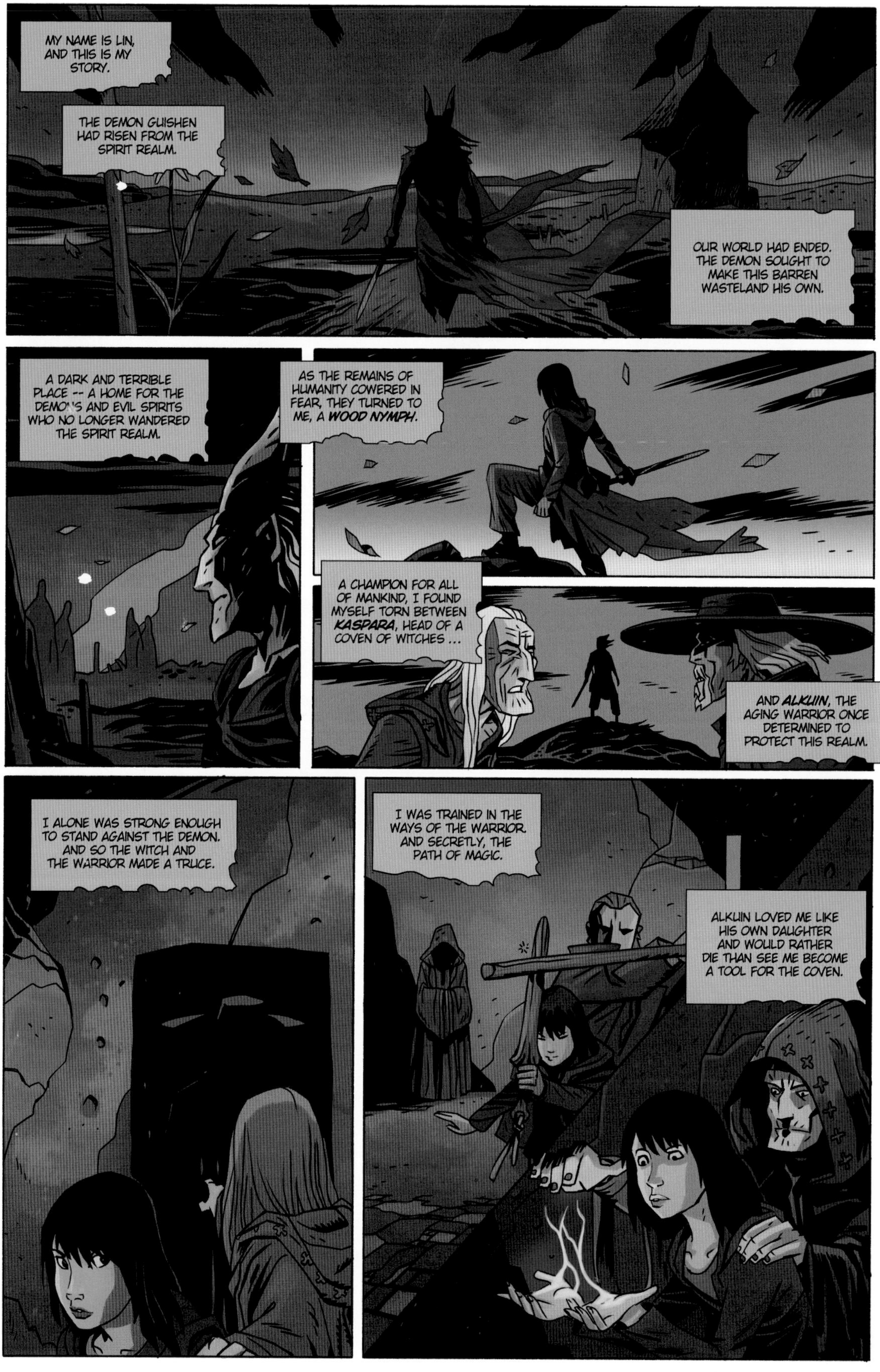
MY NAME IS LIN, AND THIS IS MY STORY.
THE DEMON GUISHEN HAD RISEN FROM THE SPIRIT REALM.
OUR WORLD HAD ENDED. THE DEMON SOUGHT TO MAKE THIS BARREN WASTELAND HIS OWN.
A DARK AND TERRIBLE PLACE -- A HOME FOR THE DEMONS AND EVIL SPIRITS WHO NO LONGER WANDERED THE SPIRIT REALM.
AS THE REMAINS OF HUMANITY COWERED IN FEAR, THEY TURNED TO ME, A WOOD NYMPH.
A CHAMPION FOR ALL OF MANKIND, I FOUND MYSELF TORN BETWEEN KASPARA, HEAD OF A COVEN OF WITCHES ...
AND ALKUIN, THE AGING WARRIOR ONCE DETERMINED TO PROTECT THIS REALM.
I ALONE WAS STRONG ENOUGH TO STAND AGAINST THE DEMON. AND SO THE WITCH AND THE WARRIOR MADE A TRUCE.
I WAS TRAINED IN THE WAYS OF THE WARRIOR. AND SECRETLY, THE PATH OF MAGIC.
ALKUIN LOVED ME LIKE HIS OWN DAUGHTER AND WOULD RATHER DIE THAN SEE ME BECOME A TOOL FOR THE COVEN.

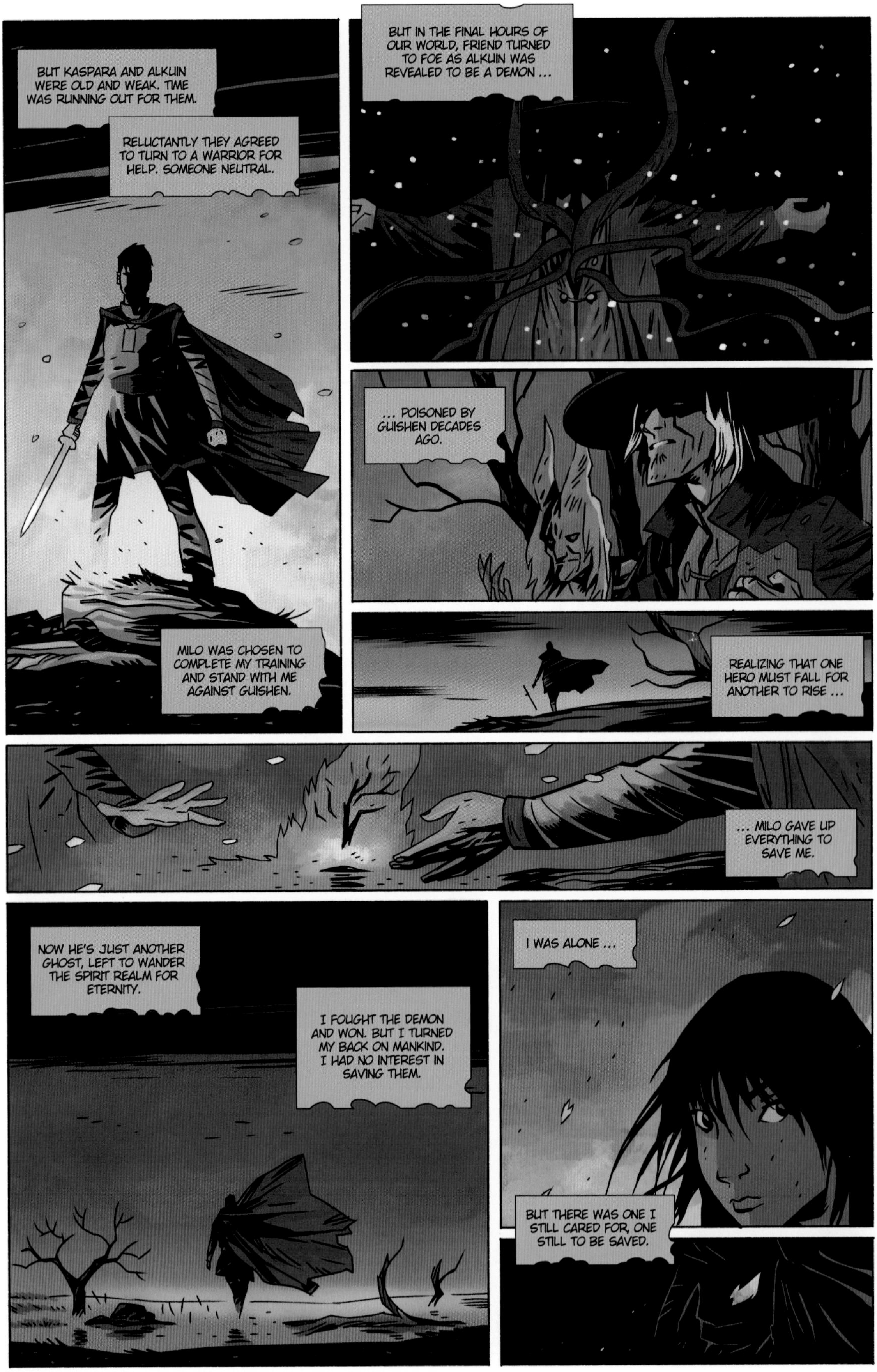

BUT KASPARA AND ALKUIN WERE OLD AND WEAK. TIME WAS RUNNING OUT FOR THEM.
RELUCTANTLY THEY AGREED TO TURN TO A WARRIOR FOR HELP. SOMEONE NEUTRAL.
MILO WAS CHOSEN TO COMPLETE MY TRAINING AND STAND WITH ME AGAINST GUISHEN.
BUT IN THE FINAL HOURS OF OUR WORLD, FRIEND TURNED TO FOE AS ALKUIN WAS REVEALED TO BE A DEMON ...
... POISONED BY GUISHEN DECADES AGO.
REALIZING THAT ONE HERO MUST FALL FOR ANOTHER TO RISE ...
... MILO GAVE UP EVERYTHING TO SAVE ME.
NOW HE'S JUST ANOTHER GHOST, LEFT TO WANDER THE SPIRIT REALM FOR ETERNITY.
I FOUGHT THE DEMON AND WON. BUT I TURNED MY BACK ON MANKIND. I HAD NO INTEREST IN SAVING THEM.
I WAS ALONE ...
BUT THERE WAS ONE I STILL CARED FOR, ONE STILL TO BE SAVED.

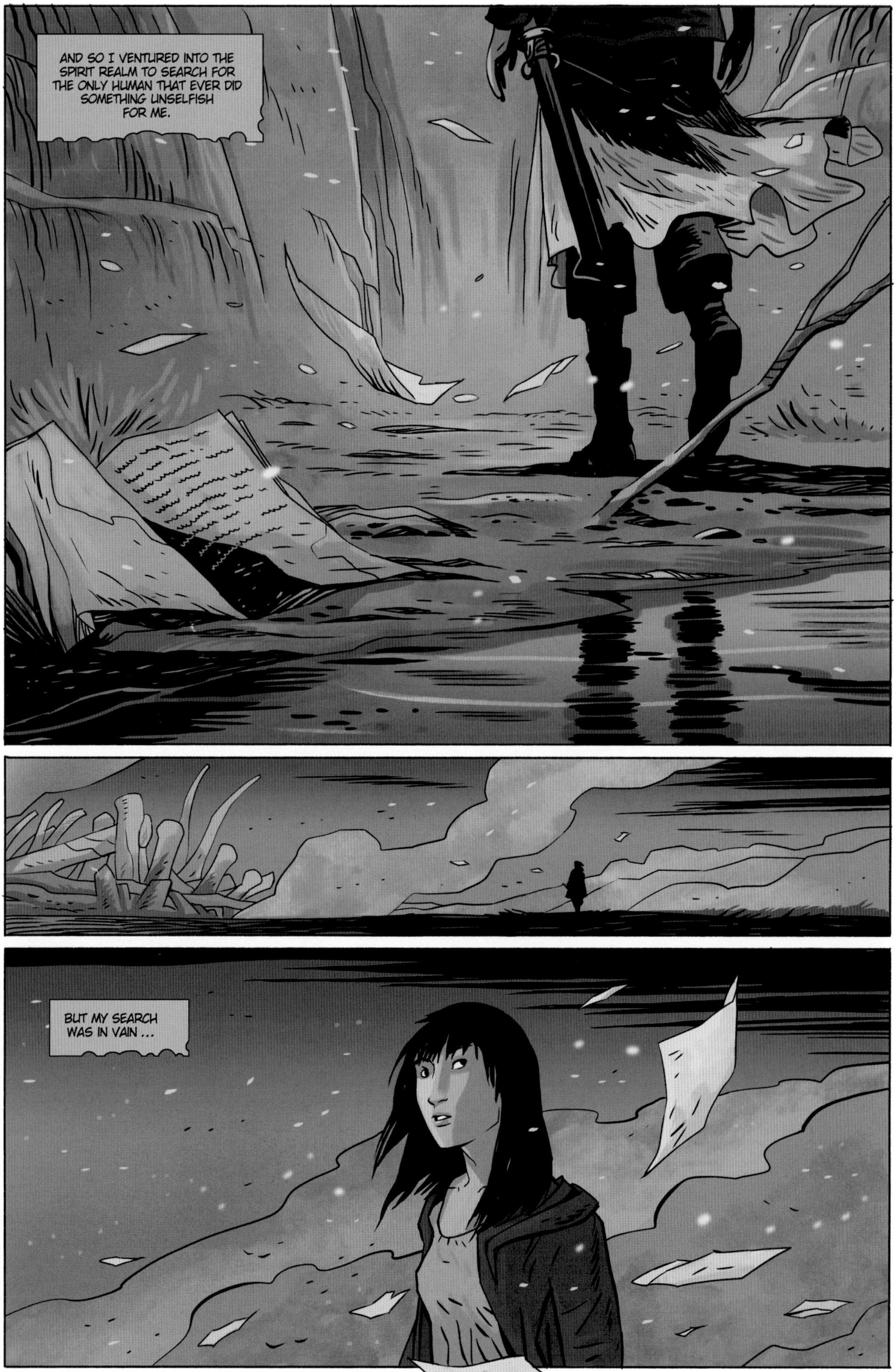
AND SO I VENTURED INTO THE SPIRIT REALM TO SEARCH FOR THE ONLY HUMAN THAT EVER DID SOMETHING UNSELFISH FOR ME.
BUT MY SEARCH WAS IN VAIN ...

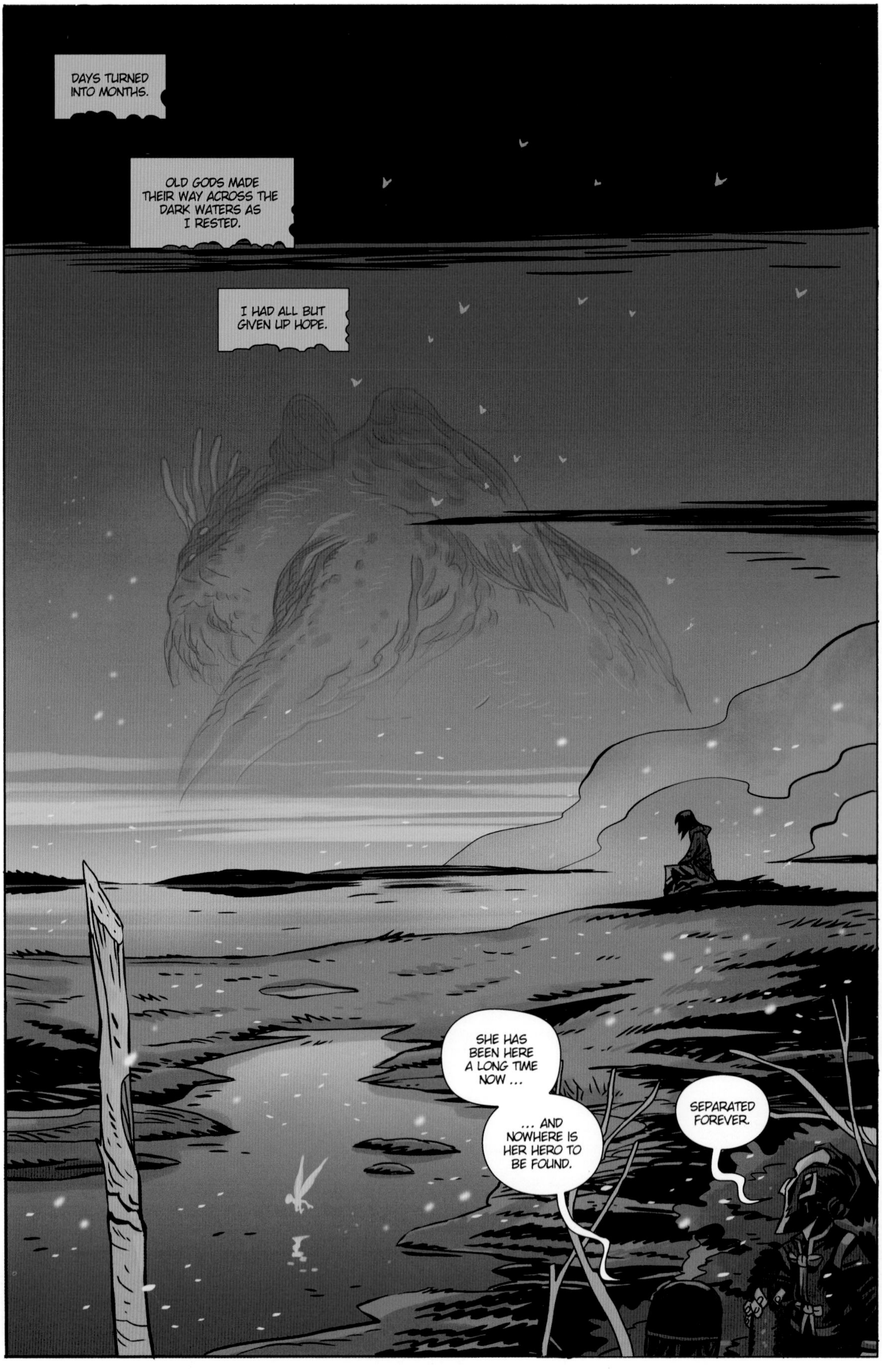
DAYS TURNED INTO MONTHS.
OLD GODS MADE THEIR WAY ACROSS THE DARK WATERS AS I RESTED.
I HAD ALL BUT GIVEN UP HOPE.
SHE HAS BEEN HERE A LONG TIME NOW ...
... AND NOWHERE IS HER HERO TO BE FOUND.
SEPARATED FOREVER.

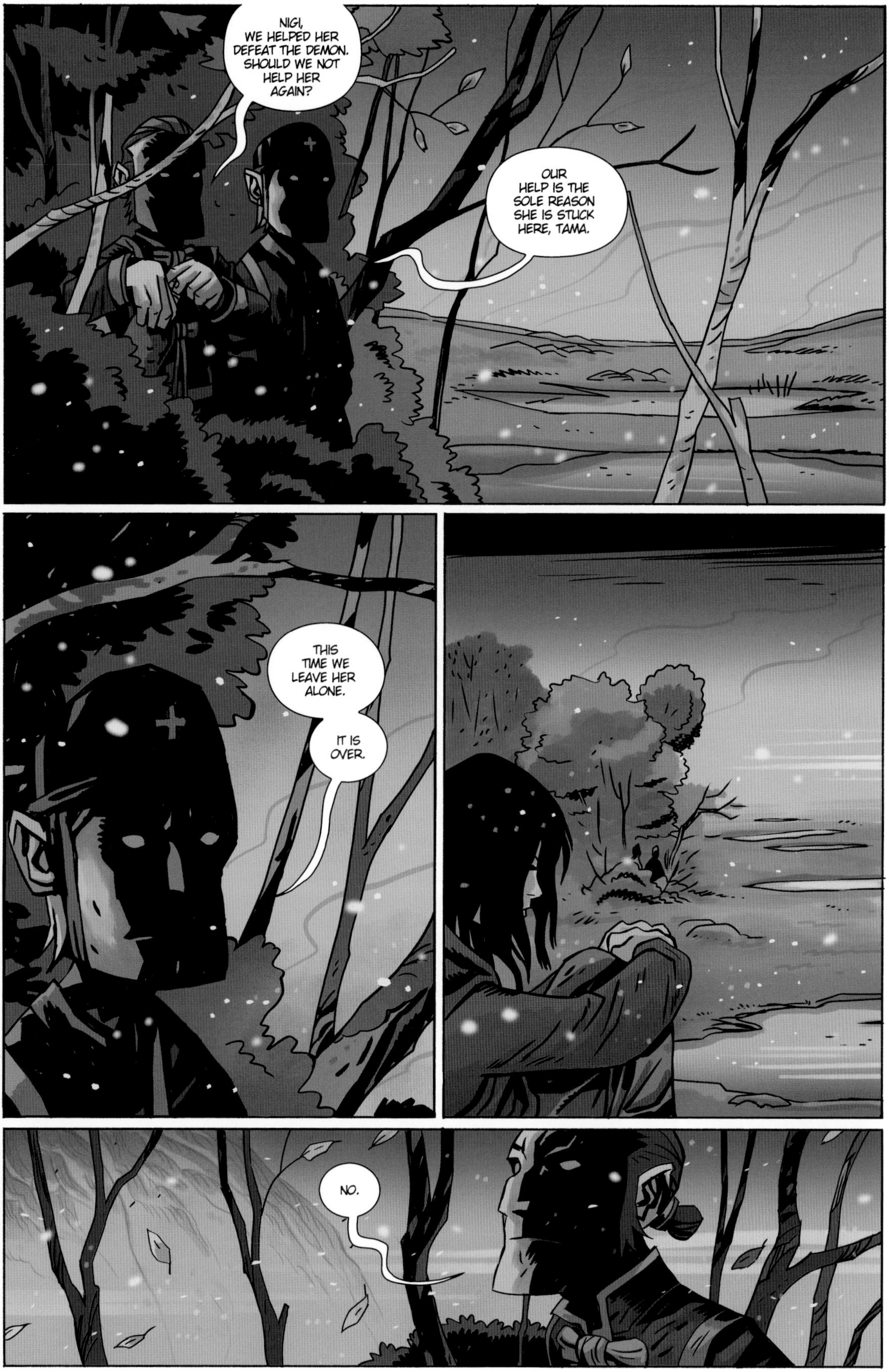
NIGI, WE HELPED HER DEFEAT THE DEMON. SHOULD WE NOT HELP HER AGAIN?
OUR HELP IS THE SOLE REASON SHE IS STUCK HERE, TAMA.
THIS TIME WE LEAVE HER ALONE.
IT IS OVER.
NO.

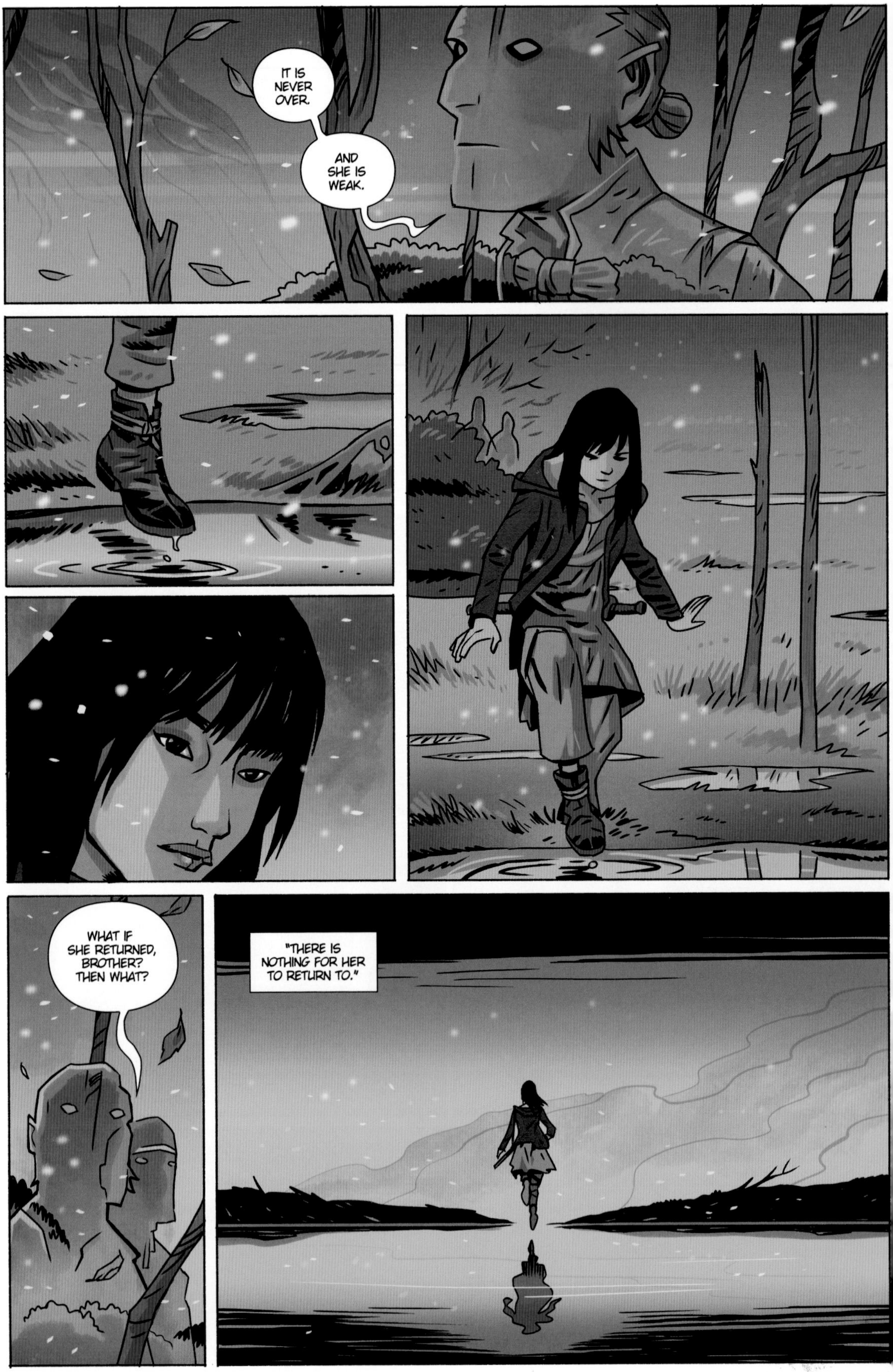
IT IS NEVER OVER.
AND SHE IS WEAK.
WHAT IF SHE RETURNED, BROTHER? THEN WHAT?
"THERE IS NOTHING FOR HER TO RETURN TO."

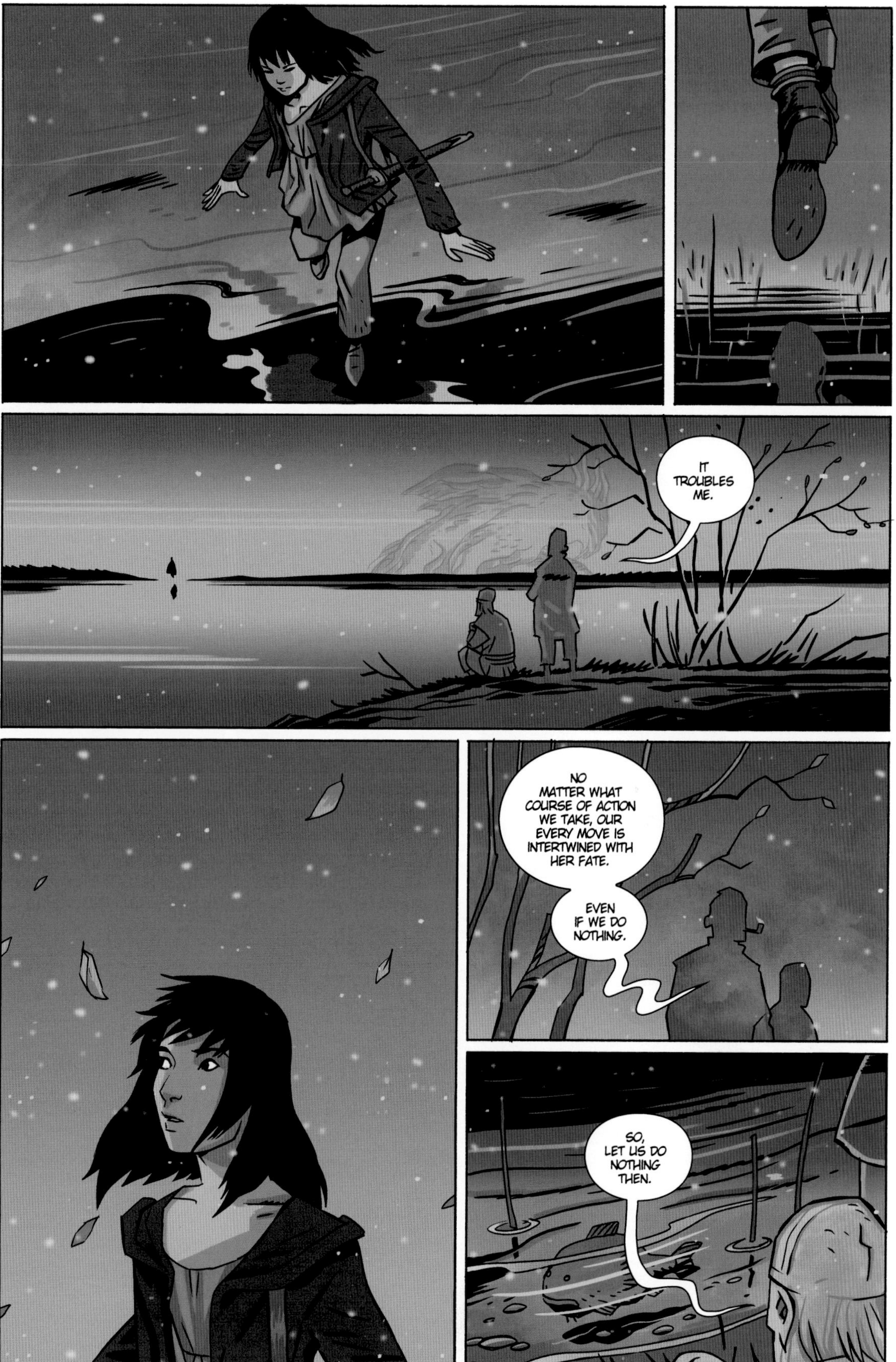
IT TROUBLES ME.
NO MATTER WHAT COURSE OF ACTION WE TAKE, OUR EVERY MOVE IS INTERTWINED WITH HER FATE.
EVEN IF WE DO NOTHING.
SO, LET US DO NOTHING THEN.

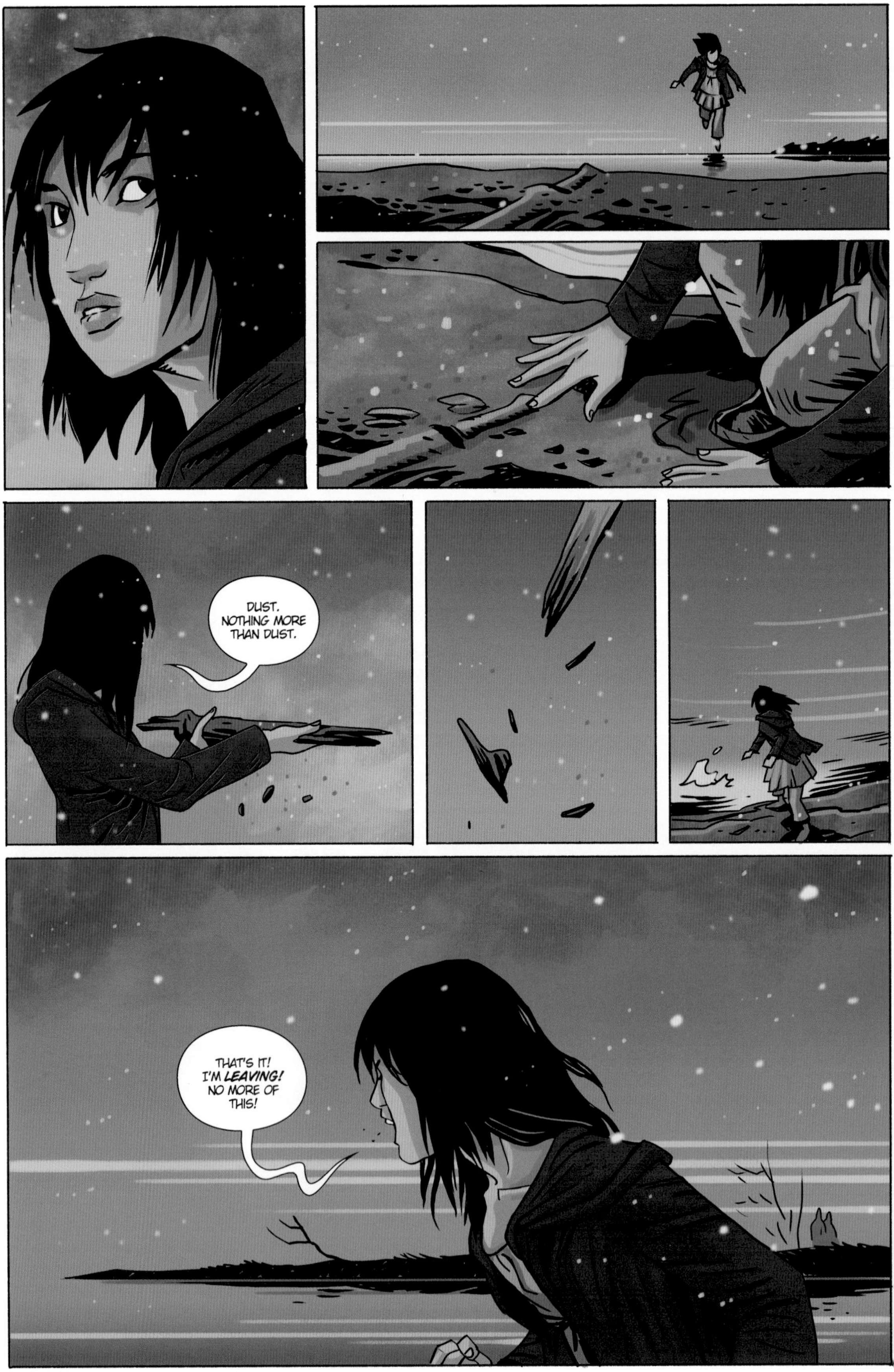
DUST. NOTHING MORE THAN DUST.
THAT'S IT! I'M ***LEAVING!*** NO MORE OF THIS!

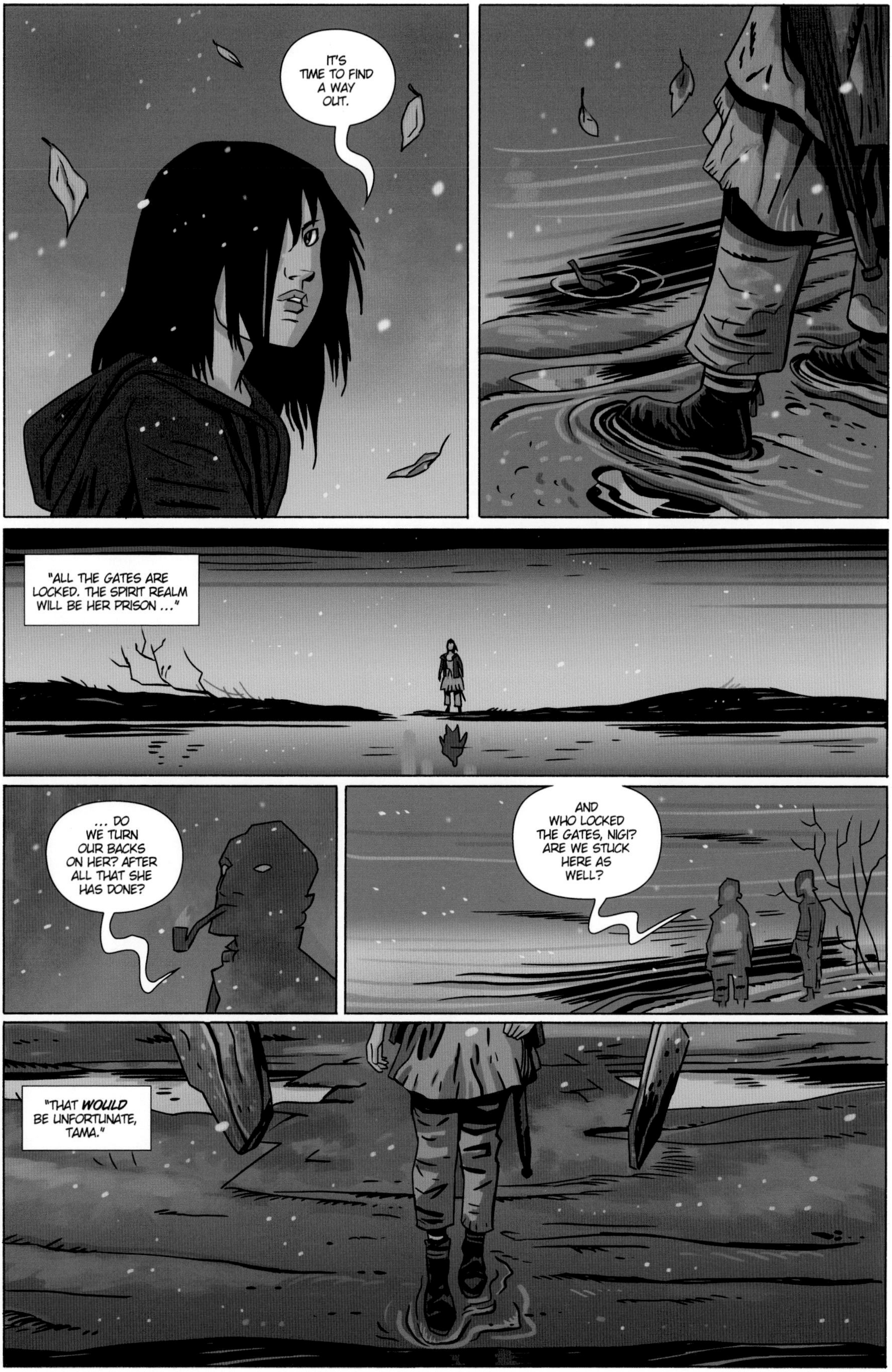
IT'S TIME TO FIND A WAY OUT.
"ALL THE GATES ARE LOCKED. THE SPIRIT REALM WILL BE HER PRISON ..."
... DO WE TURN OUR BACKS ON HER? AFTER ALL THAT SHE HAS DONE?
AND WHO LOCKED THE GATES, NIGI? ARE WE STUCK HERE AS WELL?
"THAT *WOULD* BE UNFORTUNATE, TAMA."

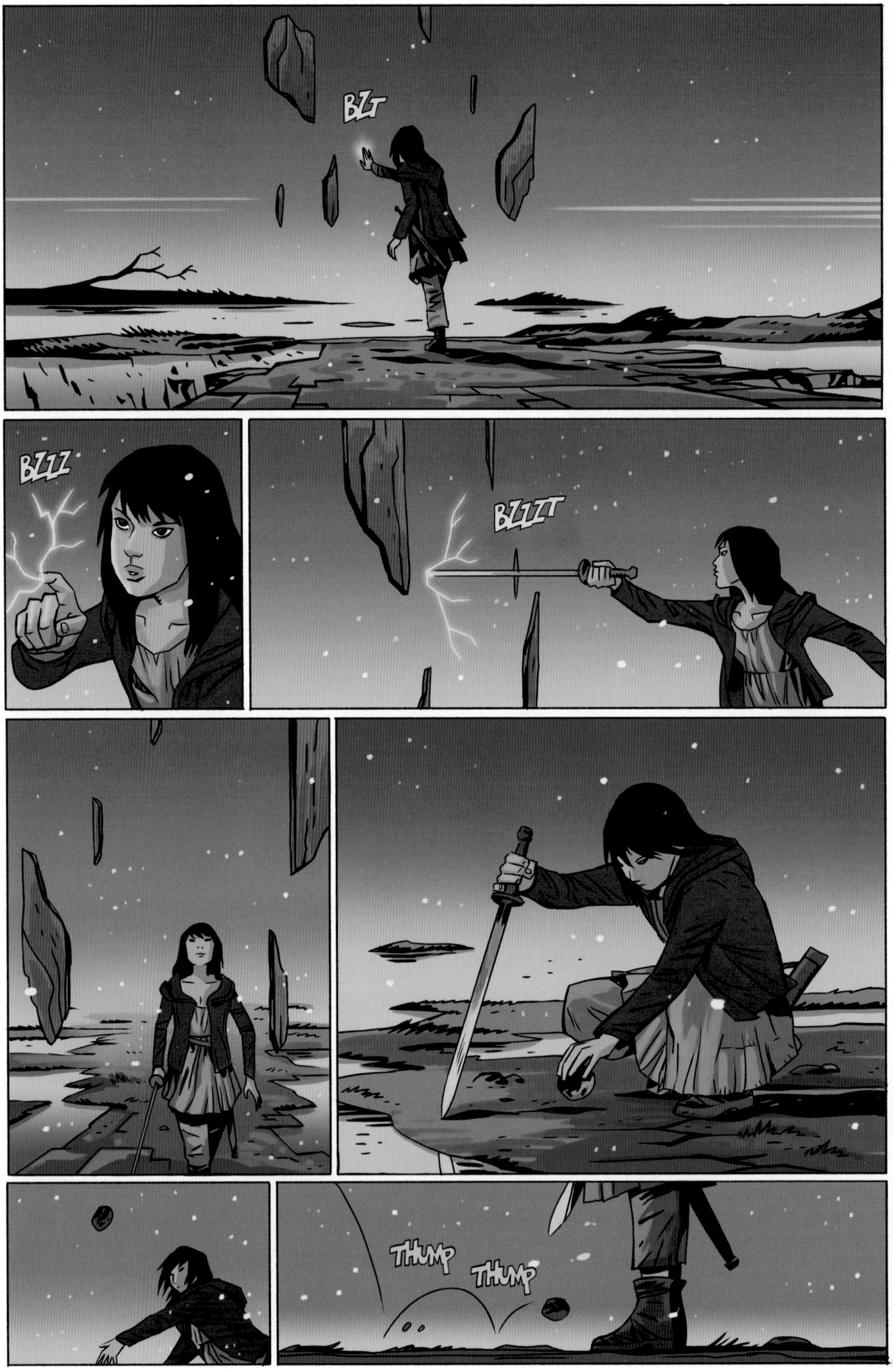
BZT
BZZZ
BZZZT
THUMP
THUMP

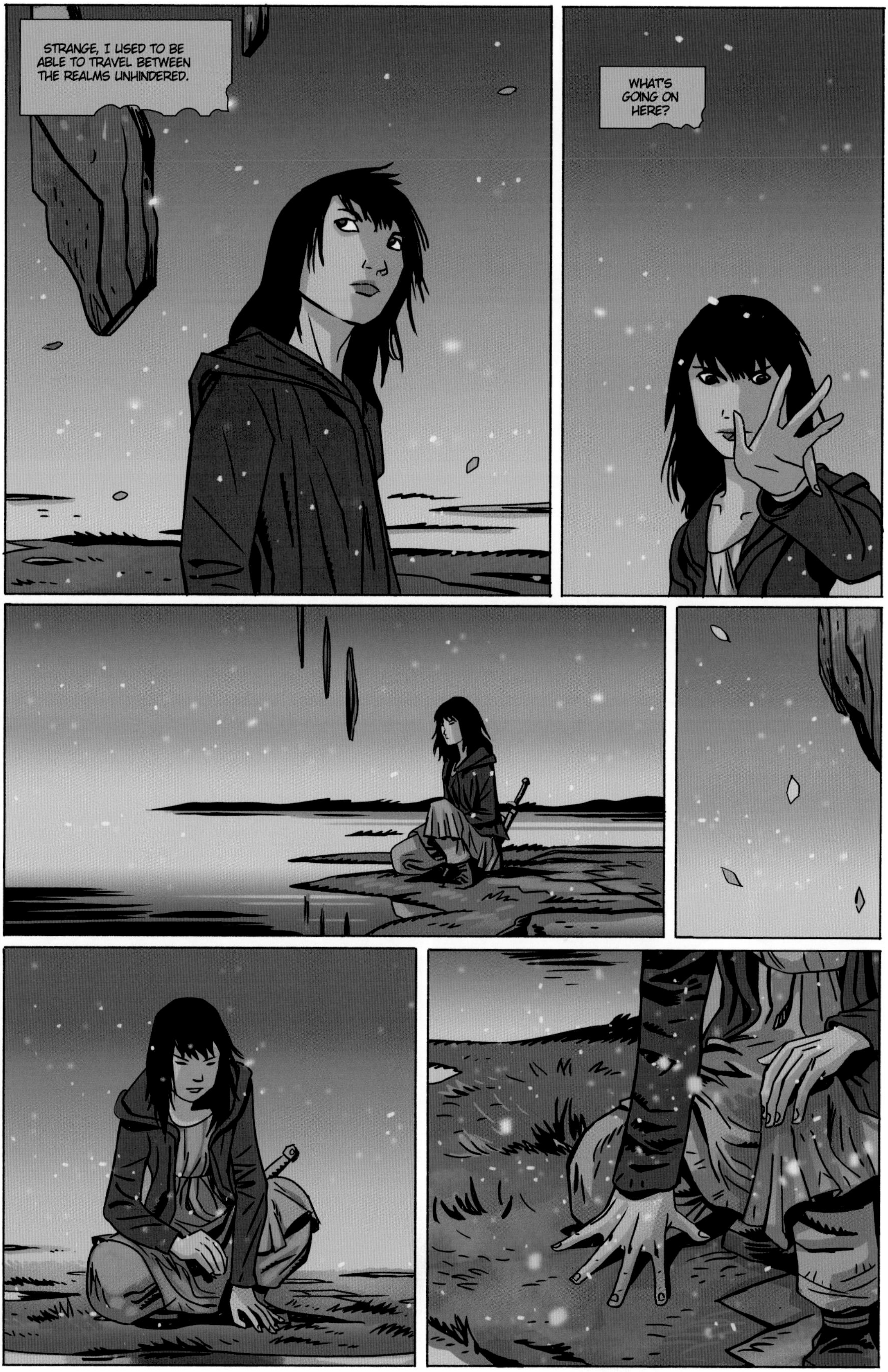
STRANGE, I USED TO BE ABLE TO TRAVEL BETWEEN THE REALMS UNHINDERED.
WHAT'S GOING ON HERE?

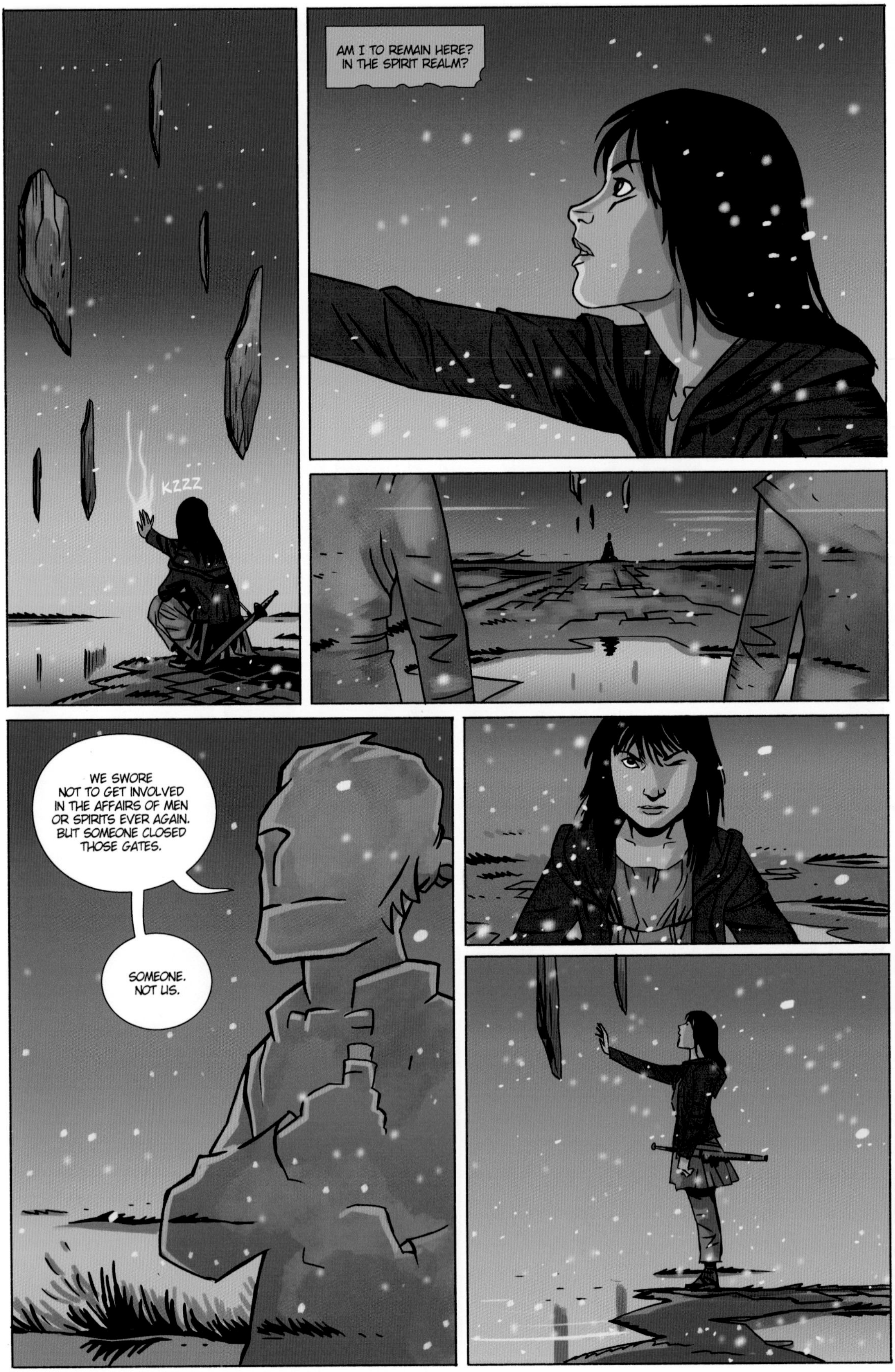
KZZZ
AM I TO REMAIN HERE? IN THE SPIRIT REALM?
WE SWORE NOT TO GET INVOLVED IN THE AFFAIRS OF MEN OR SPIRITS EVER AGAIN. BUT SOMEONE CLOSED THOSE GATES.
SOMEONE. NOT US.

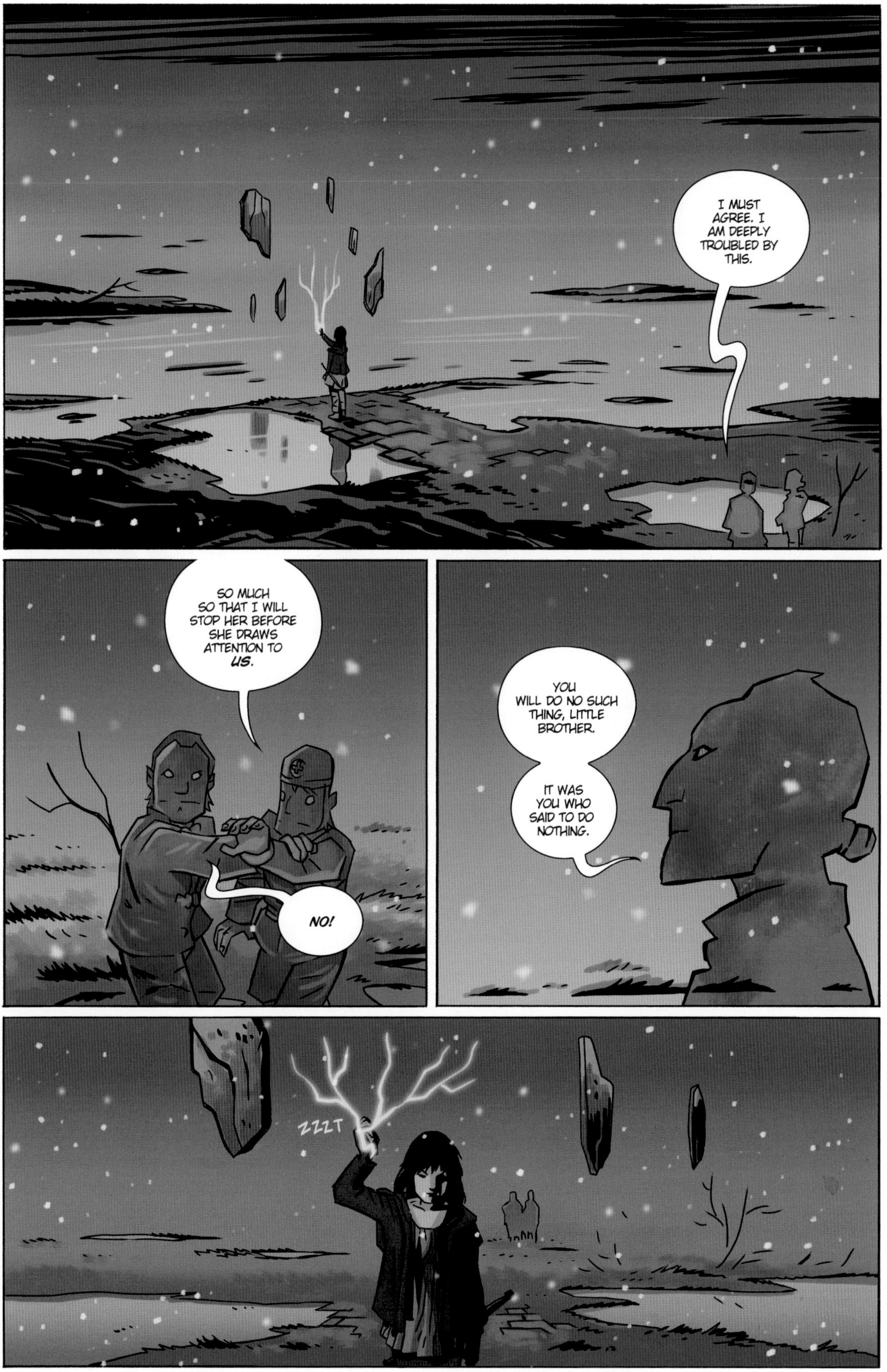
I MUST AGREE. I AM DEEPLY TROUBLED BY THIS.
SO MUCH SO THAT I WILL STOP HER BEFORE SHE DRAWS ATTENTION TO *US*.
NO!
YOU WILL DO NO SUCH THING, LITTLE BROTHER.
IT WAS YOU WHO SAID TO DO NOTHING.
ZZZT

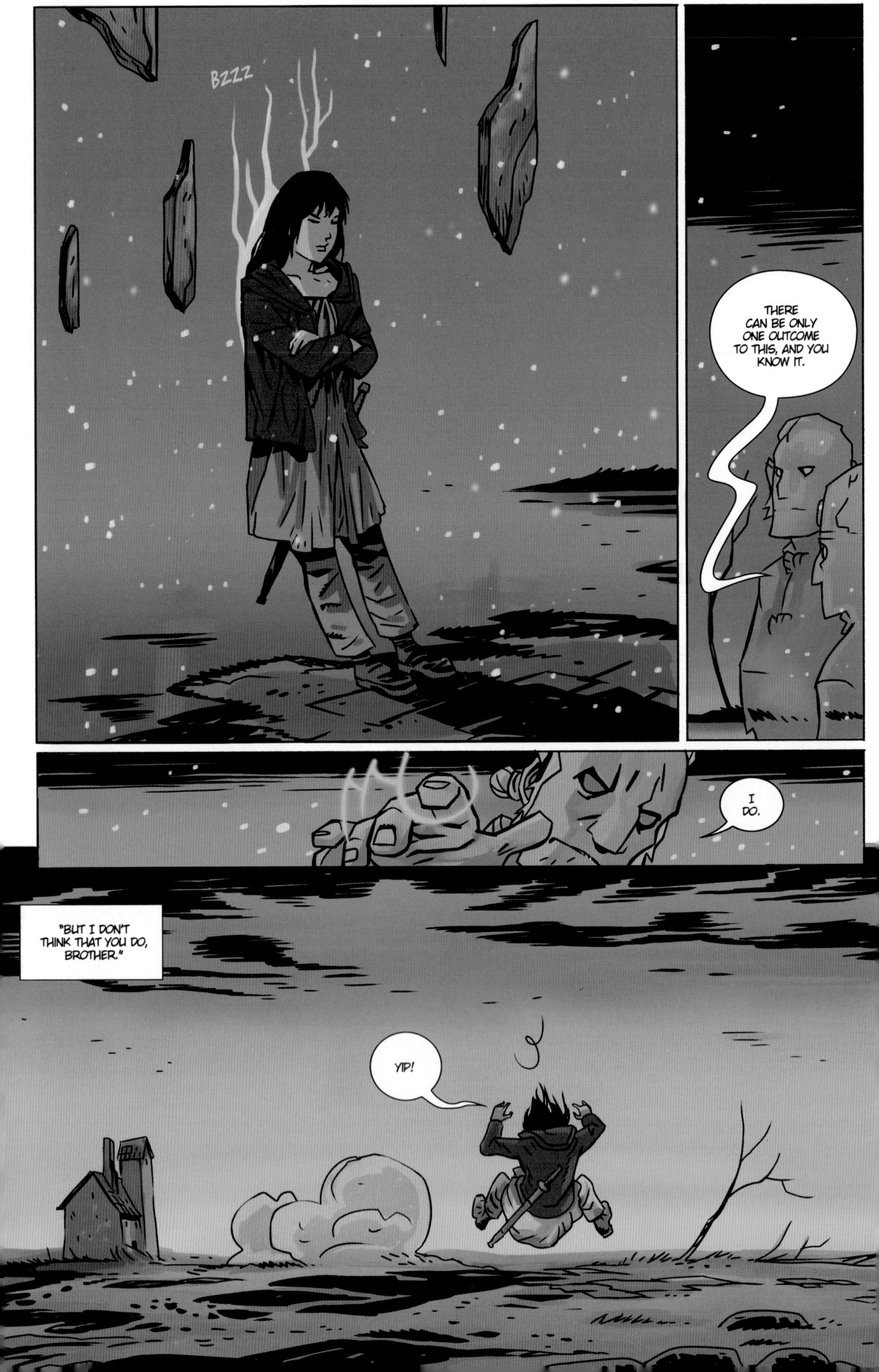
BZZZ
THERE CAN BE ONLY ONE OUTCOME TO THIS, AND YOU KNOW IT.
I DO.
"BUT I DON'T THINK THAT YOU DO, BROTHER."
YIP!

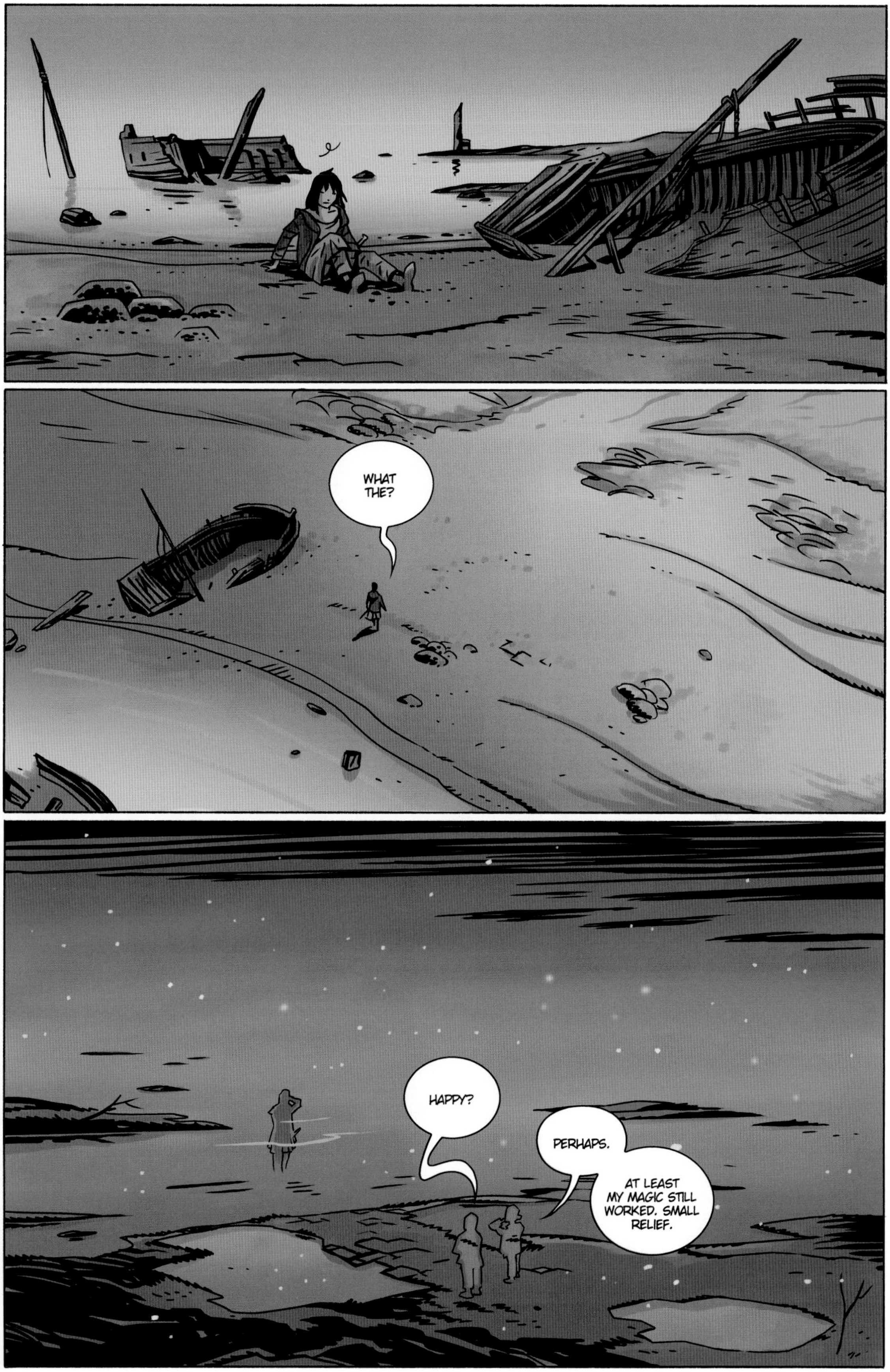
WHAT THE?
HAPPY?
PERHAPS.
AT LEAST MY MAGIC STILL WORKED. SMALL RELIEF.

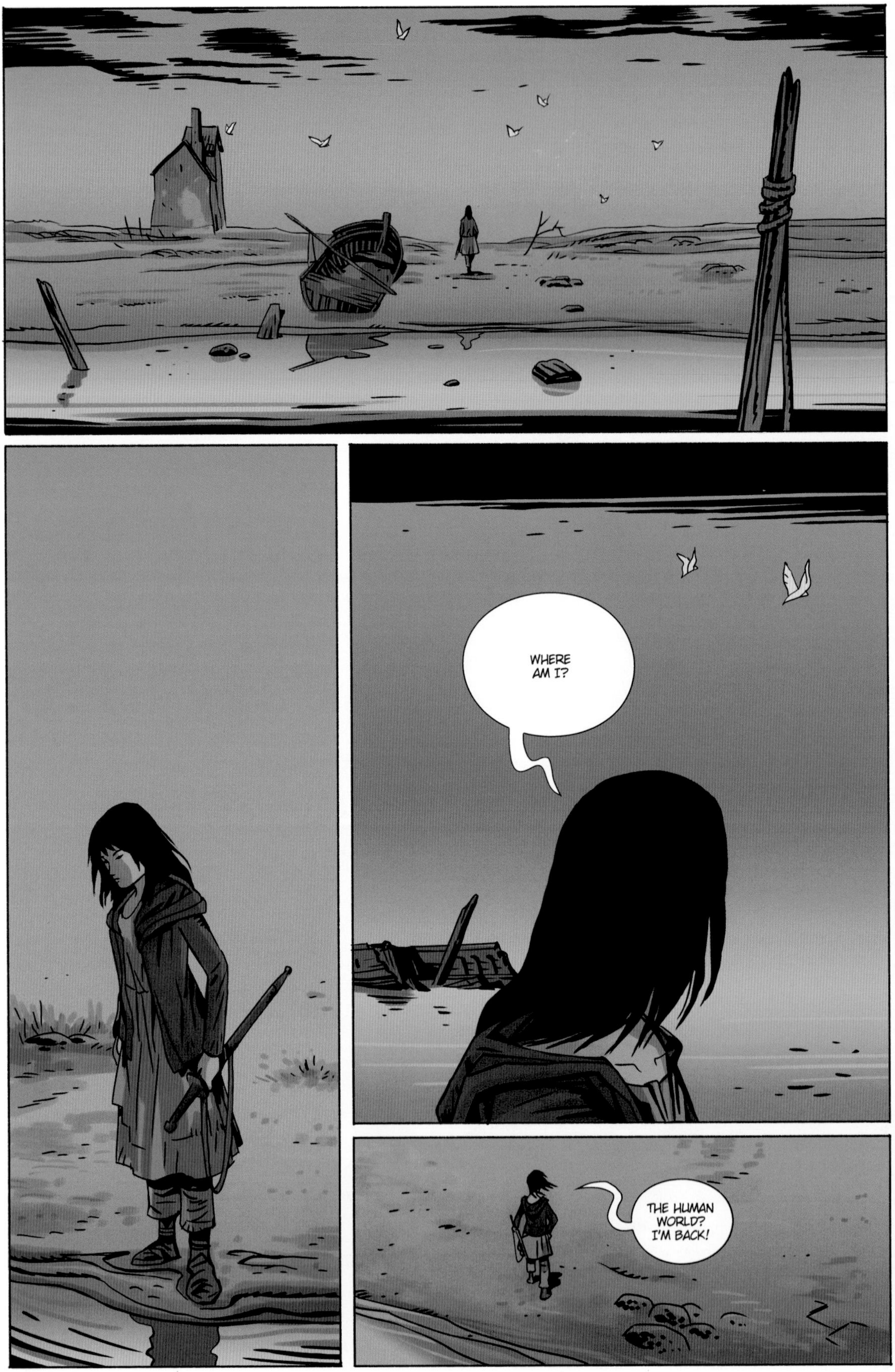
WHERE AM I?
THE HUMAN WORLD? I'M BACK!

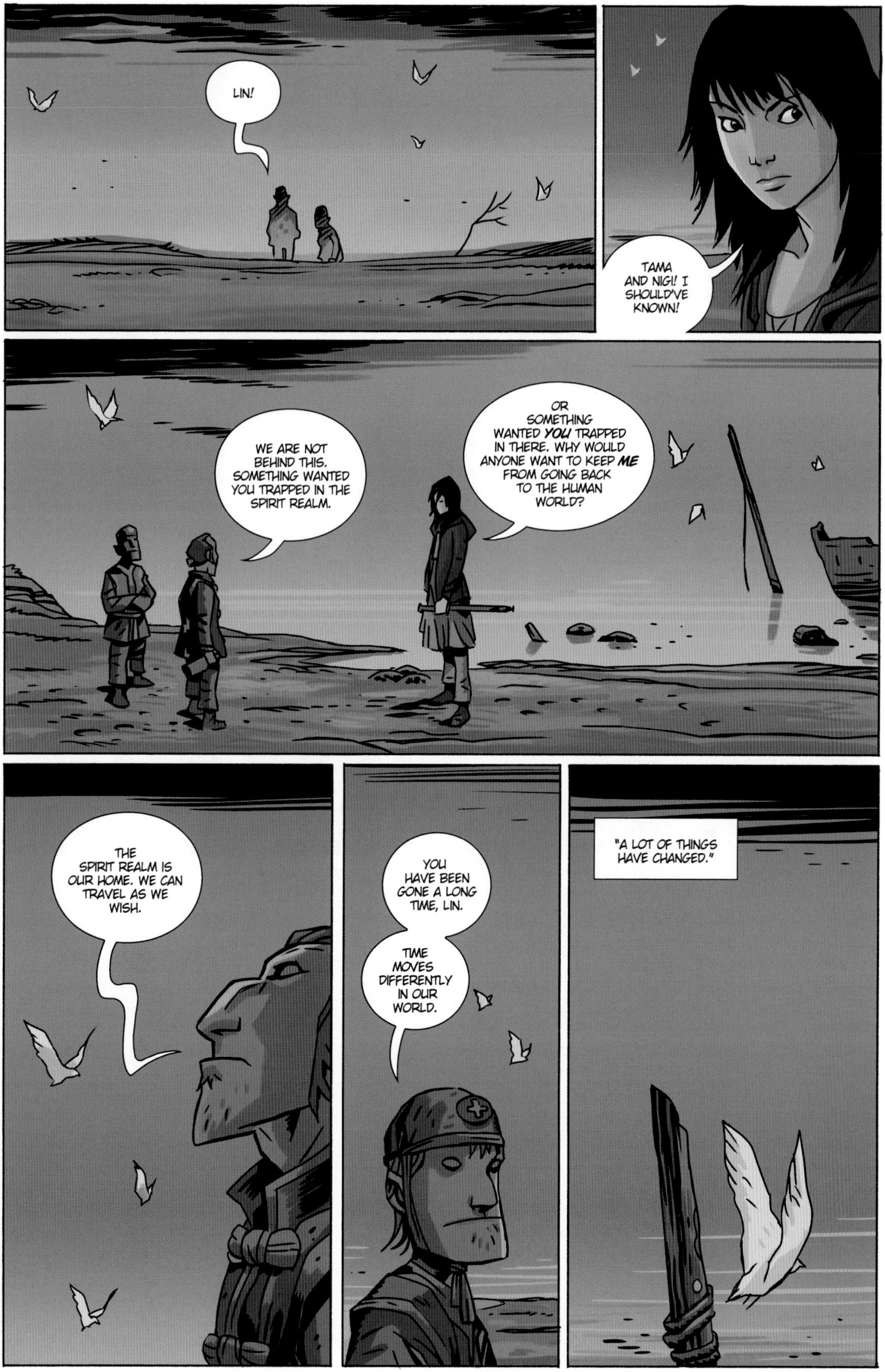
LIN!
TAMA AND NIGI! I SHOULD'VE KNOWN!
WE ARE NOT BEHIND THIS. SOMETHING WANTED YOU TRAPPED IN THE SPIRIT REALM.
OR SOMETHING WANTED **YOU** TRAPPED IN THERE. WHY WOULD ANYONE WANT TO KEEP **ME** FROM GOING BACK TO THE HUMAN WORLD?
THE SPIRIT REALM IS OUR HOME. WE CAN TRAVEL AS WE WISH.
YOU HAVE BEEN GONE A LONG TIME, LIN.
TIME MOVES DIFFERENTLY IN OUR WORLD.
"A LOT OF THINGS HAVE CHANGED."

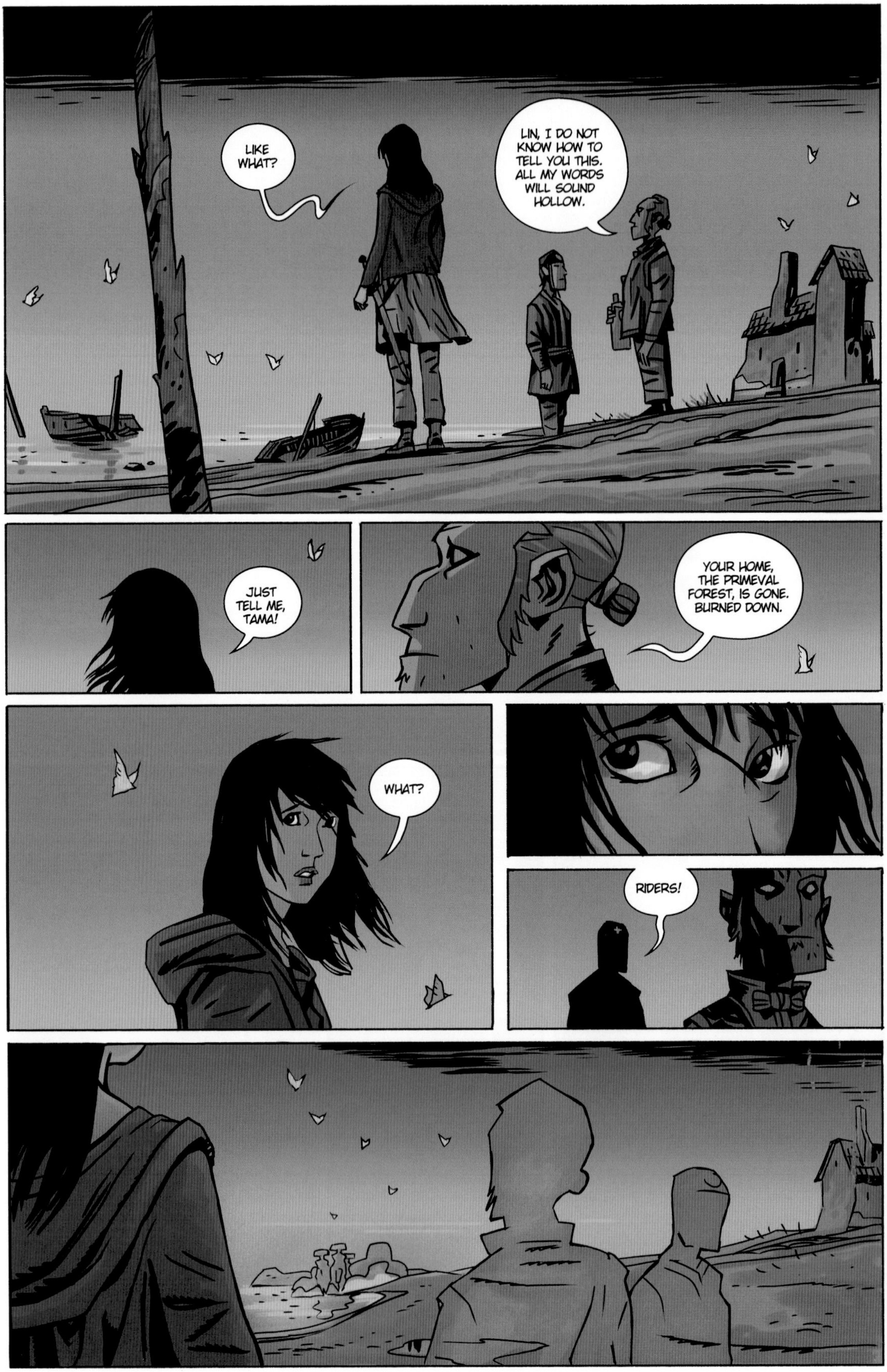
LIKE WHAT?
LIN, I DO NOT KNOW HOW TO TELL YOU THIS. ALL MY WORDS WILL SOUND HOLLOW.
JUST TELL ME, TAMA!
YOUR HOME, THE PRIMEVAL FOREST, IS GONE. BURNED DOWN.
WHAT?
RIDERS!

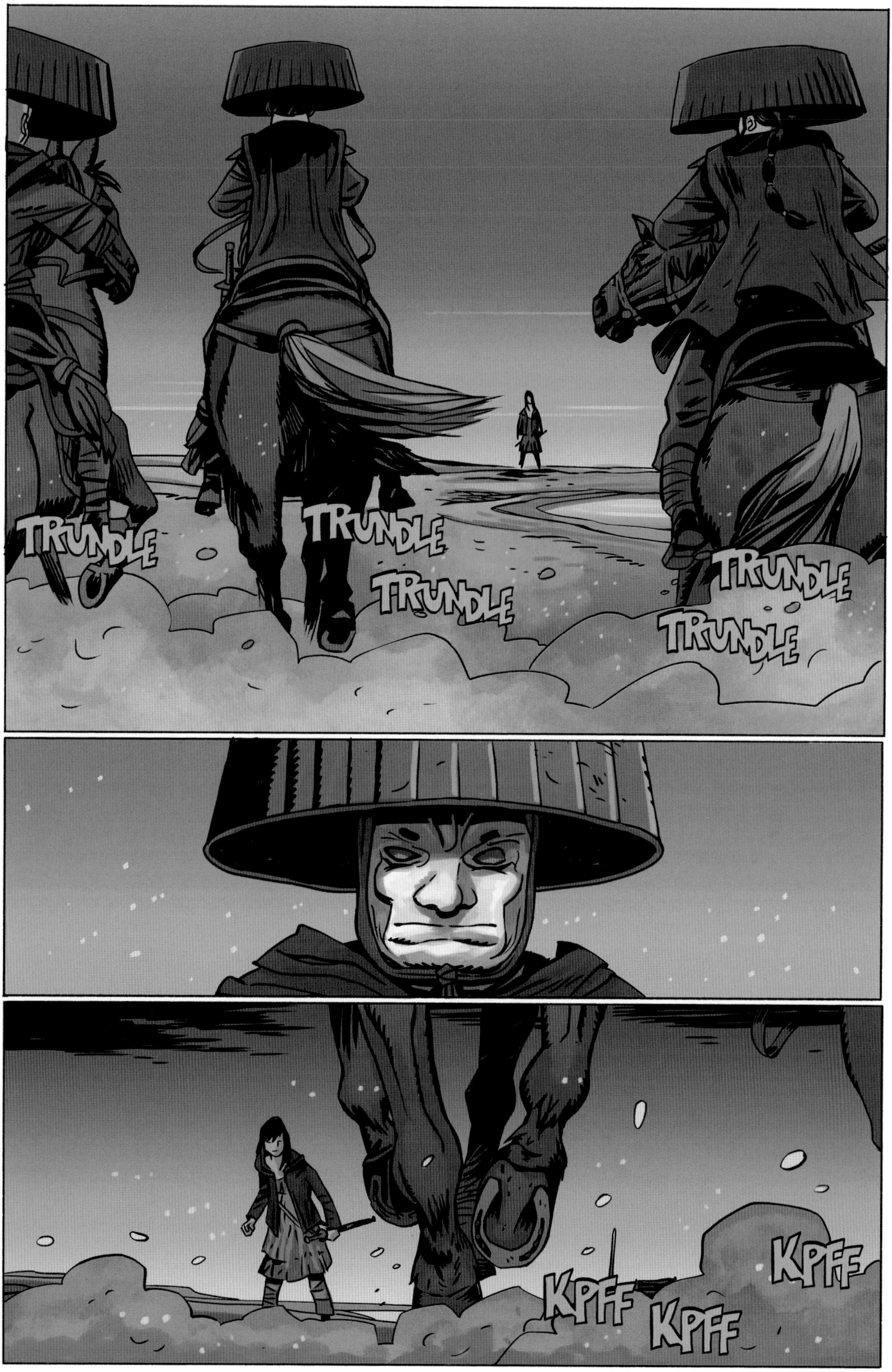
TRUNDLE
TRUNDLE
TRUNDLE
TRUNDLE
TRUNDLE
KPFF
KPFF
KPFF

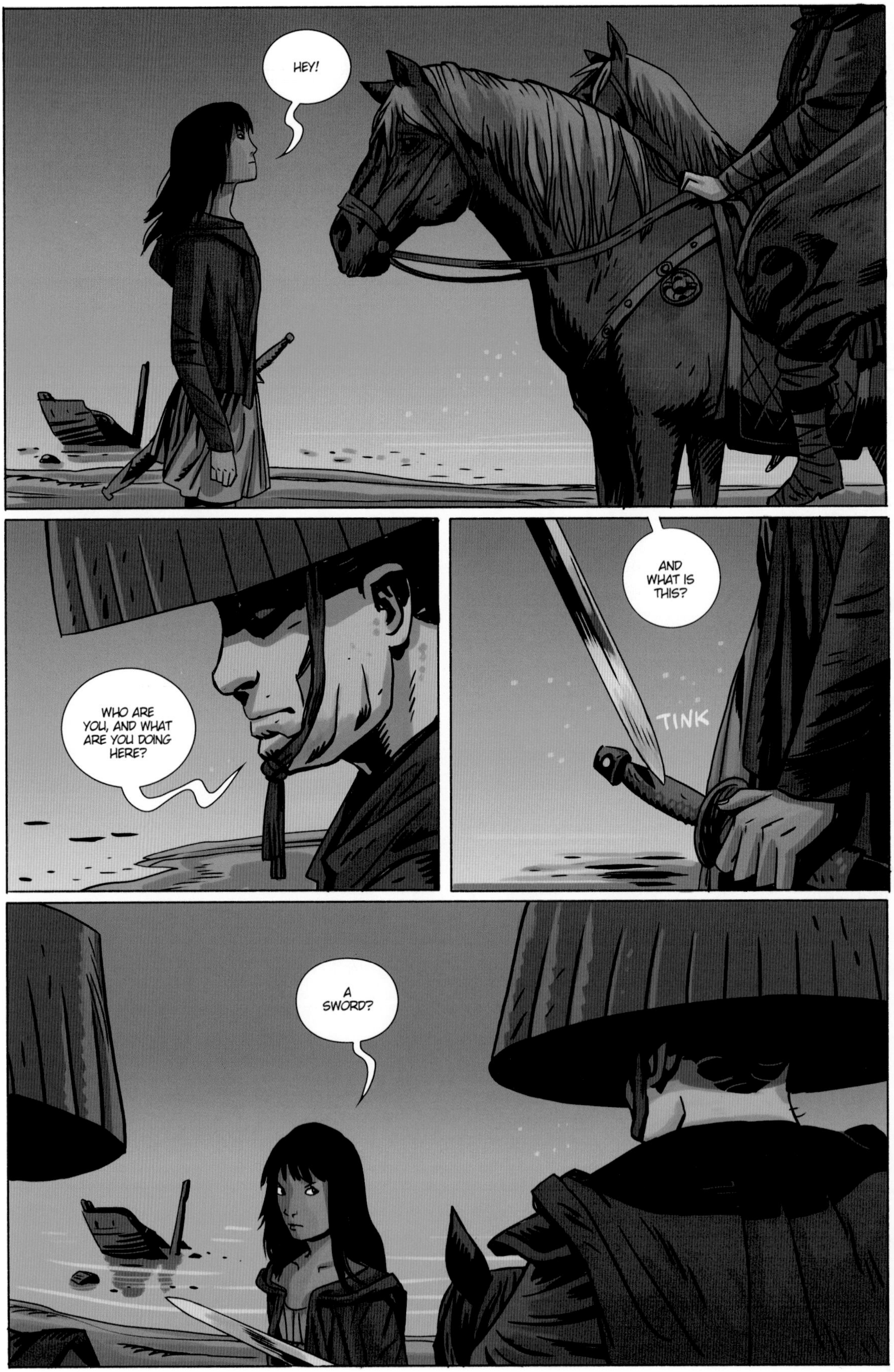
HEY!
WHO ARE YOU, AND WHAT ARE YOU DOING HERE?
AND WHAT IS THIS?
TINK
A SWORD?

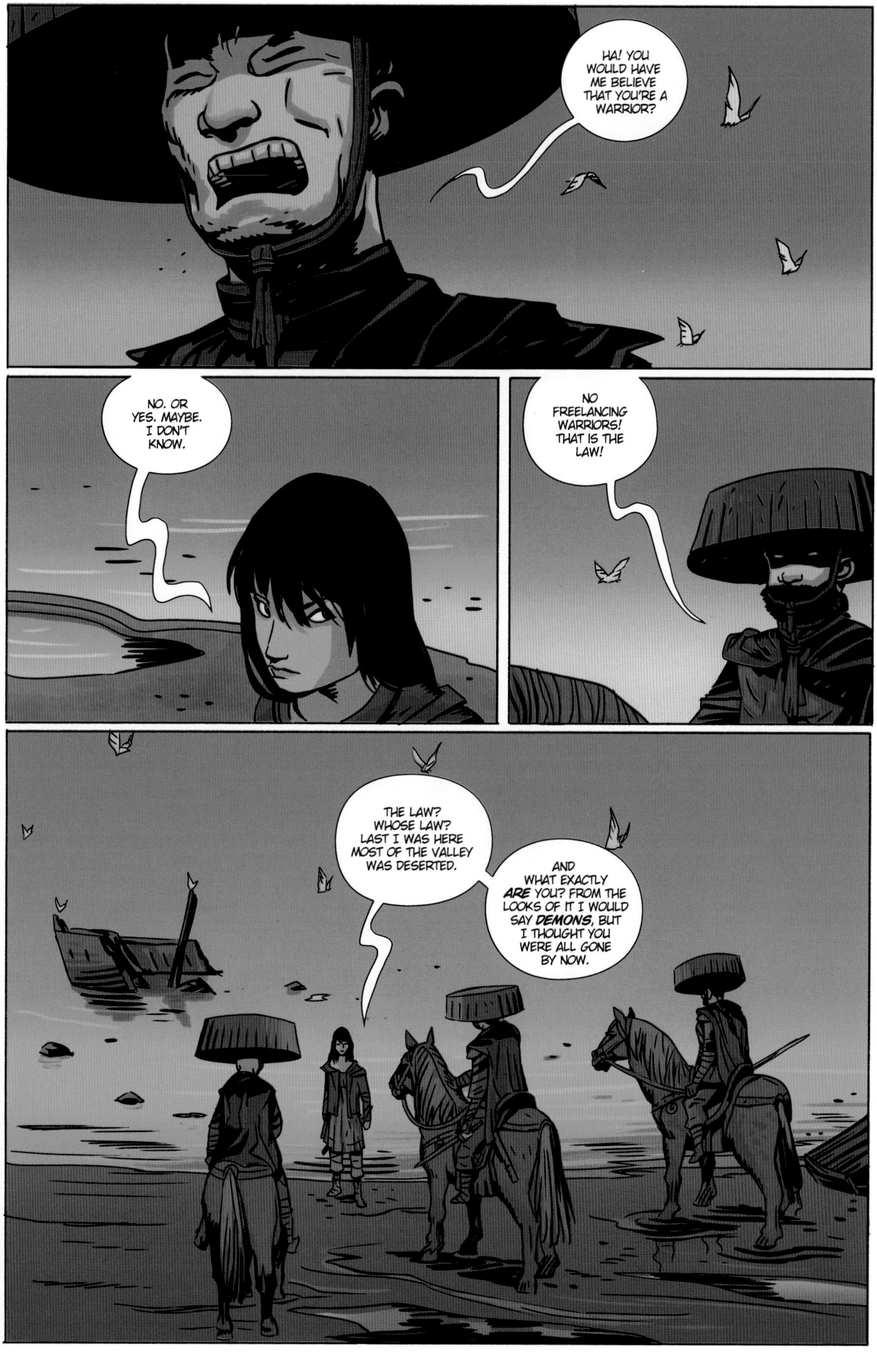
HA! YOU WOULD HAVE ME BELIEVE THAT YOU'RE A WARRIOR?
NO. OR YES. MAYBE. I DON'T KNOW.
NO FREELANCING WARRIORS! THAT IS THE LAW!
THE LAW? WHOSE LAW? LAST I WAS HERE MOST OF THE VALLEY WAS DESERTED.
AND WHAT EXACTLY ***ARE*** YOU? FROM THE LOOKS OF IT I WOULD SAY ***DEMONS***, BUT I THOUGHT YOU WERE ALL GONE BY NOW.

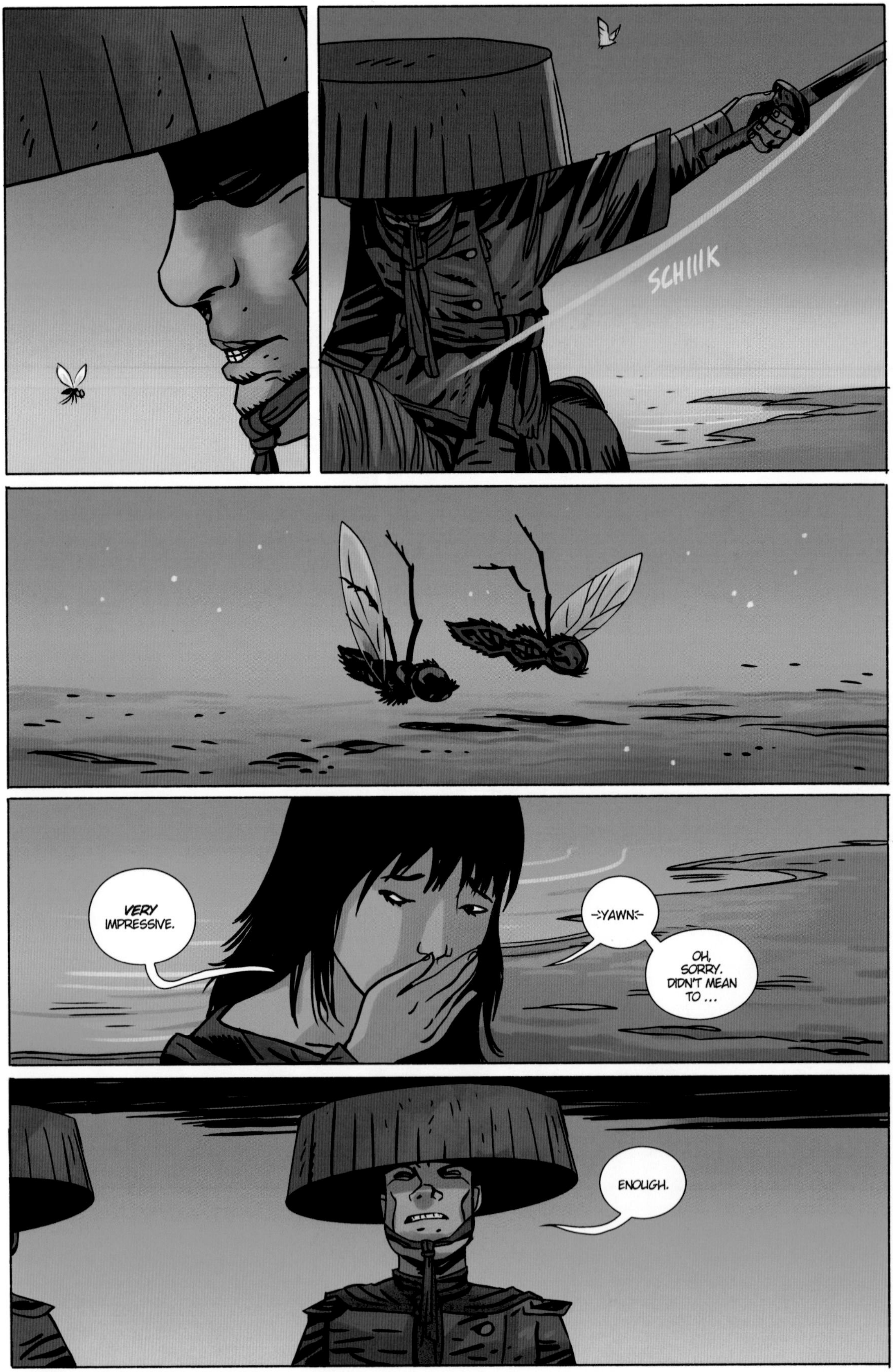
SCHIIIK
VERY IMPRESSIVE.
~YAWN~
OH, SORRY. DIDN'T MEAN TO ...
ENOUGH.

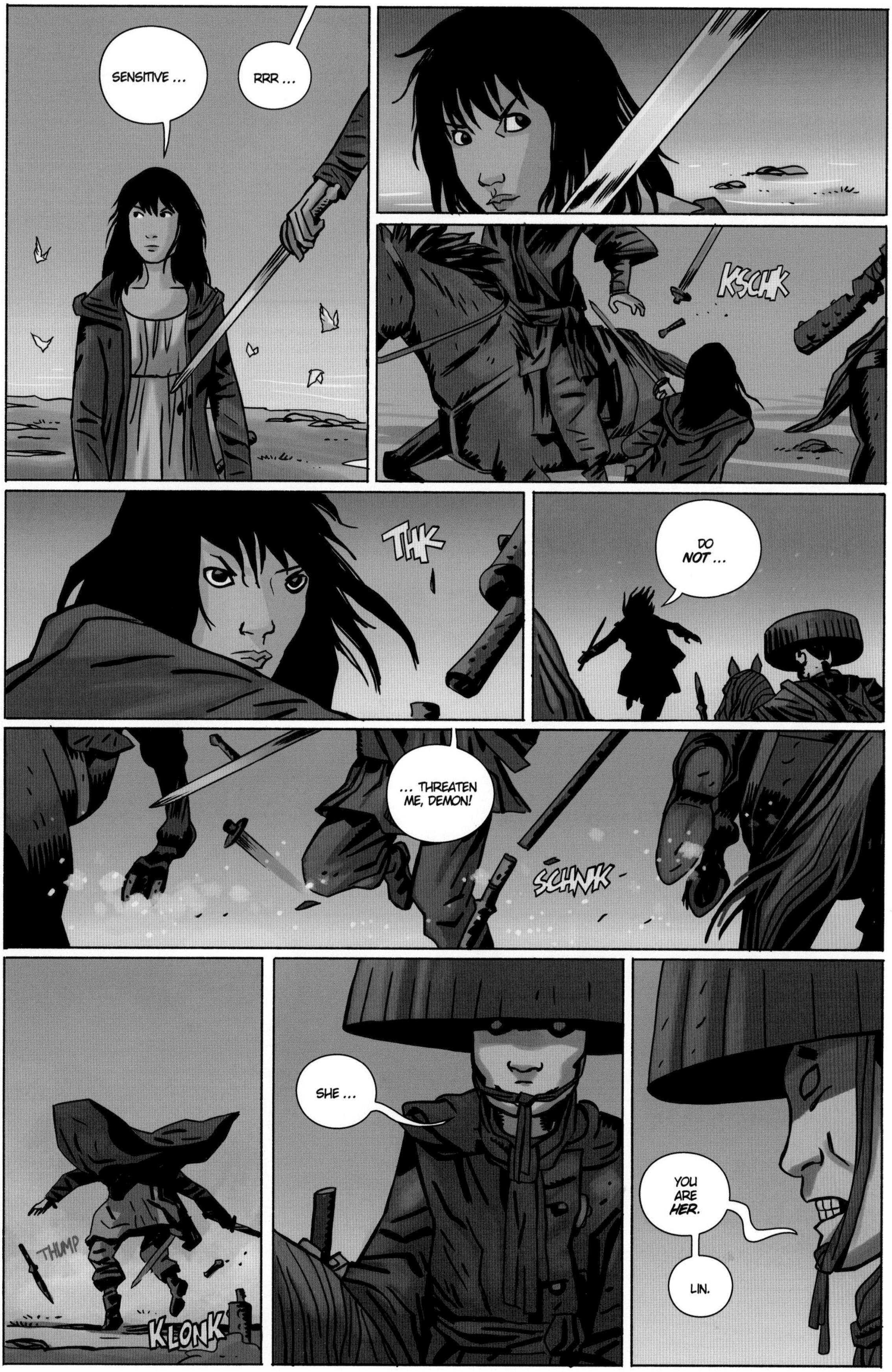
SENSITIVE ...
RRR ...
KSCHK
THK
DO NOT ...
... THREATEN ME, DEMON!
SCHNK
THUMP
KLONK
SHE ...
YOU ARE HER.
LIN.

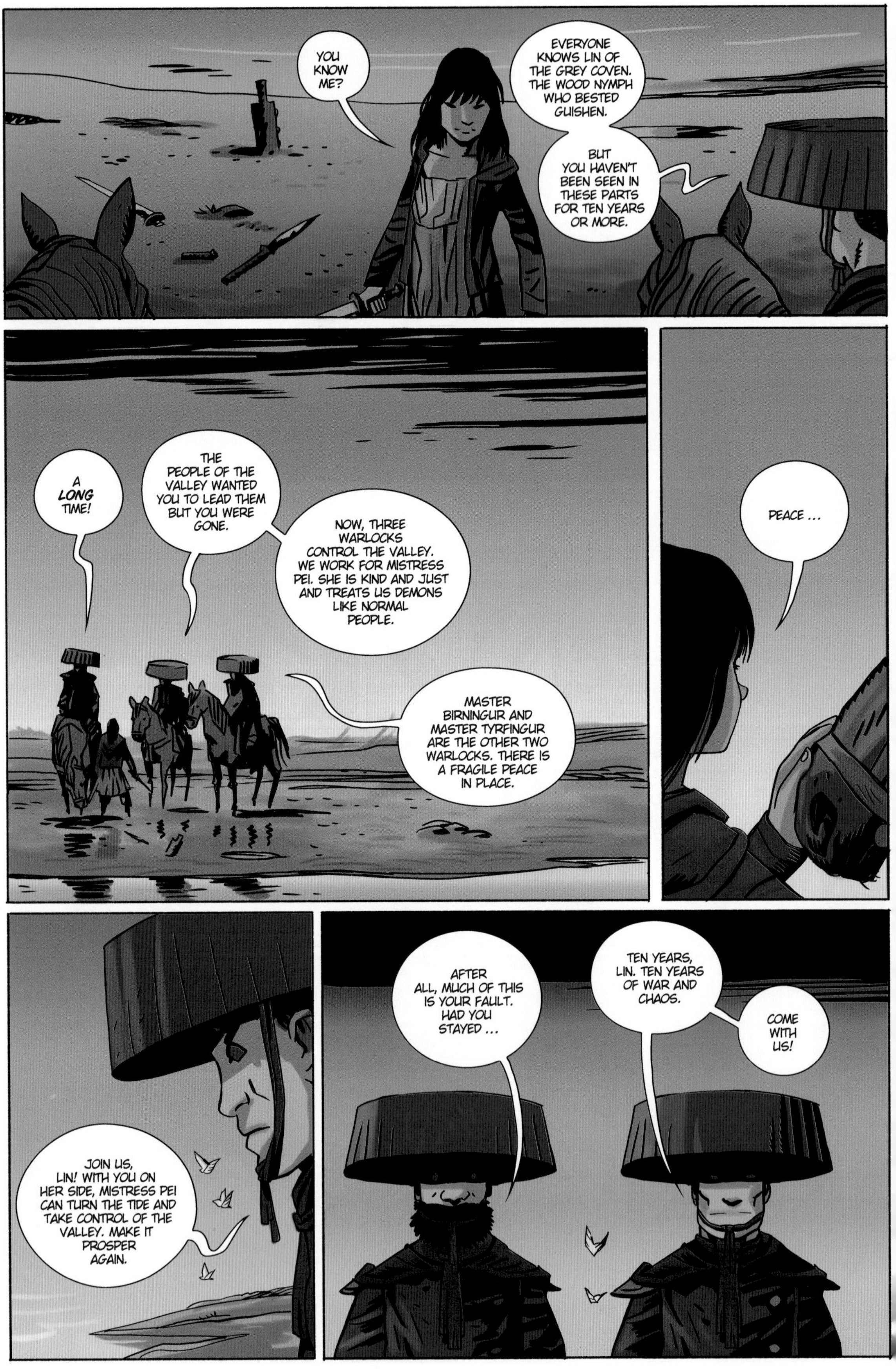
YOU KNOW ME?
EVERYONE KNOWS LIN OF THE GREY COVEN. THE WOOD NYMPH WHO BESTED GUISHEN.
BUT YOU HAVEN'T BEEN SEEN IN THESE PARTS FOR TEN YEARS OR MORE.
A LONG TIME!
THE PEOPLE OF THE VALLEY WANTED YOU TO LEAD THEM BUT YOU WERE GONE.
NOW, THREE WARLOCKS CONTROL THE VALLEY. WE WORK FOR MISTRESS PEI. SHE IS KIND AND JUST AND TREATS US DEMONS LIKE NORMAL PEOPLE.
MASTER BIRNINGUR AND MASTER TYRFINGUR ARE THE OTHER TWO WARLOCKS. THERE IS A FRAGILE PEACE IN PLACE.
PEACE ...
JOIN US, LIN! WITH YOU ON HER SIDE, MISTRESS PEI CAN TURN THE TIDE AND TAKE CONTROL OF THE VALLEY. MAKE IT PROSPER AGAIN.
AFTER ALL, MUCH OF THIS IS YOUR FAULT. HAD YOU STAYED ...
TEN YEARS, LIN. TEN YEARS OF WAR AND CHAOS.
COME WITH US!

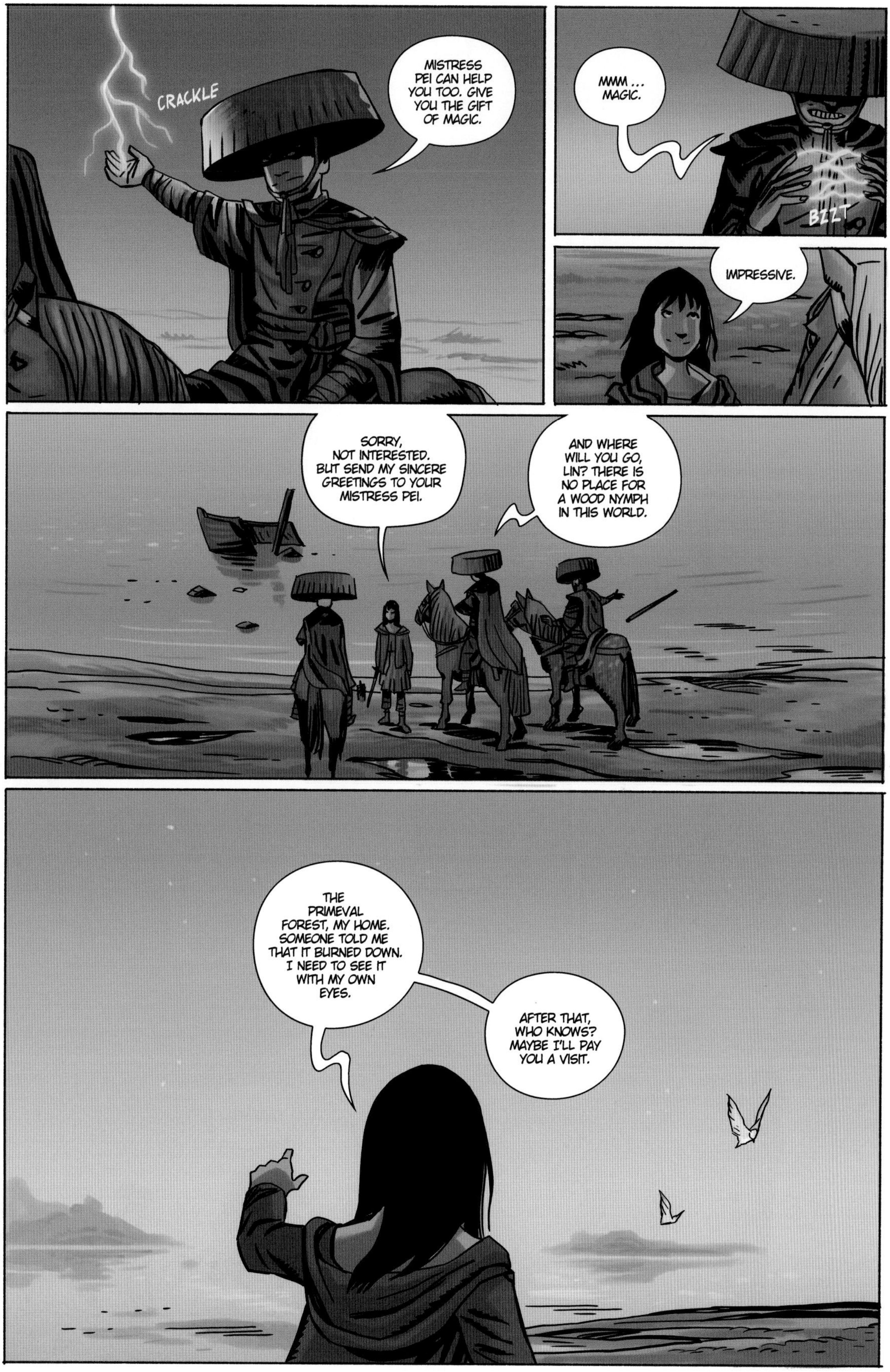
CRACKLE
MISTRESS PEI CAN HELP YOU TOO. GIVE YOU THE GIFT OF MAGIC.
MMM ... MAGIC.
BZZT
IMPRESSIVE.
SORRY, NOT INTERESTED. BUT SEND MY SINCERE GREETINGS TO YOUR MISTRESS PEI.
AND WHERE WILL YOU GO, LIN? THERE IS NO PLACE FOR A WOOD NYMPH IN THIS WORLD.
THE PRIMEVAL FOREST, MY HOME. SOMEONE TOLD ME THAT IT BURNED DOWN. I NEED TO SEE IT WITH MY OWN EYES.
AFTER THAT, WHO KNOWS? MAYBE I'LL PAY YOU A VISIT.

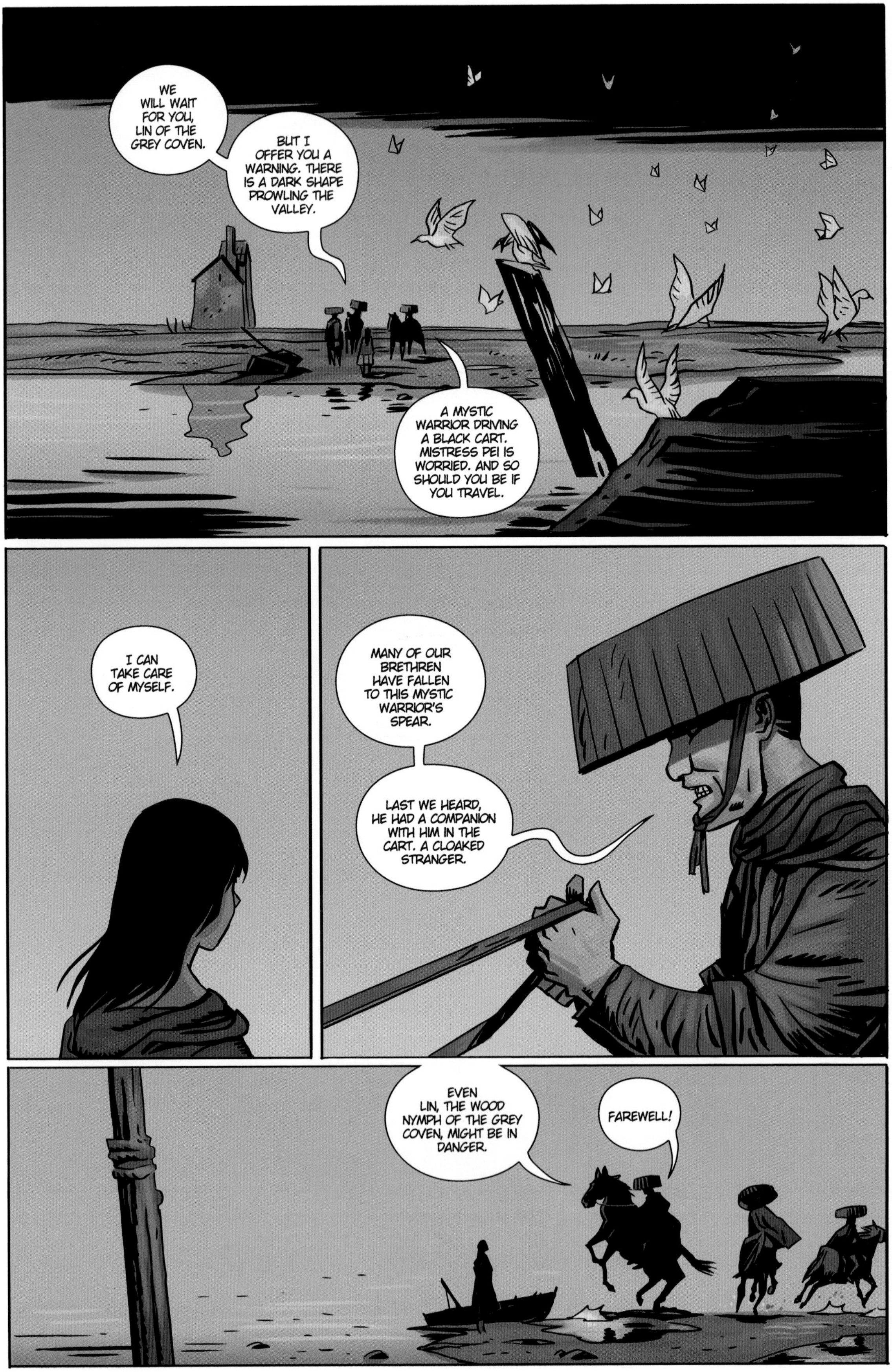
WE WILL WAIT FOR YOU, LIN OF THE GREY COVEN.
BUT I OFFER YOU A WARNING. THERE IS A DARK SHAPE PROWLING THE VALLEY.
A MYSTIC WARRIOR DRIVING A BLACK CART. MISTRESS PEI IS WORRIED. AND SO SHOULD YOU BE IF YOU TRAVEL.
I CAN TAKE CARE OF MYSELF.
MANY OF OUR BRETHREN HAVE FALLEN TO THIS MYSTIC WARRIOR'S SPEAR.
LAST WE HEARD, HE HAD A COMPANION WITH HIM IN THE CART. A CLOAKED STRANGER.
EVEN LIN, THE WOOD NYMPH OF THE GREY COVEN, MIGHT BE IN DANGER.
FAREWELL!

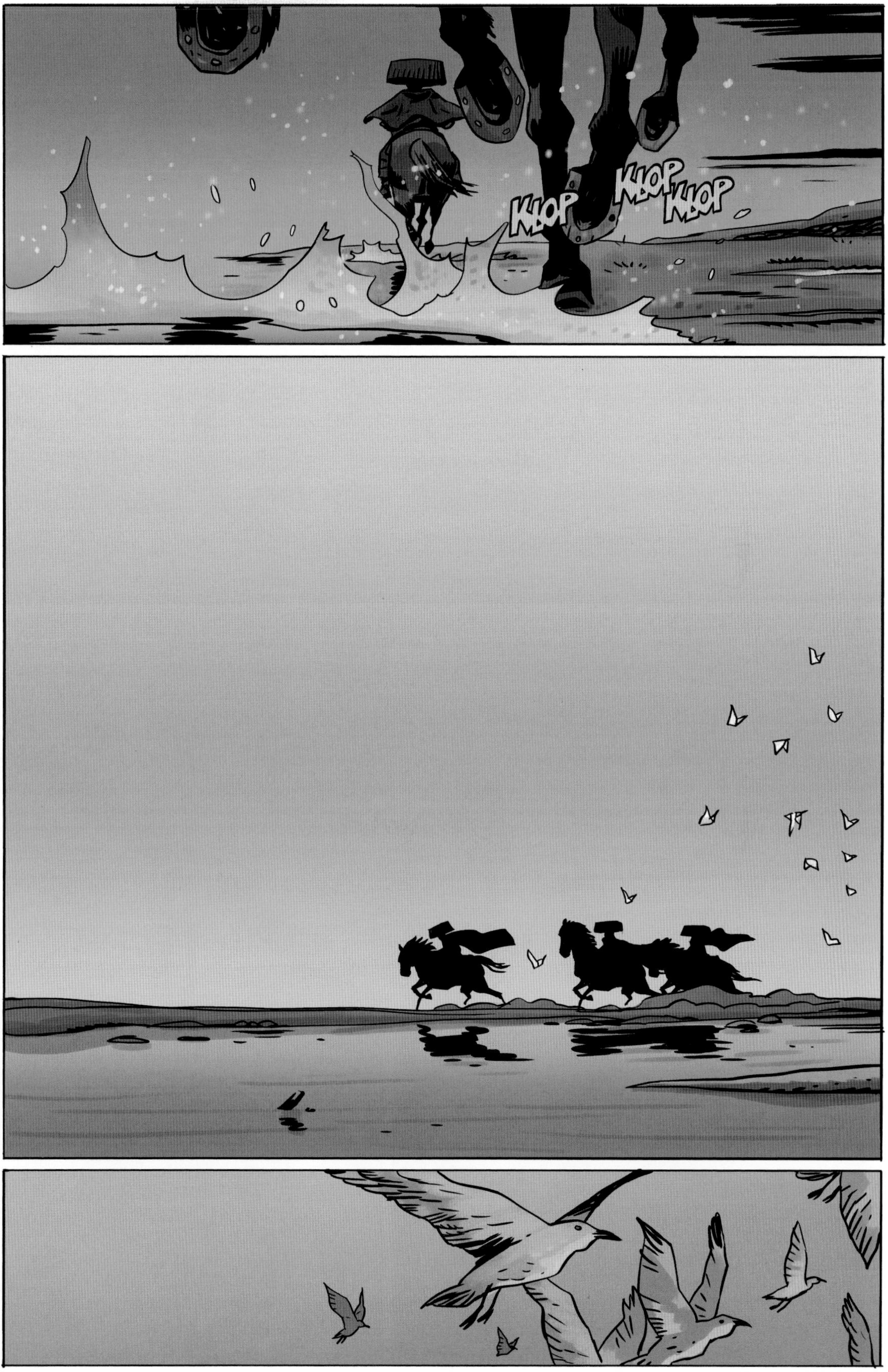
KLOP
KLOP
KLOP

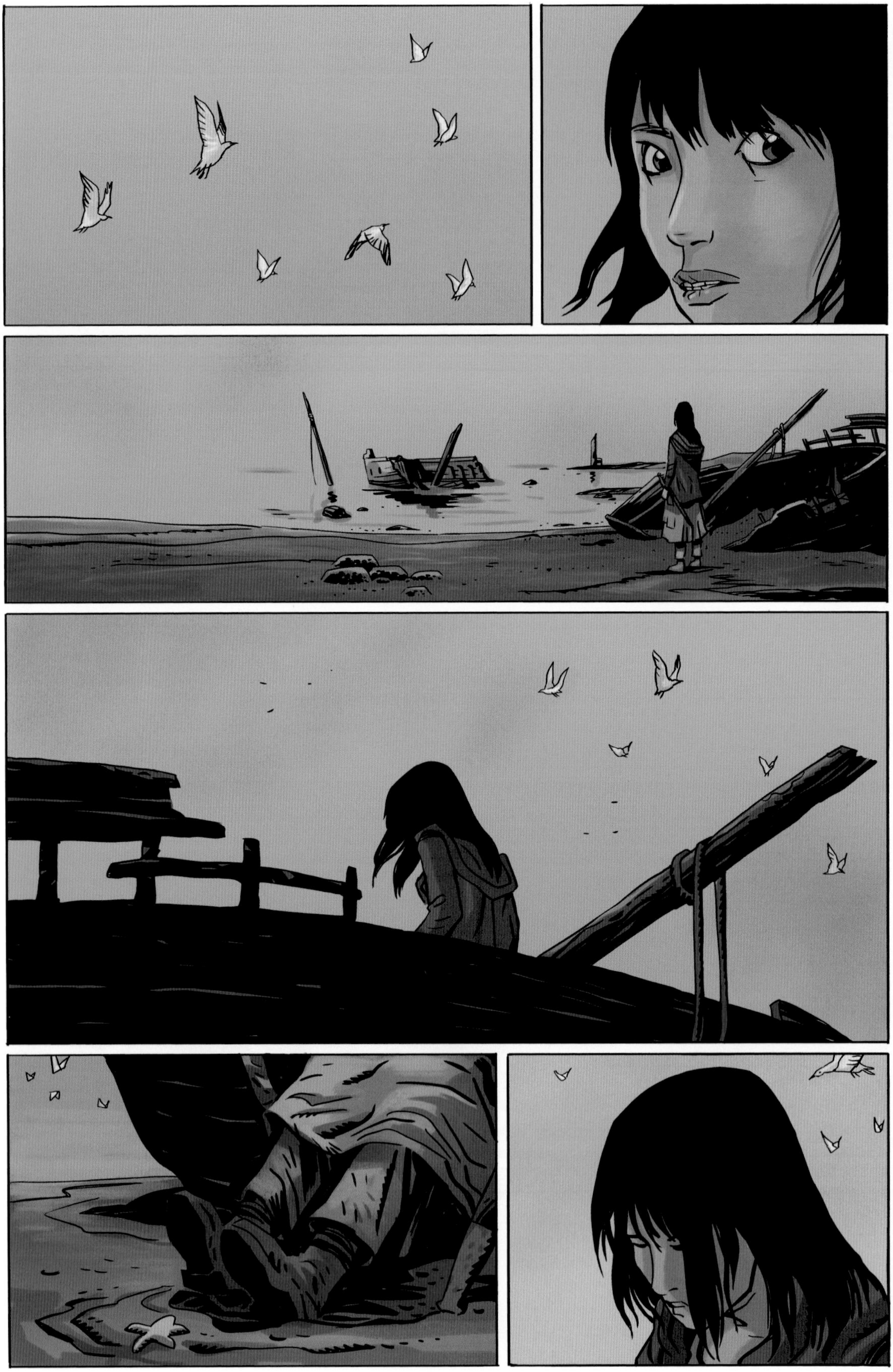

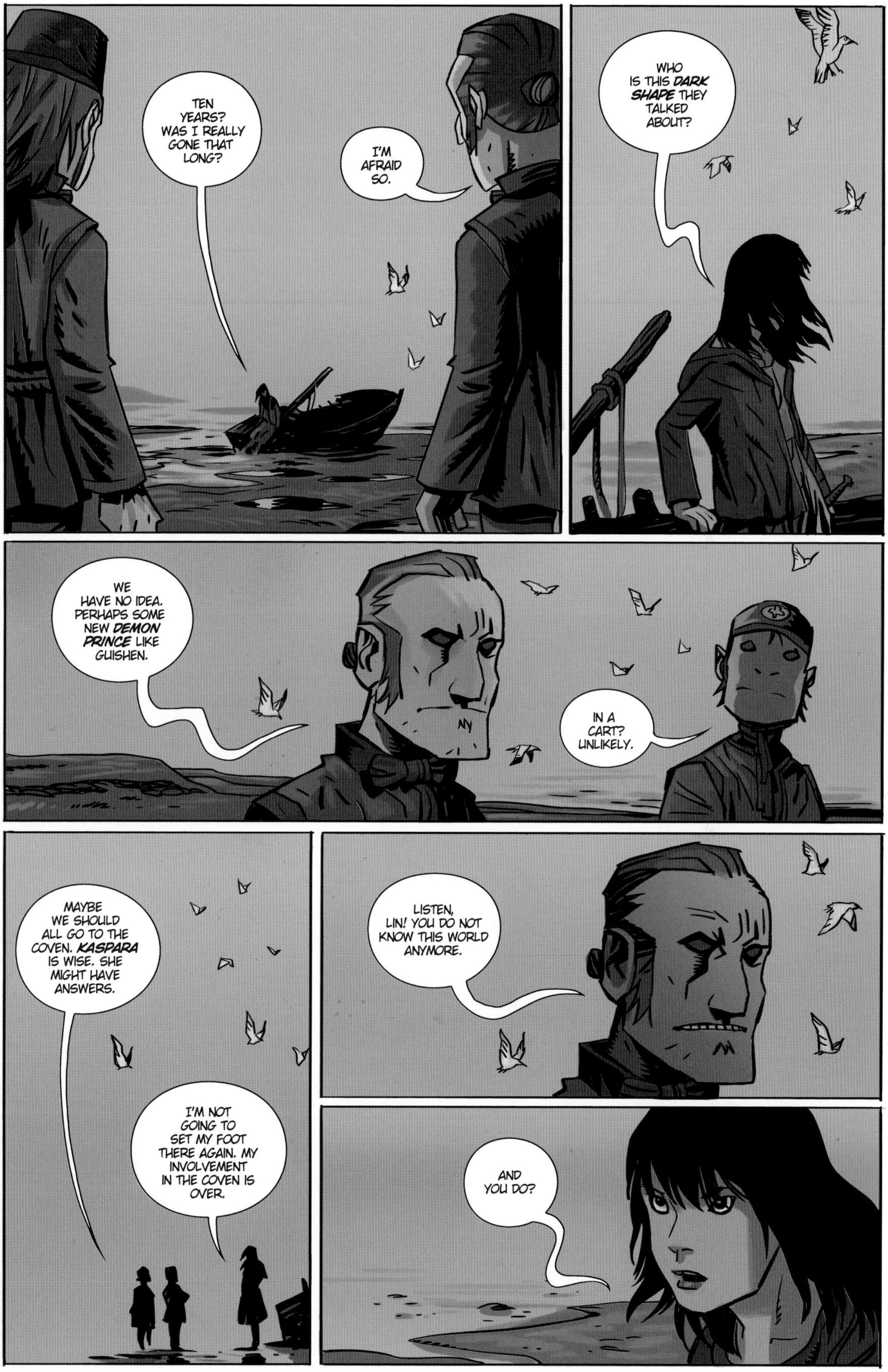
TEN YEARS? WAS I REALLY GONE THAT LONG?
I'M AFRAID SO.
WHO IS THIS DARK SHAPE THEY TALKED ABOUT?
WE HAVE NO IDEA. PERHAPS SOME NEW DEMON PRINCE LIKE GUISHEN.
IN A CART? UNLIKELY.
MAYBE WE SHOULD ALL GO TO THE COVEN. KASPARA IS WISE. SHE MIGHT HAVE ANSWERS.
I'M NOT GOING TO SET MY FOOT THERE AGAIN. MY INVOLVEMENT IN THE COVEN IS OVER.
LISTEN, LIN! YOU DO NOT KNOW THIS WORLD ANYMORE.
AND YOU DO?

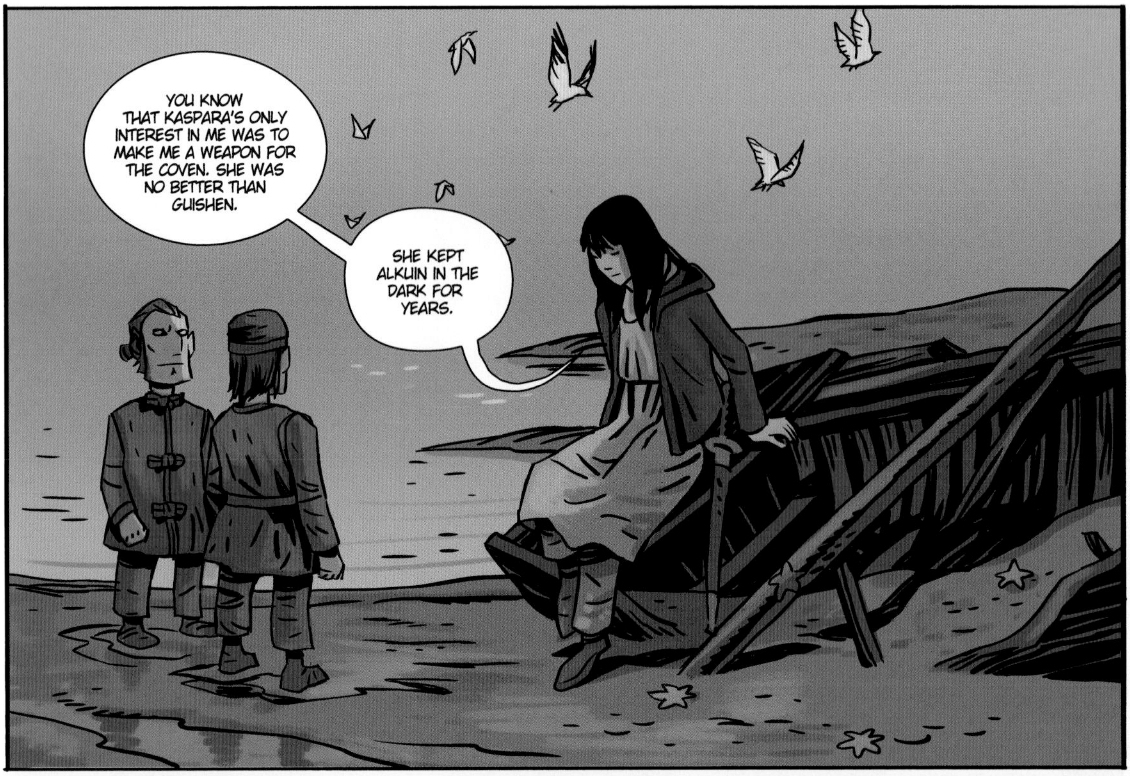
YOU KNOW THAT KASPARA'S ONLY INTEREST IN ME WAS TO MAKE ME A WEAPON FOR THE COVEN. SHE WAS NO BETTER THAN GUISHEN.
SHE KEPT ALKUIN IN THE DARK FOR YEARS.

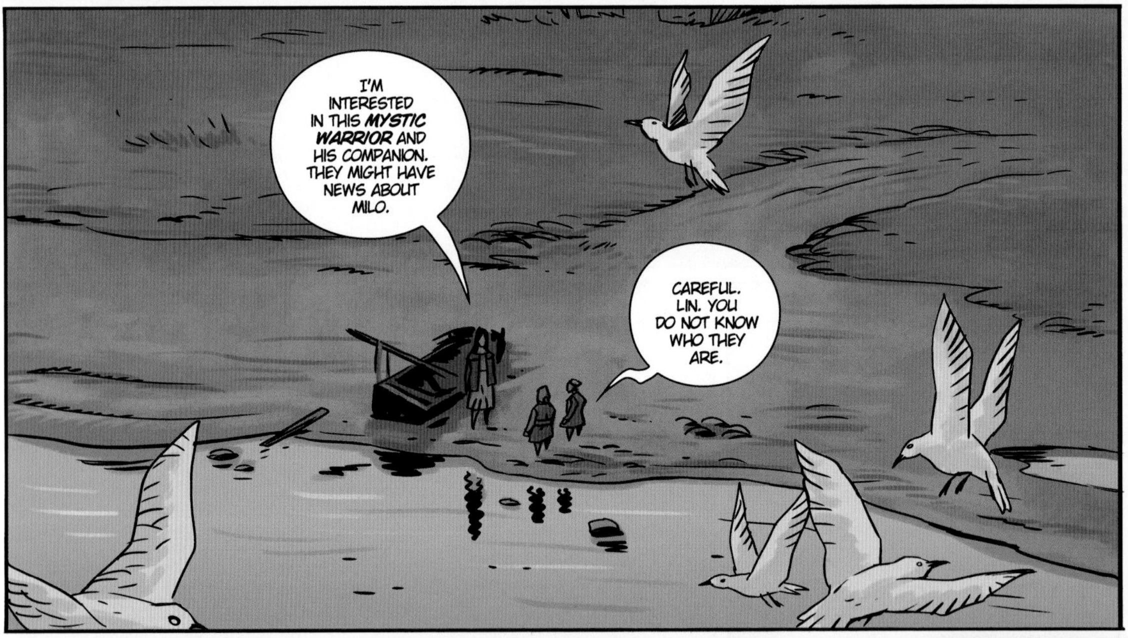
I'M INTERESTED IN THIS ***MYSTIC WARRIOR*** AND HIS COMPANION. THEY MIGHT HAVE NEWS ABOUT MILO.
CAREFUL. LIN. YOU DO NOT KNOW WHO THEY ARE.

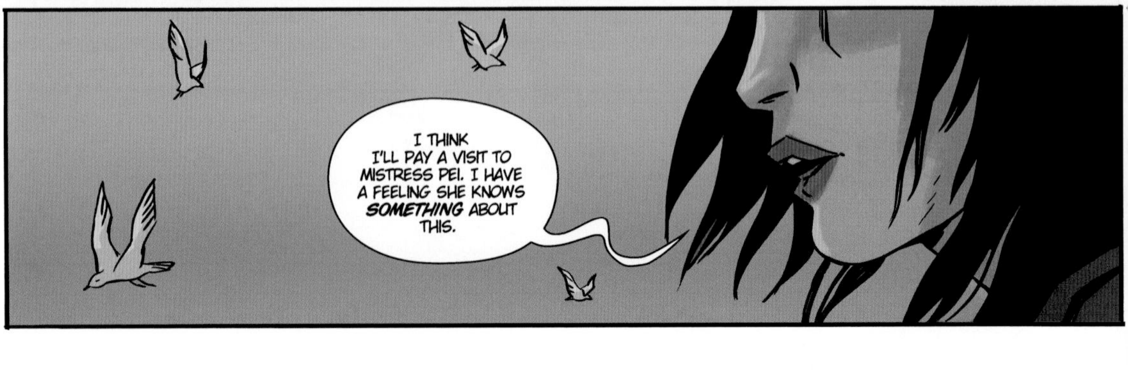
I THINK I'LL PAY A VISIT TO MISTRESS PEI. I HAVE A FEELING SHE KNOWS ***SOMETHING*** ABOUT THIS.

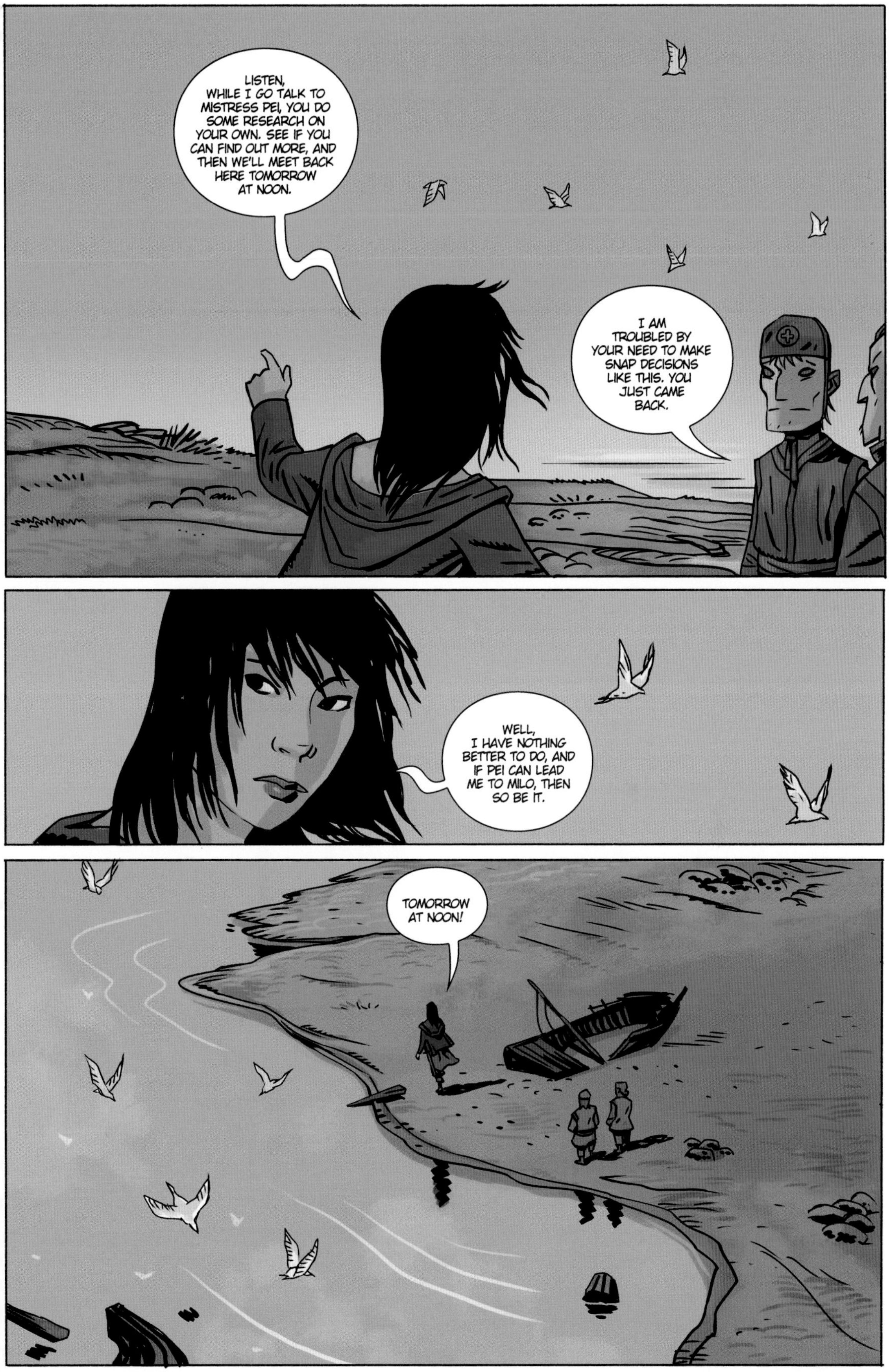
LISTEN, WHILE I GO TALK TO MISTRESS PEI, YOU DO SOME RESEARCH ON YOUR OWN. SEE IF YOU CAN FIND OUT MORE, AND THEN WE'LL MEET BACK HERE TOMORROW AT NOON.
I AM TROUBLED BY YOUR NEED TO MAKE SNAP DECISIONS LIKE THIS. YOU JUST CAME BACK.
WELL, I HAVE NOTHING BETTER TO DO, AND IF PEI CAN LEAD ME TO MILO, THEN SO BE IT.
TOMORROW AT NOON!

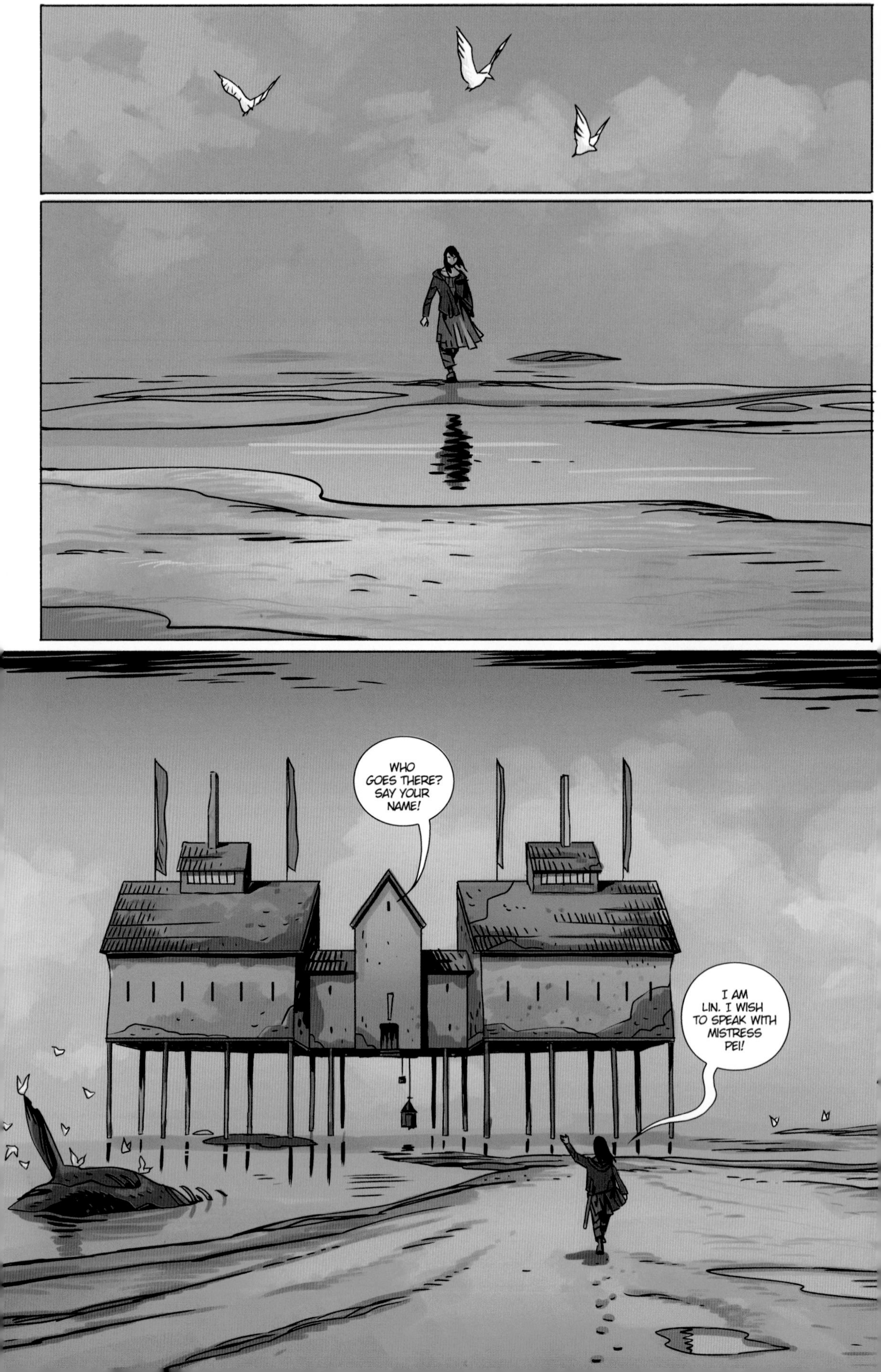
WHO GOES THERE? SAY YOUR NAME!
I AM LIN. I WISH TO SPEAK WITH MISTRESS PEI!

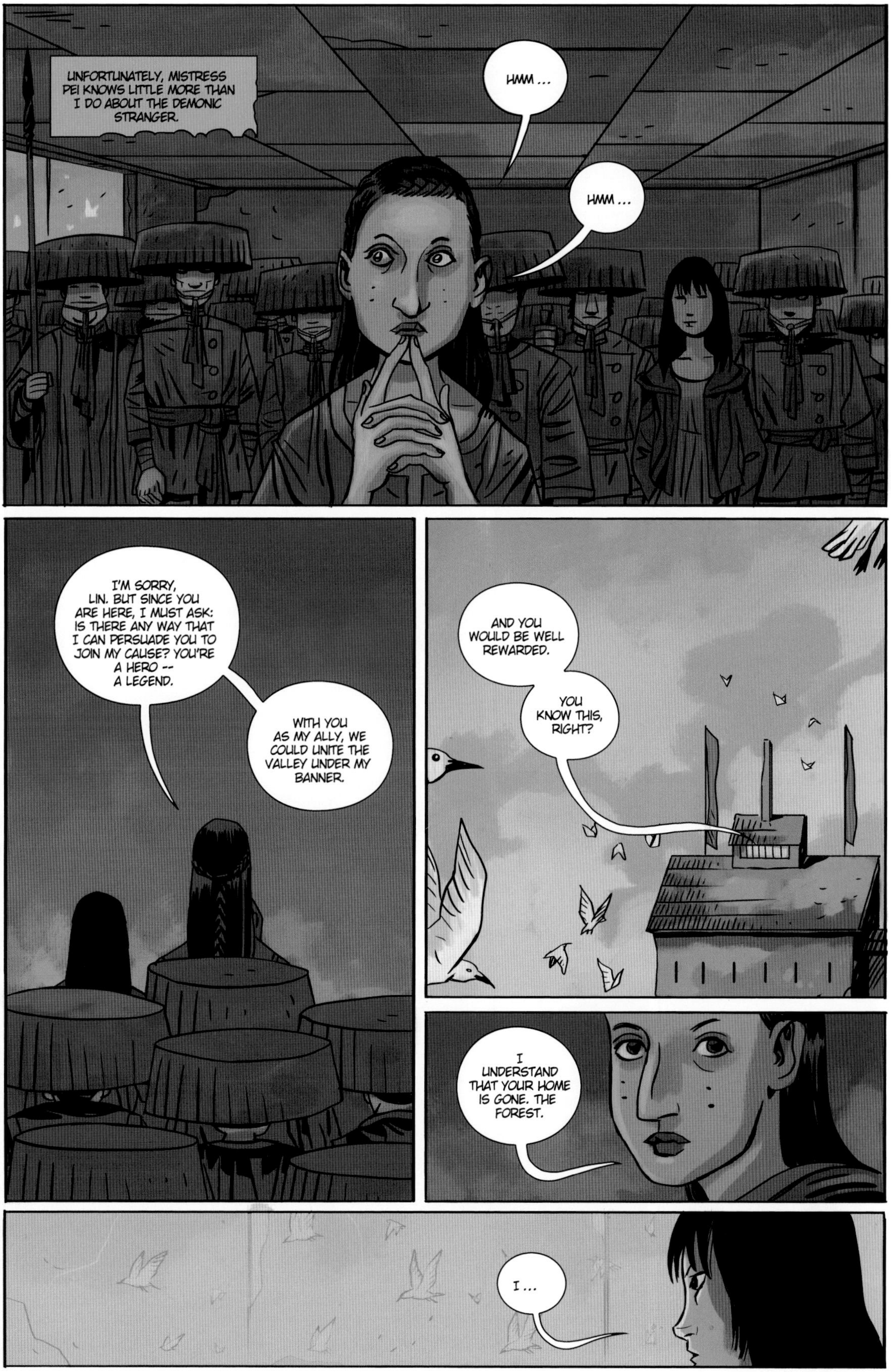
UNFORTUNATELY, MISTRESS PEI KNOWS LITTLE MORE THAN I DO ABOUT THE DEMONIC STRANGER.
HMM ...
HMM ...
I'M SORRY, LIN. BUT SINCE YOU ARE HERE, I MUST ASK: IS THERE ANY WAY THAT I CAN PERSUADE YOU TO JOIN MY CAUSE? YOU'RE A HERO -- A LEGEND.
WITH YOU AS MY ALLY, WE COULD UNITE THE VALLEY UNDER MY BANNER.
AND YOU WOULD BE WELL REWARDED.
YOU KNOW THIS, RIGHT?
I UNDERSTAND THAT YOUR HOME IS GONE. THE FOREST.
I ...

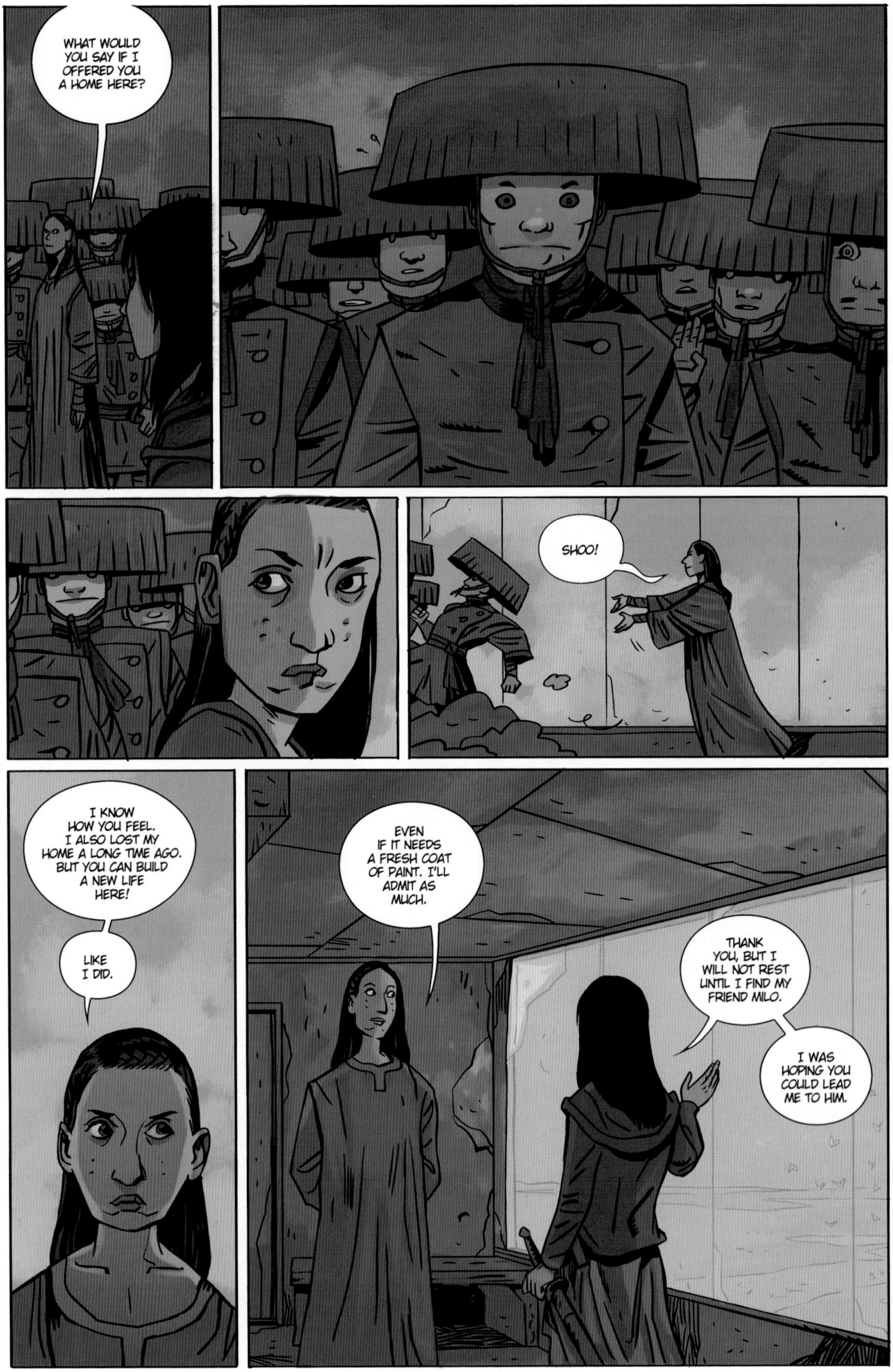
WHAT WOULD YOU SAY IF I OFFERED YOU A HOME HERE?
SHOO!
I KNOW HOW YOU FEEL. I ALSO LOST MY HOME A LONG TIME AGO. BUT YOU CAN BUILD A NEW LIFE HERE!
LIKE I DID.
EVEN IF IT NEEDS A FRESH COAT OF PAINT. I'LL ADMIT AS MUCH.
THANK YOU, BUT I WILL NOT REST UNTIL I FIND MY FRIEND MILO.
I WAS HOPING YOU COULD LEAD ME TO HIM.

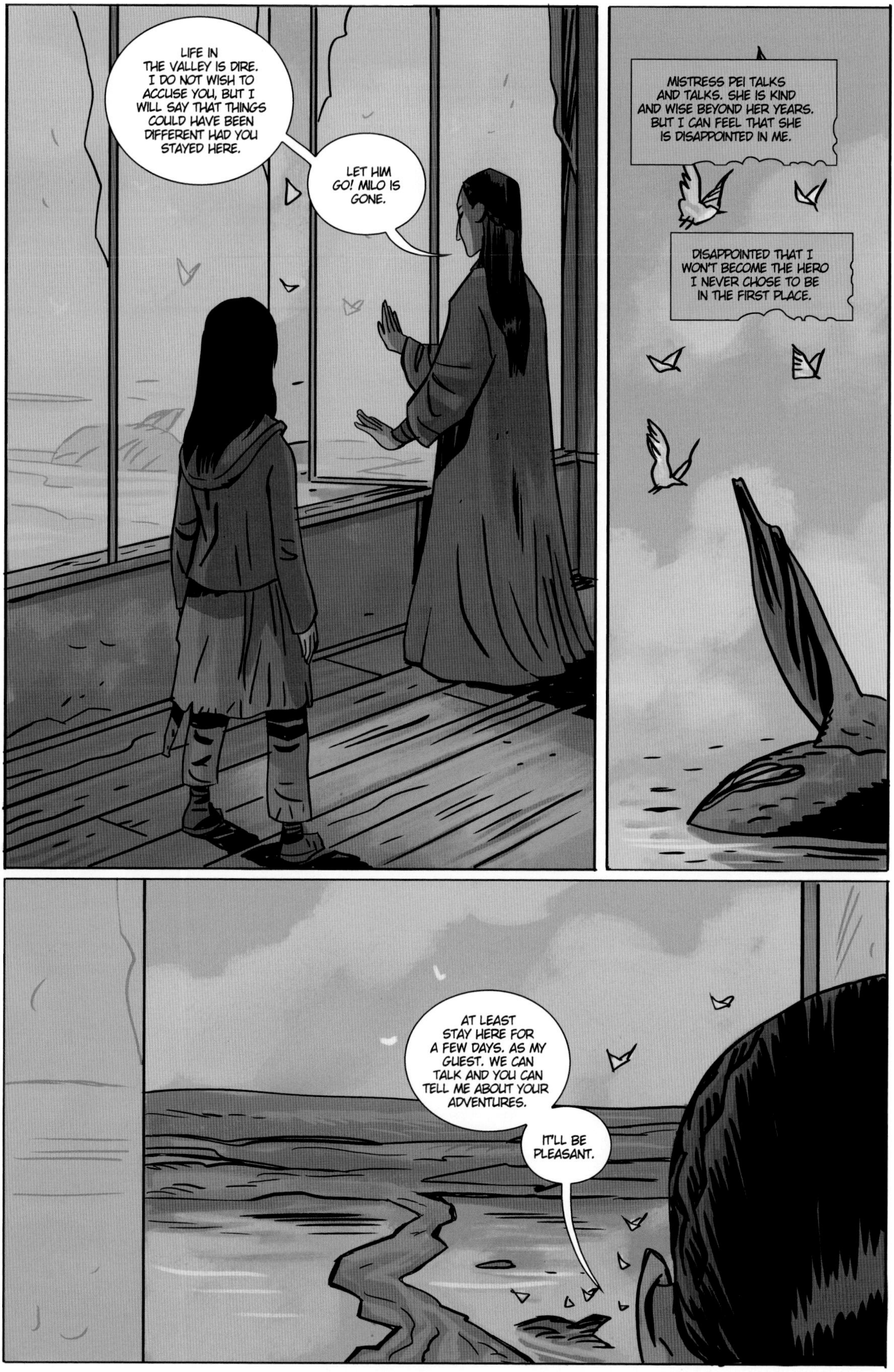
LIFE IN THE VALLEY IS DIRE. I DO NOT WISH TO ACCUSE YOU, BUT I WILL SAY THAT THINGS COULD HAVE BEEN DIFFERENT HAD YOU STAYED HERE.
LET HIM GO! MILO IS GONE.
MISTRESS PEI TALKS AND TALKS. SHE IS KIND AND WISE BEYOND HER YEARS. BUT I CAN FEEL THAT SHE IS DISAPPOINTED IN ME.
DISAPPOINTED THAT I WON'T BECOME THE HERO I NEVER CHOSE TO BE IN THE FIRST PLACE.
AT LEAST STAY HERE FOR A FEW DAYS. AS MY GUEST. WE CAN TALK AND YOU CAN TELL ME ABOUT YOUR ADVENTURES.
IT'LL BE PLEASANT.

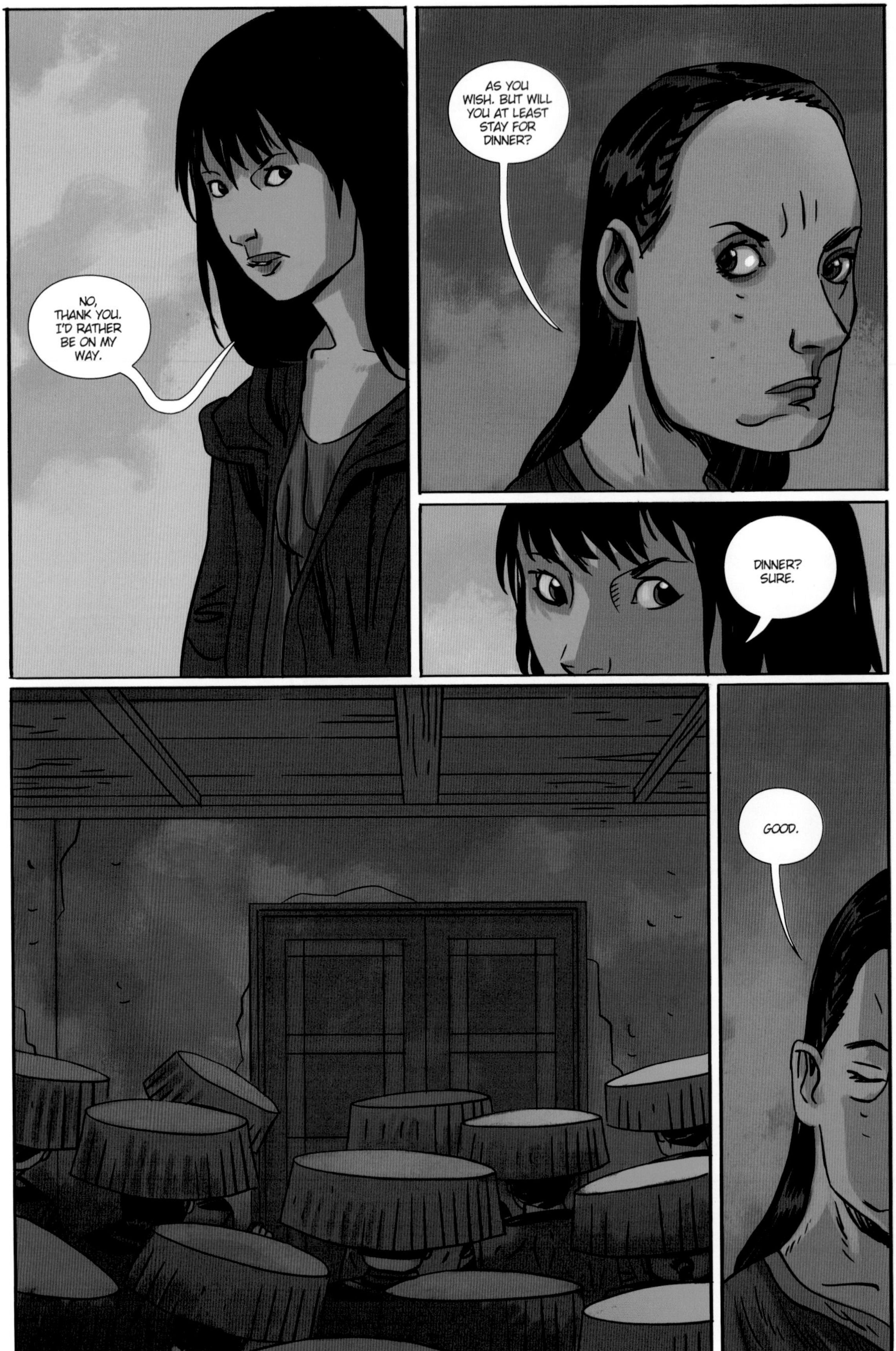
NO, THANK YOU. I'D RATHER BE ON MY WAY.
AS YOU WISH. BUT WILL YOU AT LEAST STAY FOR DINNER?
DINNER? SURE.
GOOD.

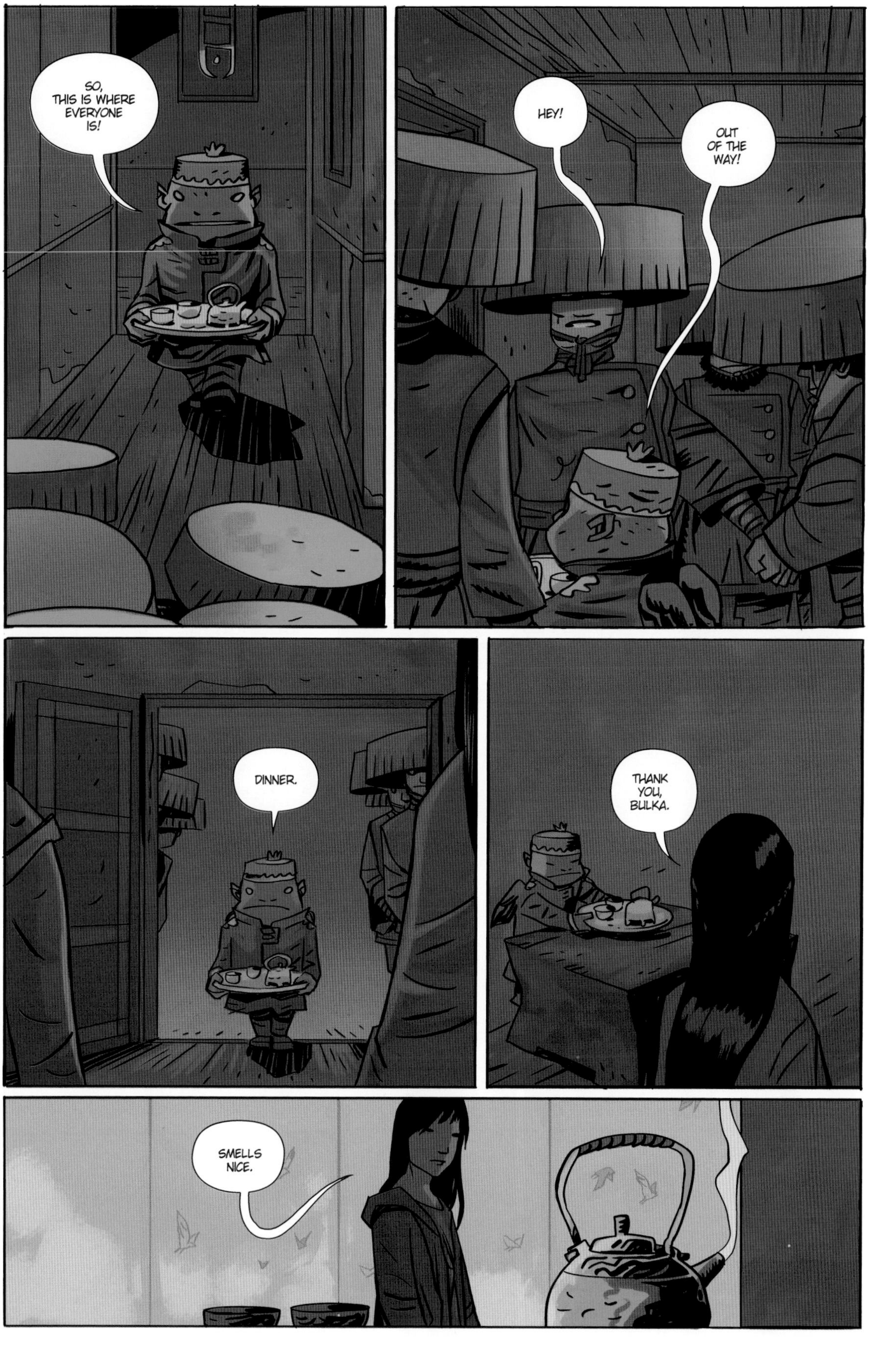
SO, THIS IS WHERE EVERYONE IS!
HEY!
OUT OF THE WAY!
DINNER.
THANK YOU, BULKA.
SMELLS NICE.

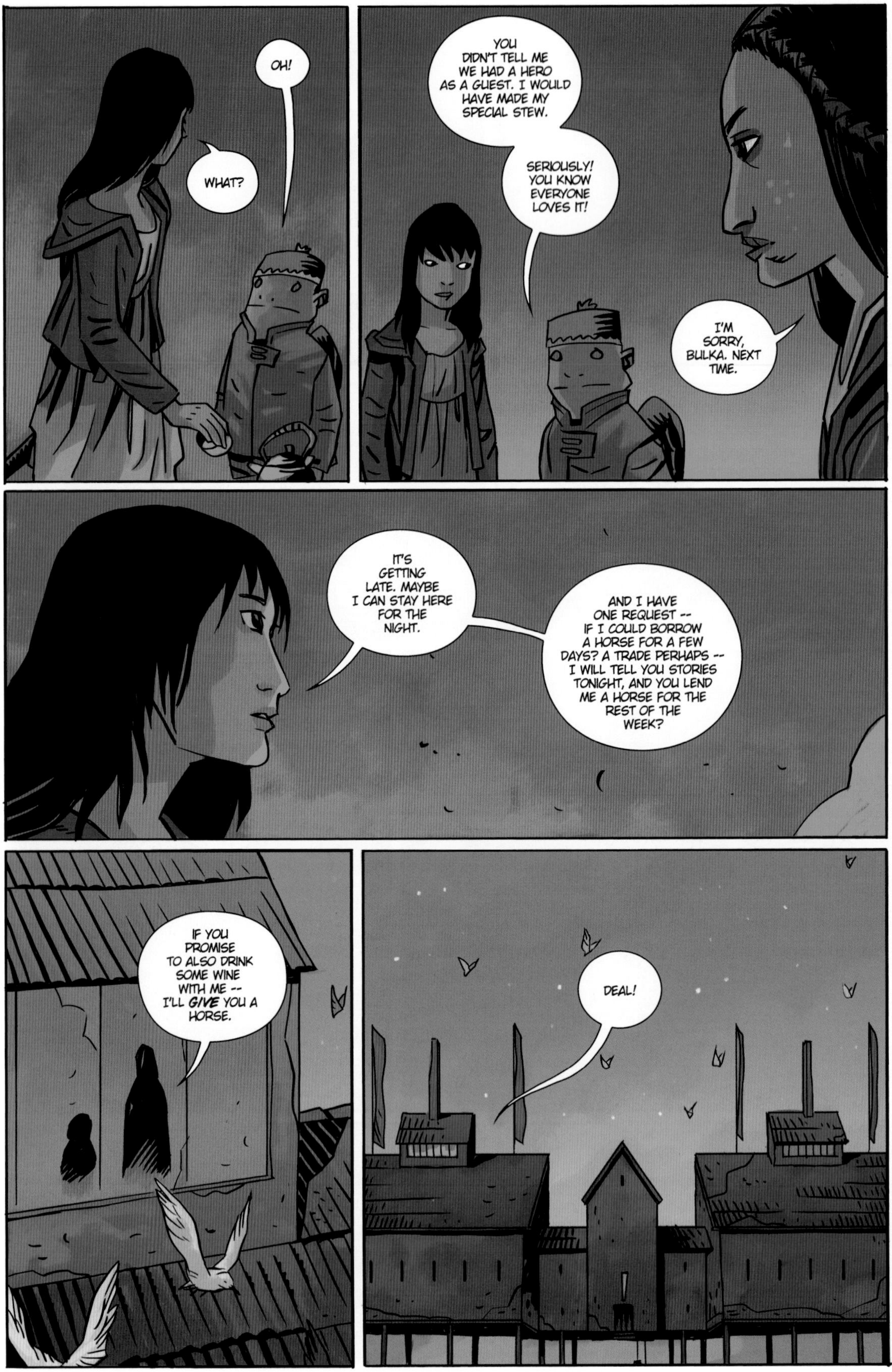
OH!
WHAT?
YOU DIDN'T TELL ME WE HAD A HERO AS A GUEST. I WOULD HAVE MADE MY SPECIAL STEW.
SERIOUSLY! YOU KNOW EVERYONE LOVES IT!
I'M SORRY, BULKA. NEXT TIME.
IT'S GETTING LATE. MAYBE I CAN STAY HERE FOR THE NIGHT.
AND I HAVE ONE REQUEST -- IF I COULD BORROW A HORSE FOR A FEW DAYS? A TRADE PERHAPS -- I WILL TELL YOU STORIES TONIGHT, AND YOU LEND ME A HORSE FOR THE REST OF THE WEEK?
IF YOU PROMISE TO ALSO DRINK SOME WINE WITH ME -- I'LL **GIVE** YOU A HORSE.
DEAL!

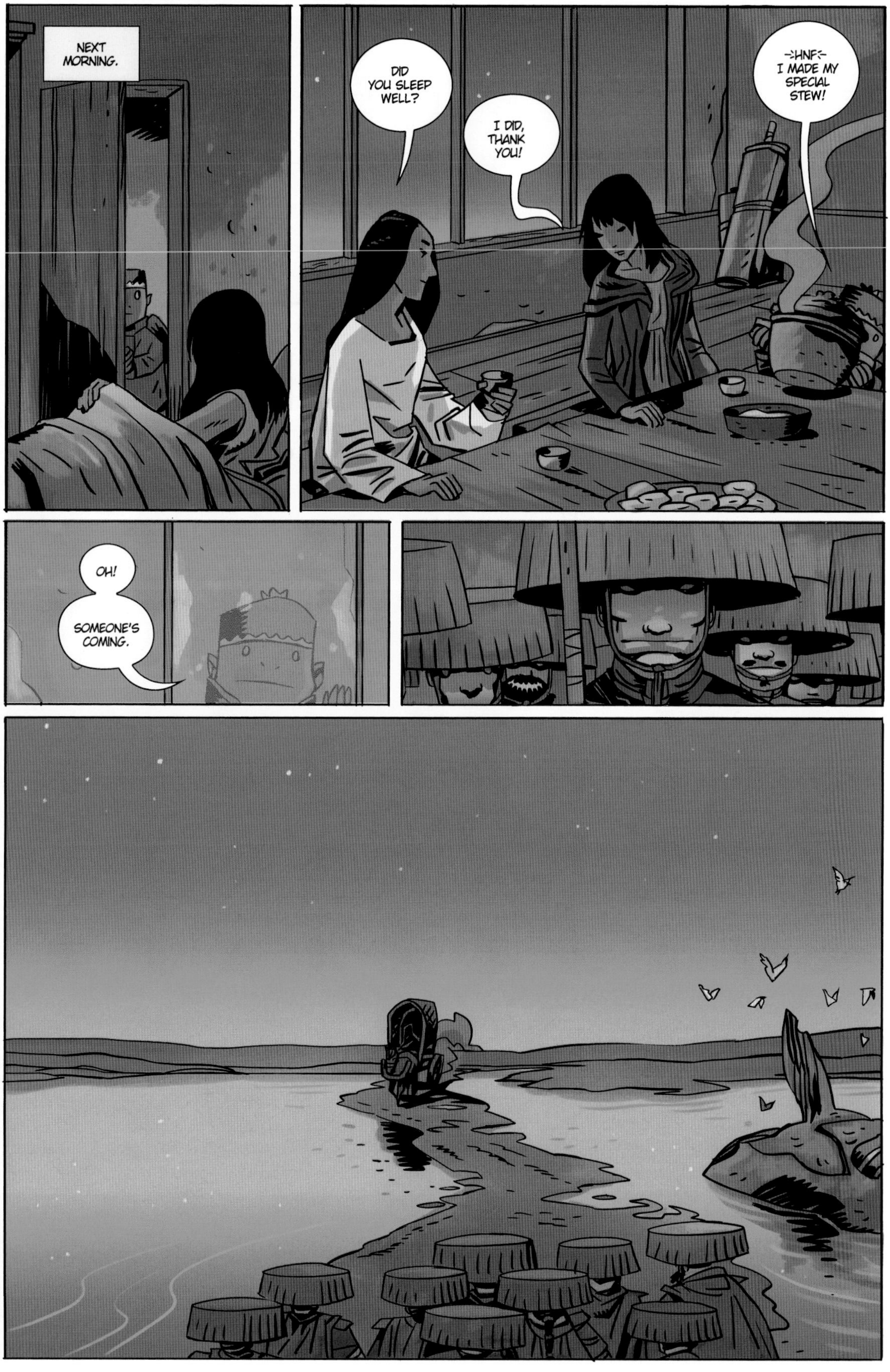
NEXT MORNING.
DID YOU SLEEP WELL?
I DID, THANK YOU!
-HNF- I MADE MY SPECIAL STEW!
OH!
SOMEONE'S COMING.

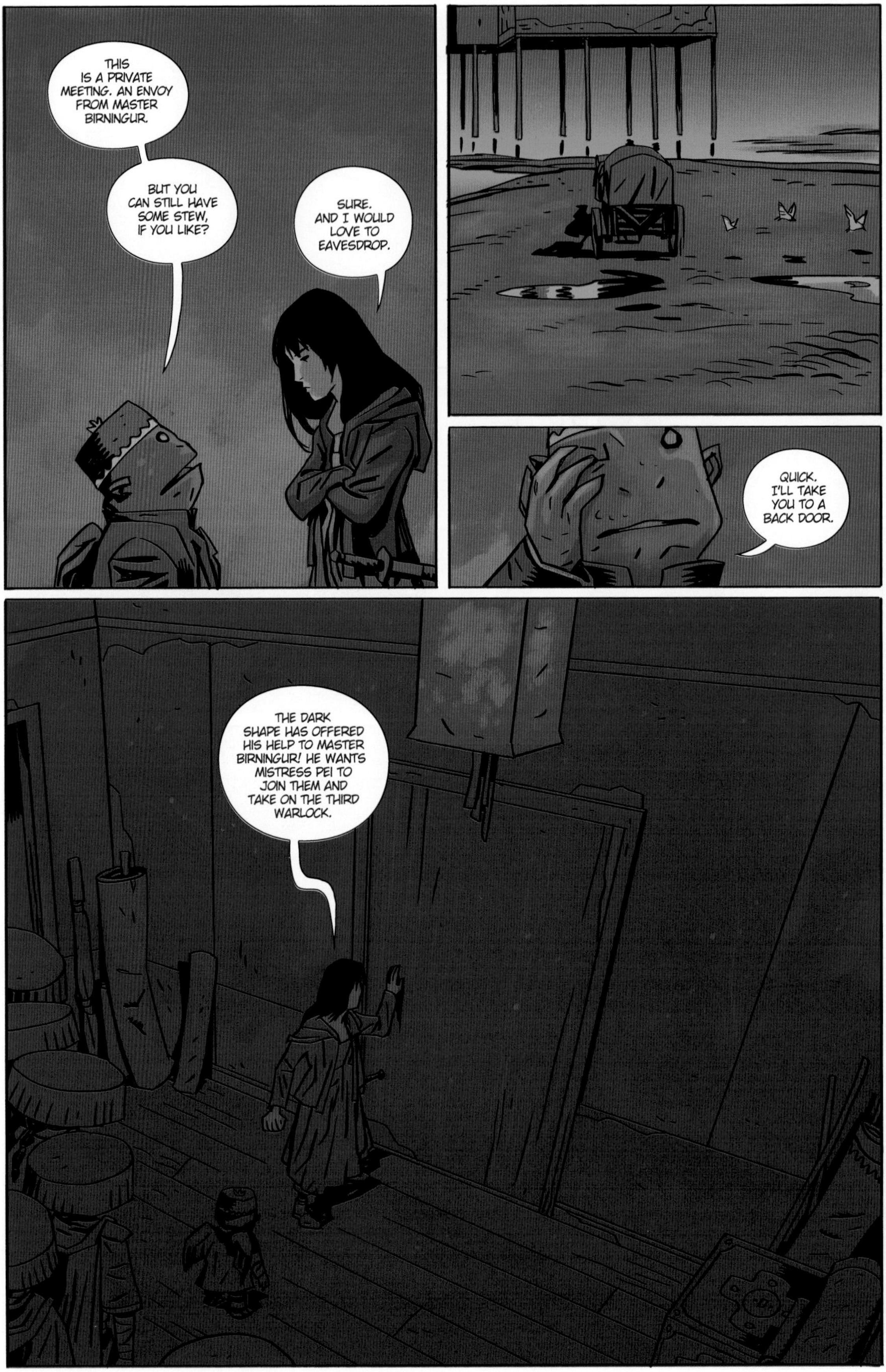
THIS IS A PRIVATE MEETING. AN ENVOY FROM MASTER BIRNINGUR.
BUT YOU CAN STILL HAVE SOME STEW, IF YOU LIKE?
SURE. AND I WOULD LOVE TO EAVESDROP.
QUICK. I'LL TAKE YOU TO A BACK DOOR.
THE DARK SHAPE HAS OFFERED HIS HELP TO MASTER BIRNINGUR! HE WANTS MISTRESS PEI TO JOIN THEM AND TAKE ON THE THIRD WARLOCK.

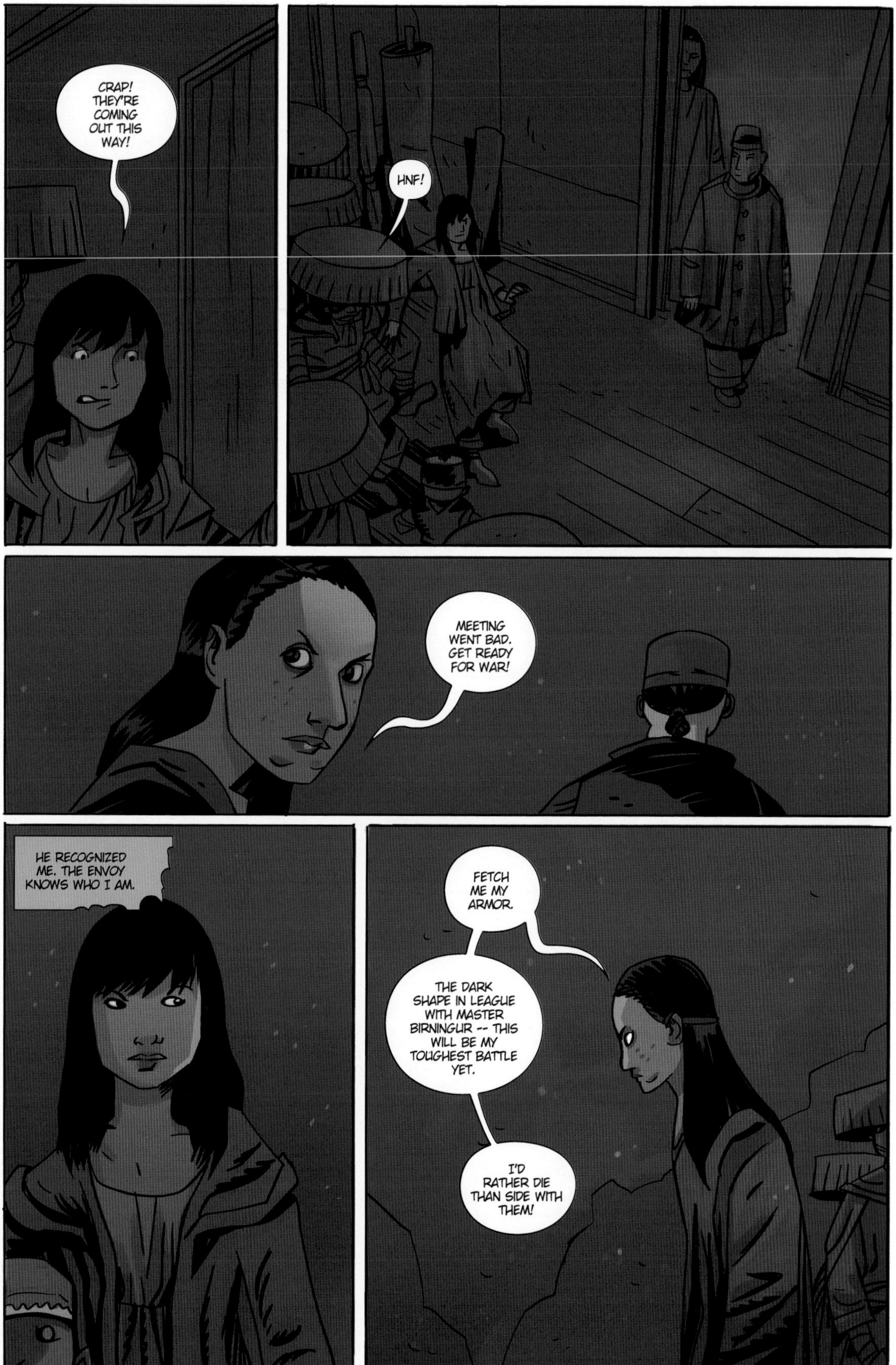
CRAP! THEY'RE COMING OUT THIS WAY!
HNF!
MEETING WENT BAD. GET READY FOR WAR!
HE RECOGNIZED ME. THE ENVOY KNOWS WHO I AM.
FETCH ME MY ARMOR.
THE DARK SHAPE IN LEAGUE WITH MASTER BIRNINGUR -- THIS WILL BE MY TOUGHEST BATTLE YET.
I'D RATHER DIE THAN SIDE WITH THEM!

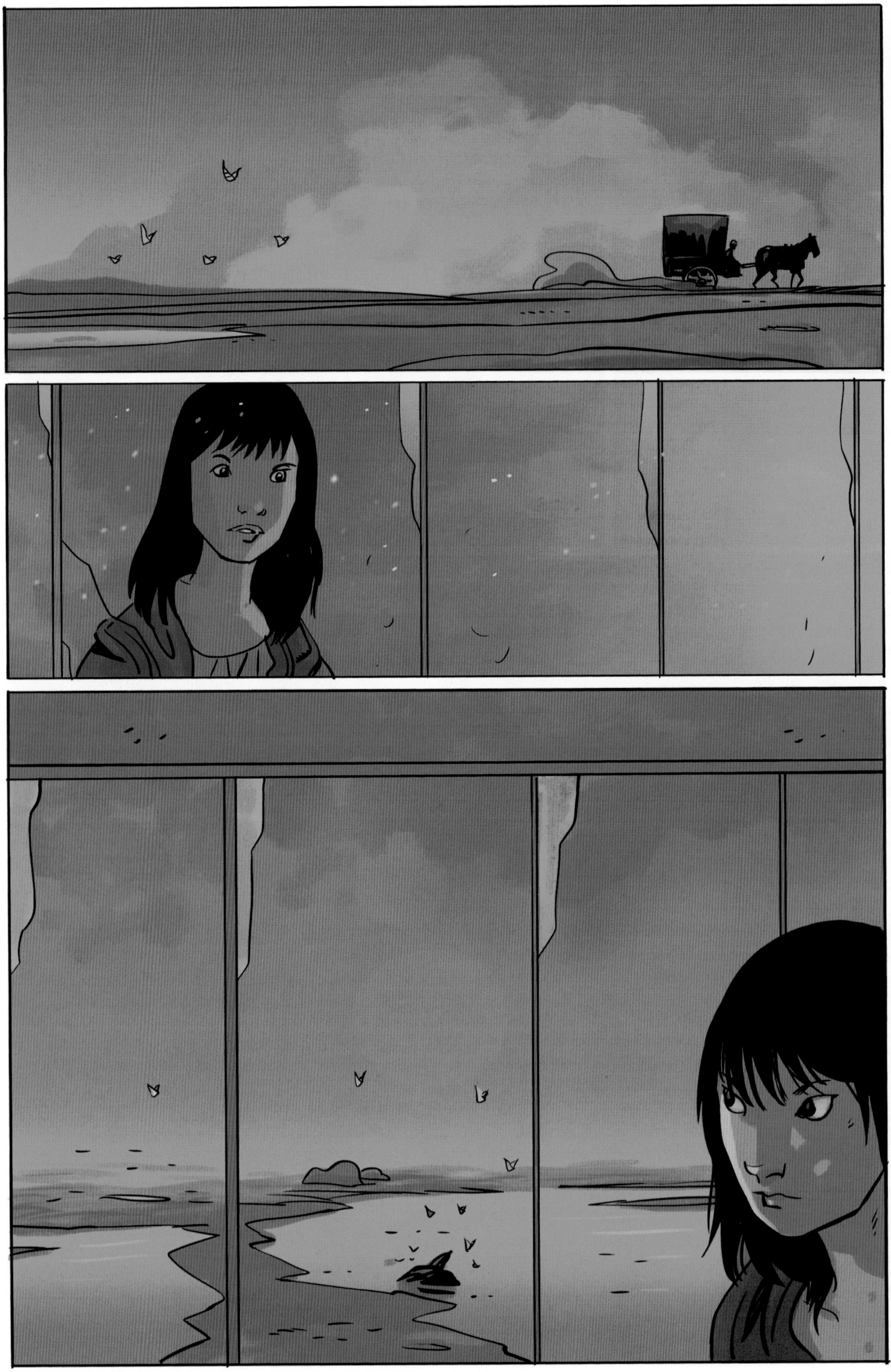

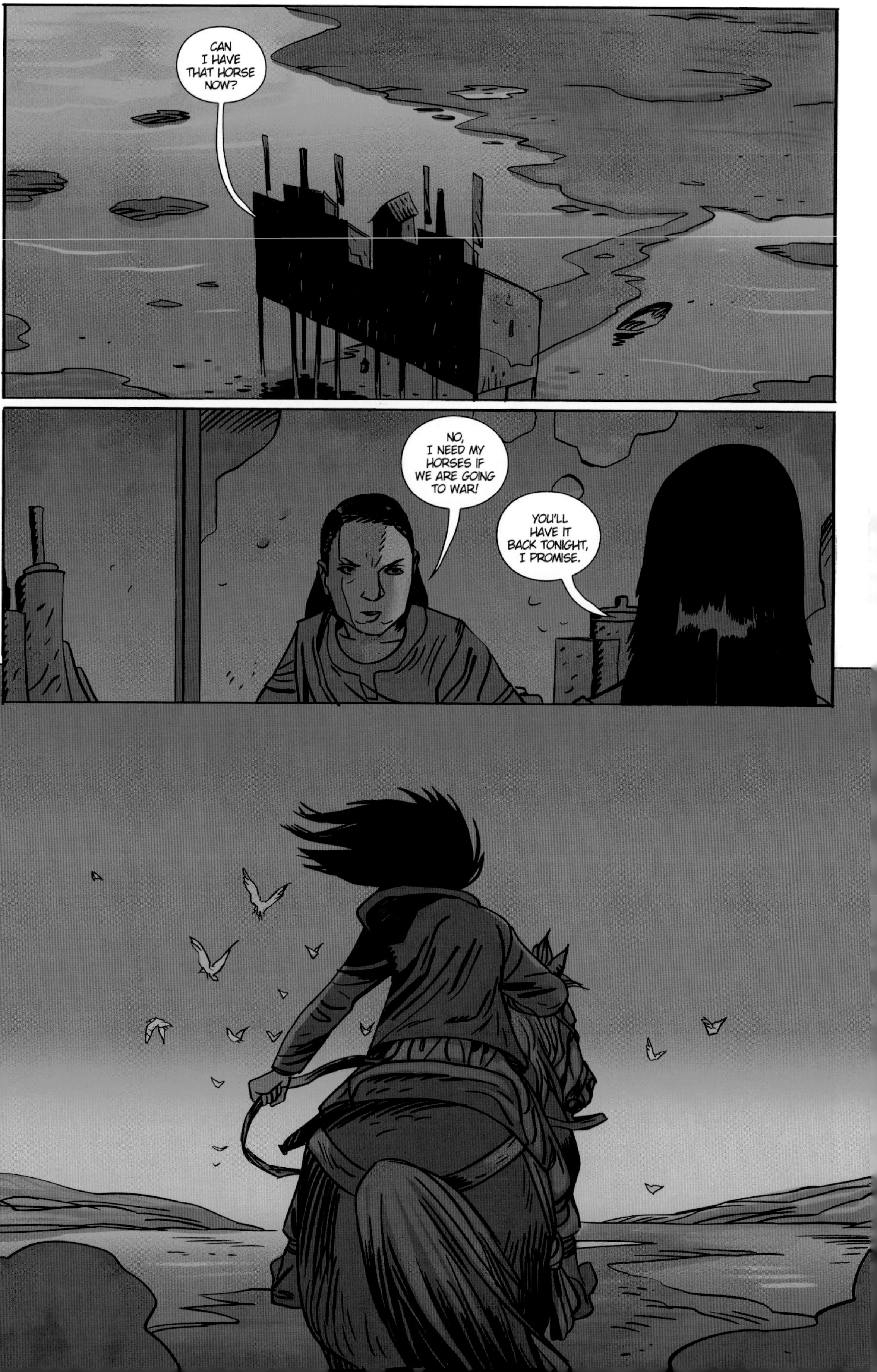
CAN I HAVE THAT HORSE NOW?
NO, I NEED MY HORSES IF WE ARE GOING TO WAR!
YOU'LL HAVE IT BACK TONIGHT, I PROMISE.

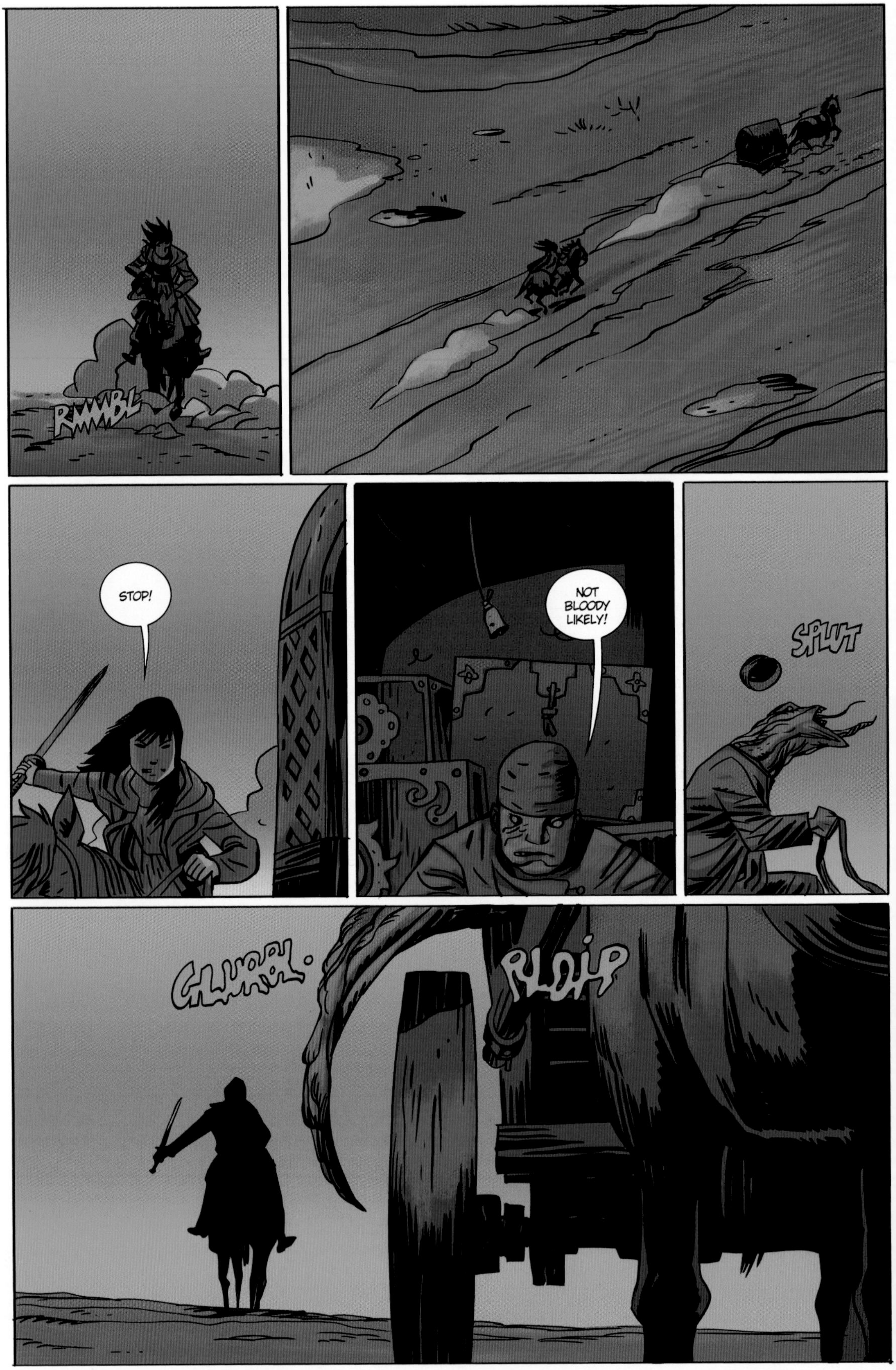
RMMBL
STOP!
NOT BLOODY LIKELY!
SPLUT
GLURRL
PLOIP

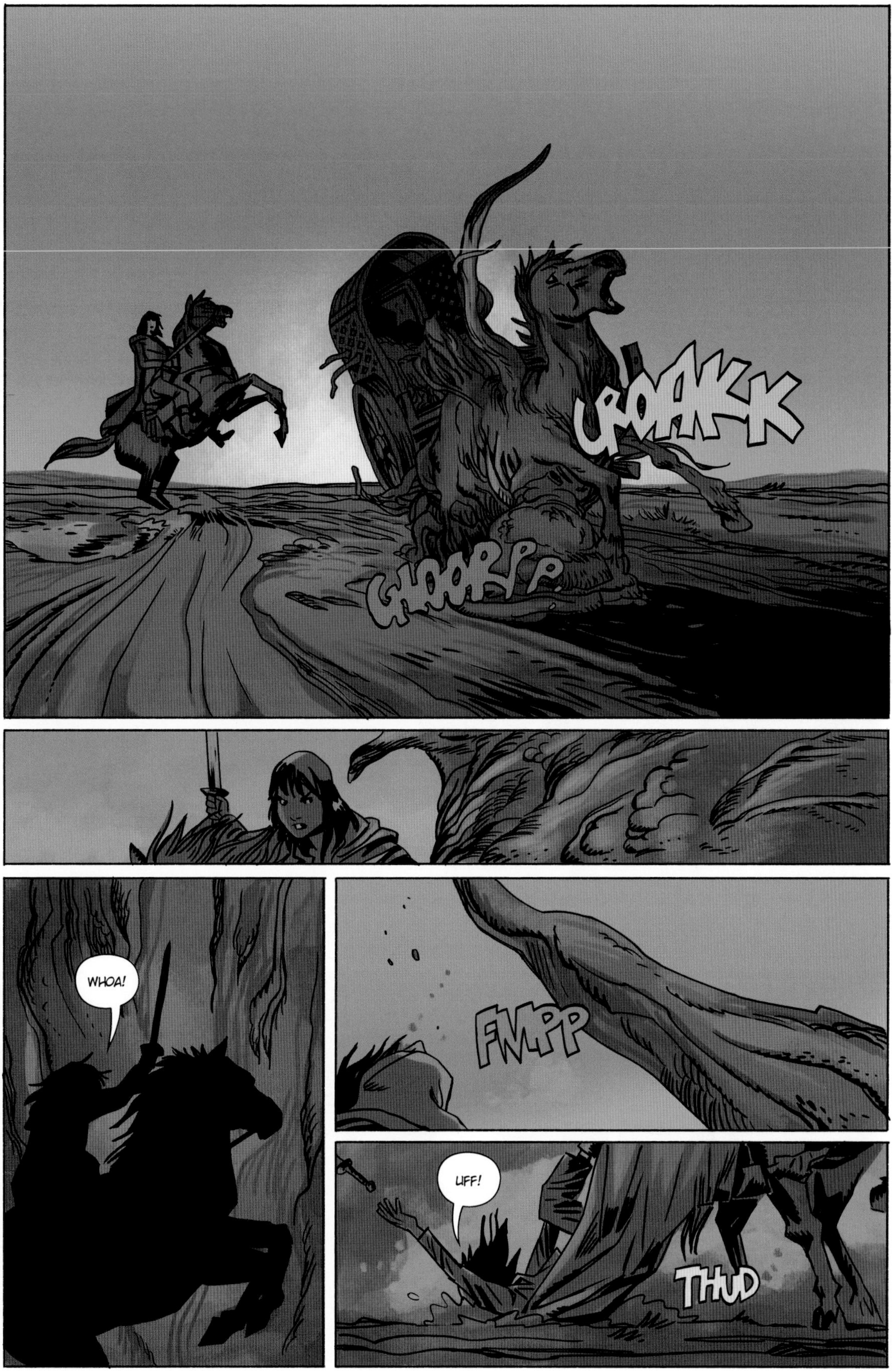
CROAKK
WHOA!
UFF!
THUD

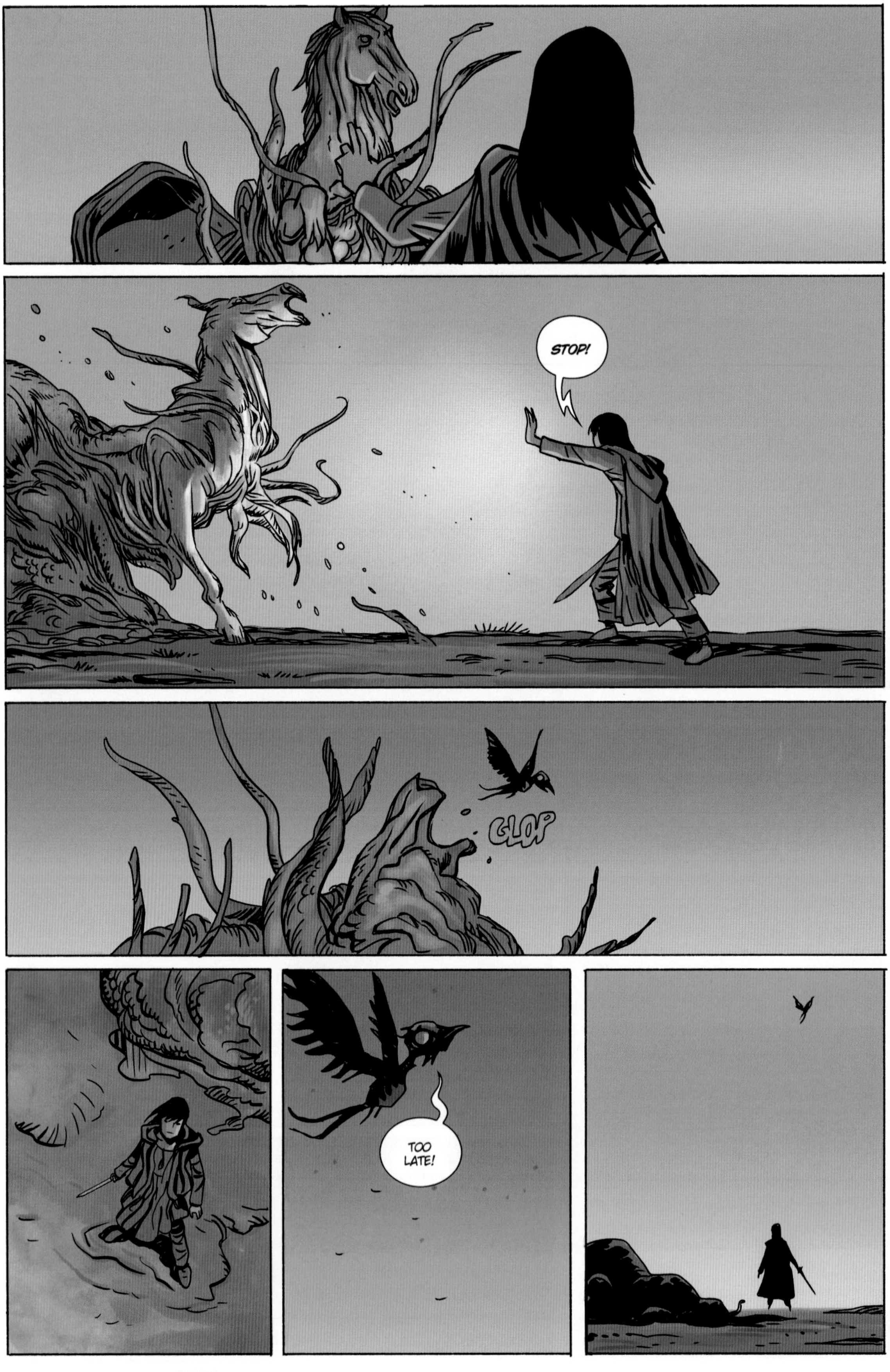
STOP!
GLOP
TOO LATE!

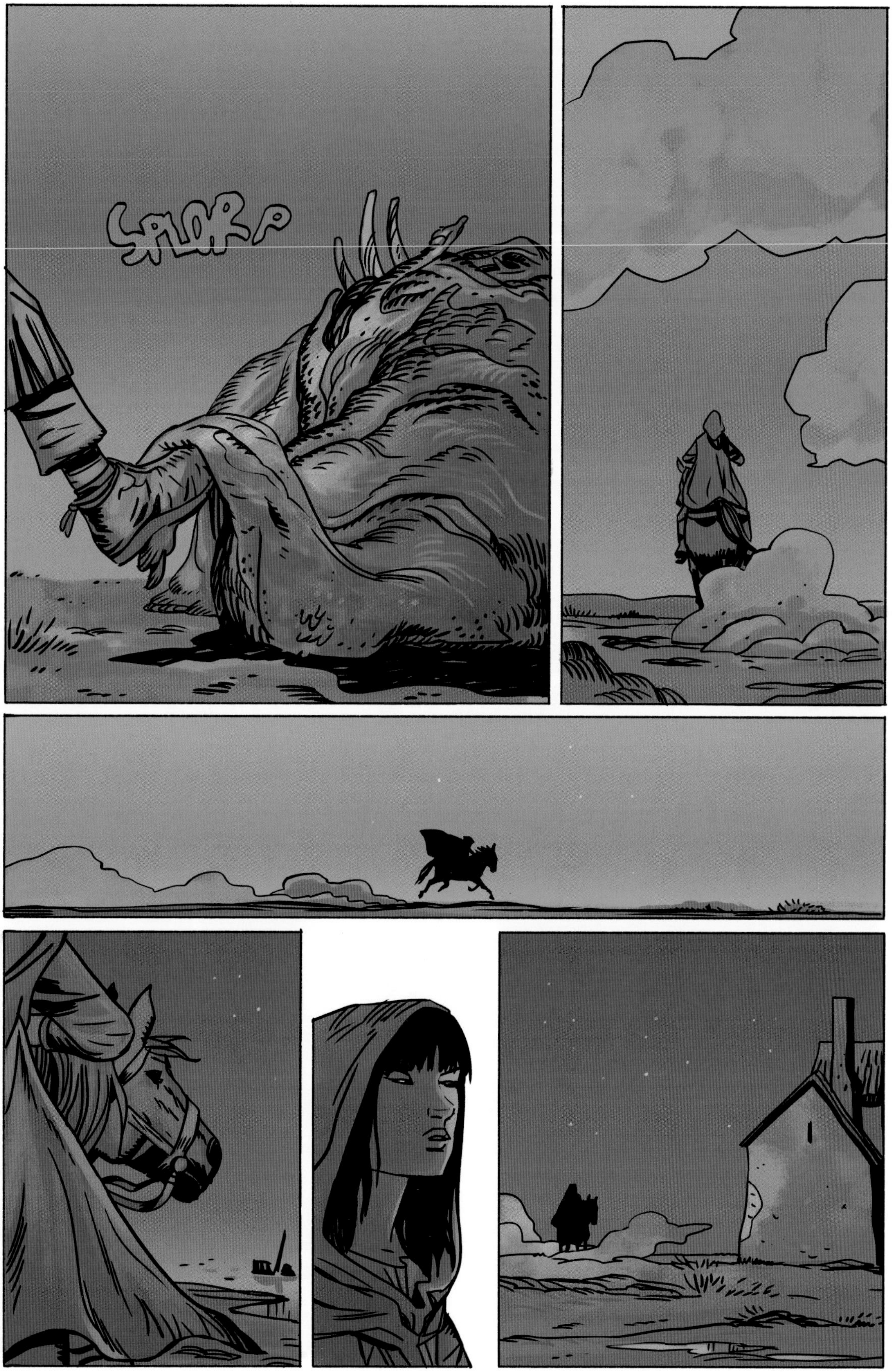
SPLORP

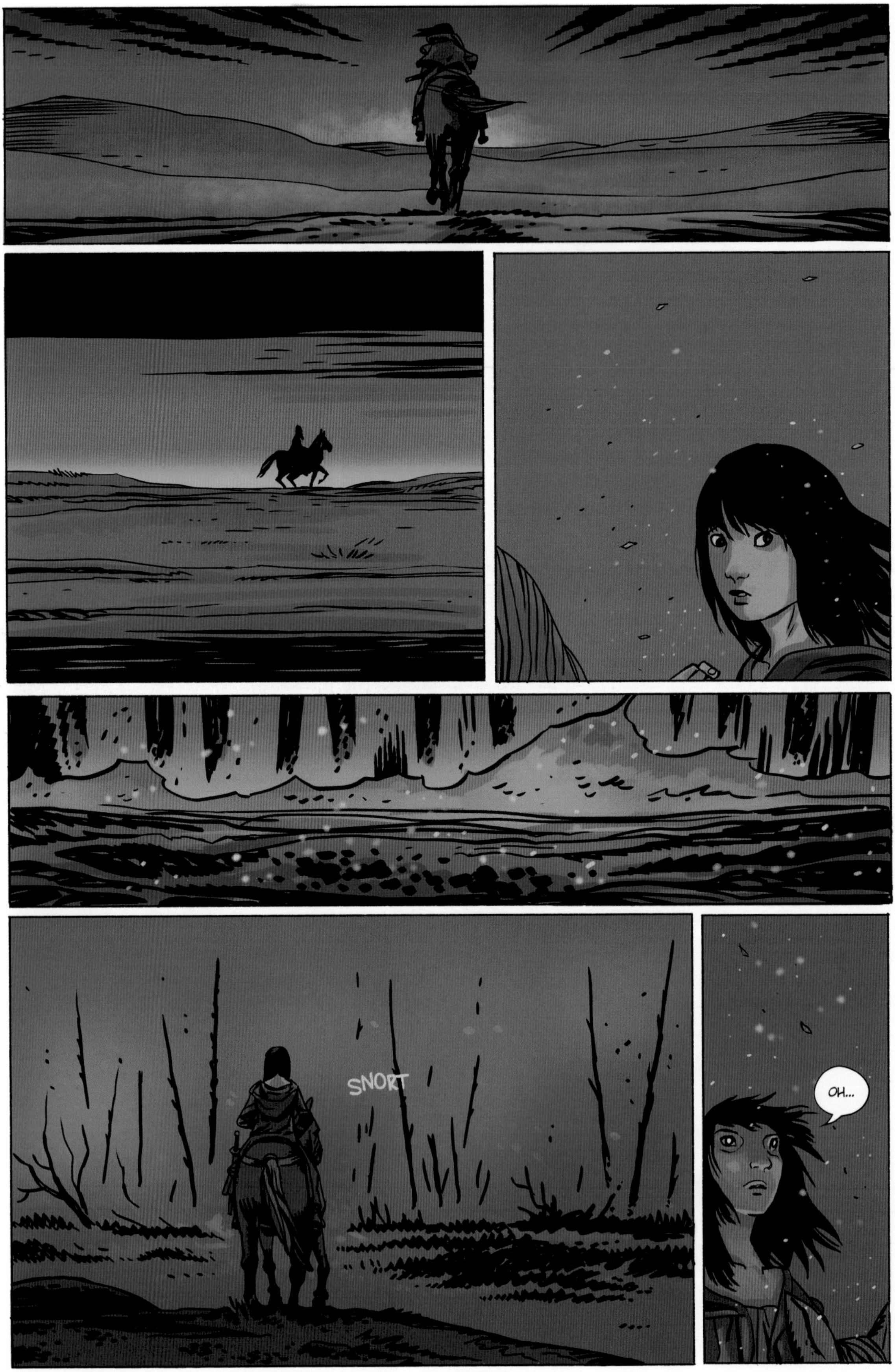
SNORT
OH...

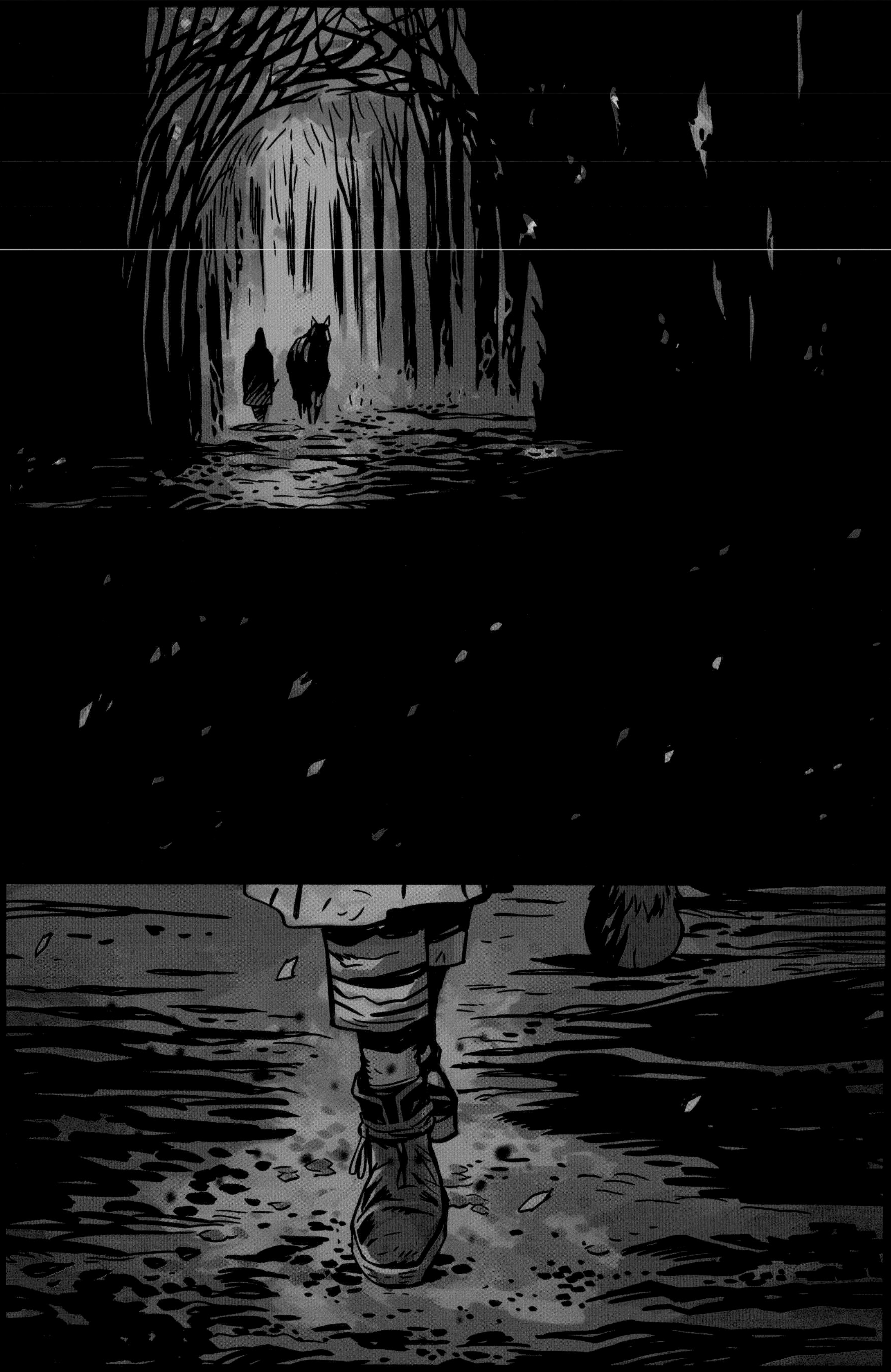

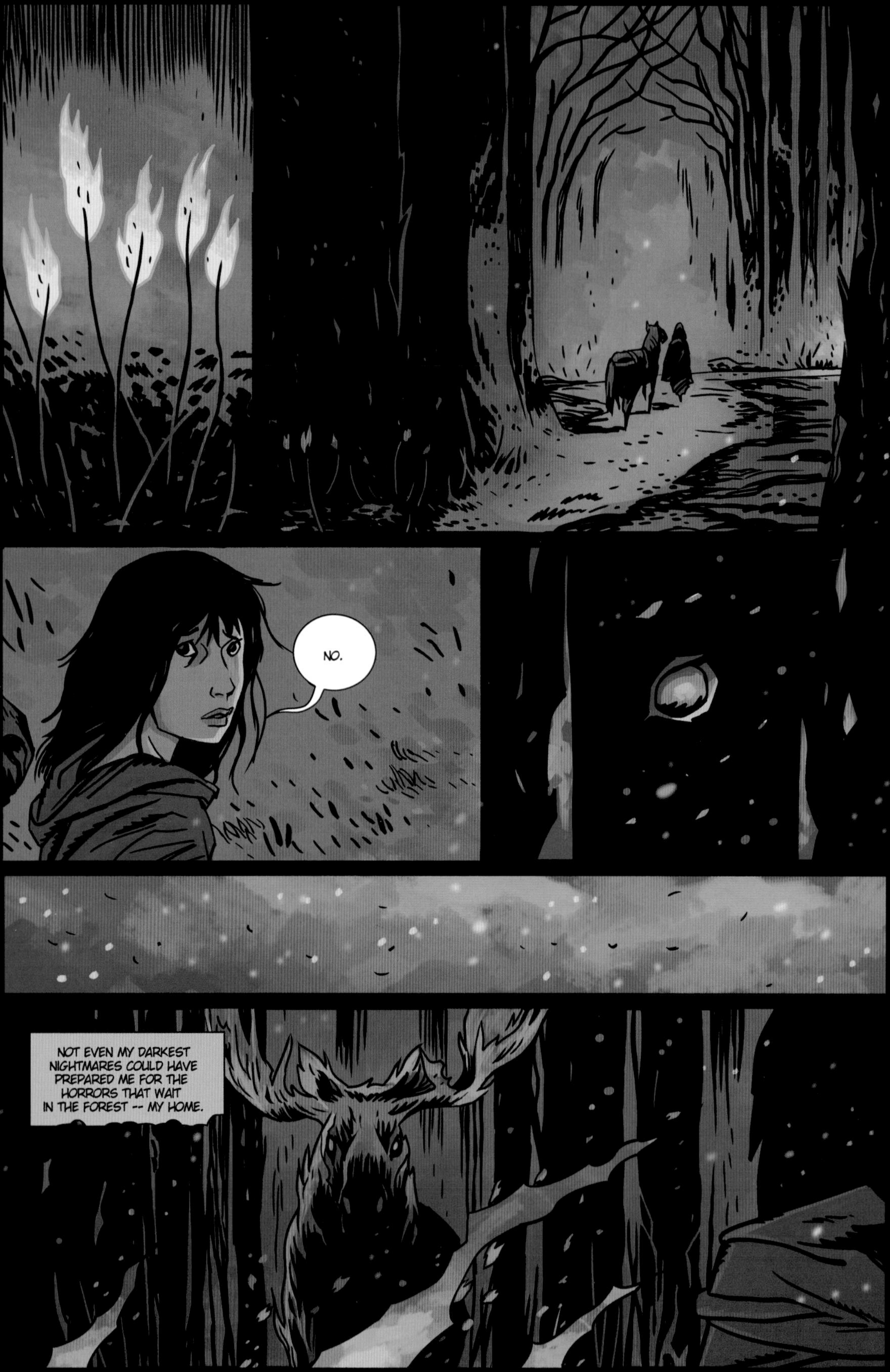
NO.
NOT EVEN MY DARKEST NIGHTMARES COULD HAVE PREPARED ME FOR THE HORRORS THAT WAIT IN THE FOREST -- MY HOME.

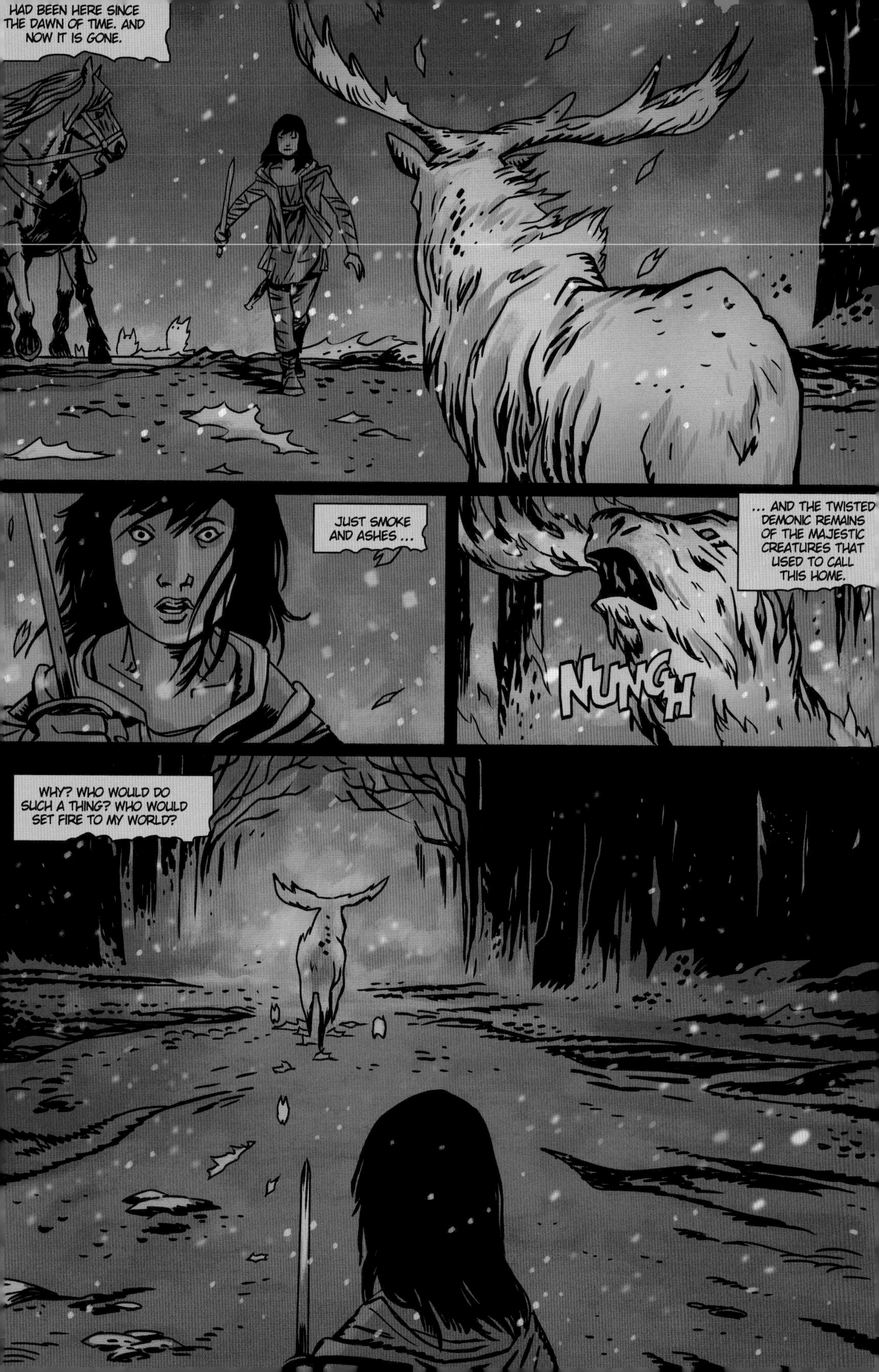
HAD BEEN HERE SINCE THE DAWN OF TIME. AND NOW IT IS GONE.
JUST SMOKE AND ASHES ...
... AND THE TWISTED DEMONIC REMAINS OF THE MAJESTIC CREATURES THAT USED TO CALL THIS HOME.
NUNCH
WHY? WHO WOULD DO SUCH A THING? WHO WOULD SET FIRE TO MY WORLD?

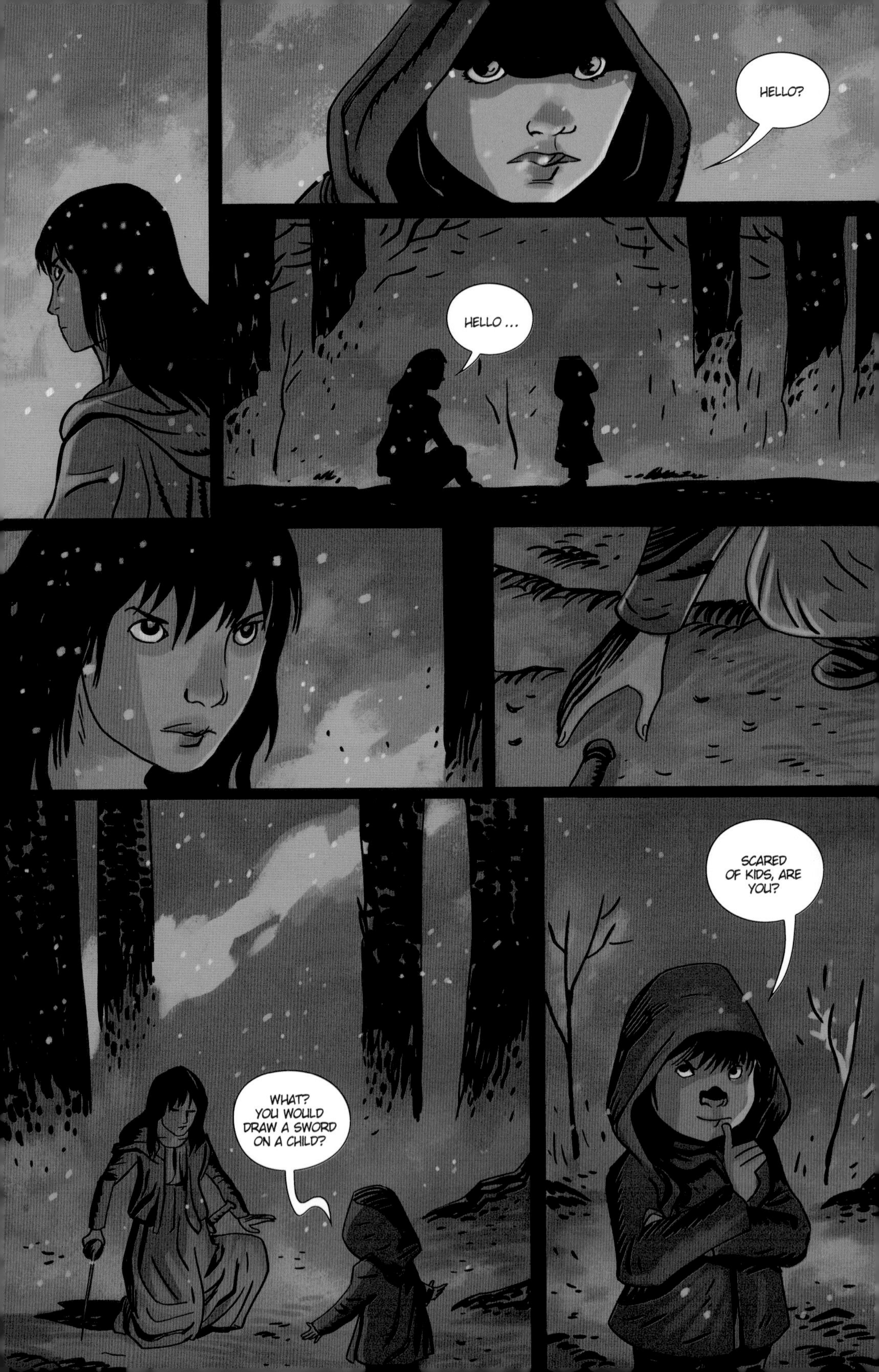
HELLO?
HELLO ...
SCARED OF KIDS, ARE YOU?
WHAT? YOU WOULD DRAW A SWORD ON A CHILD?

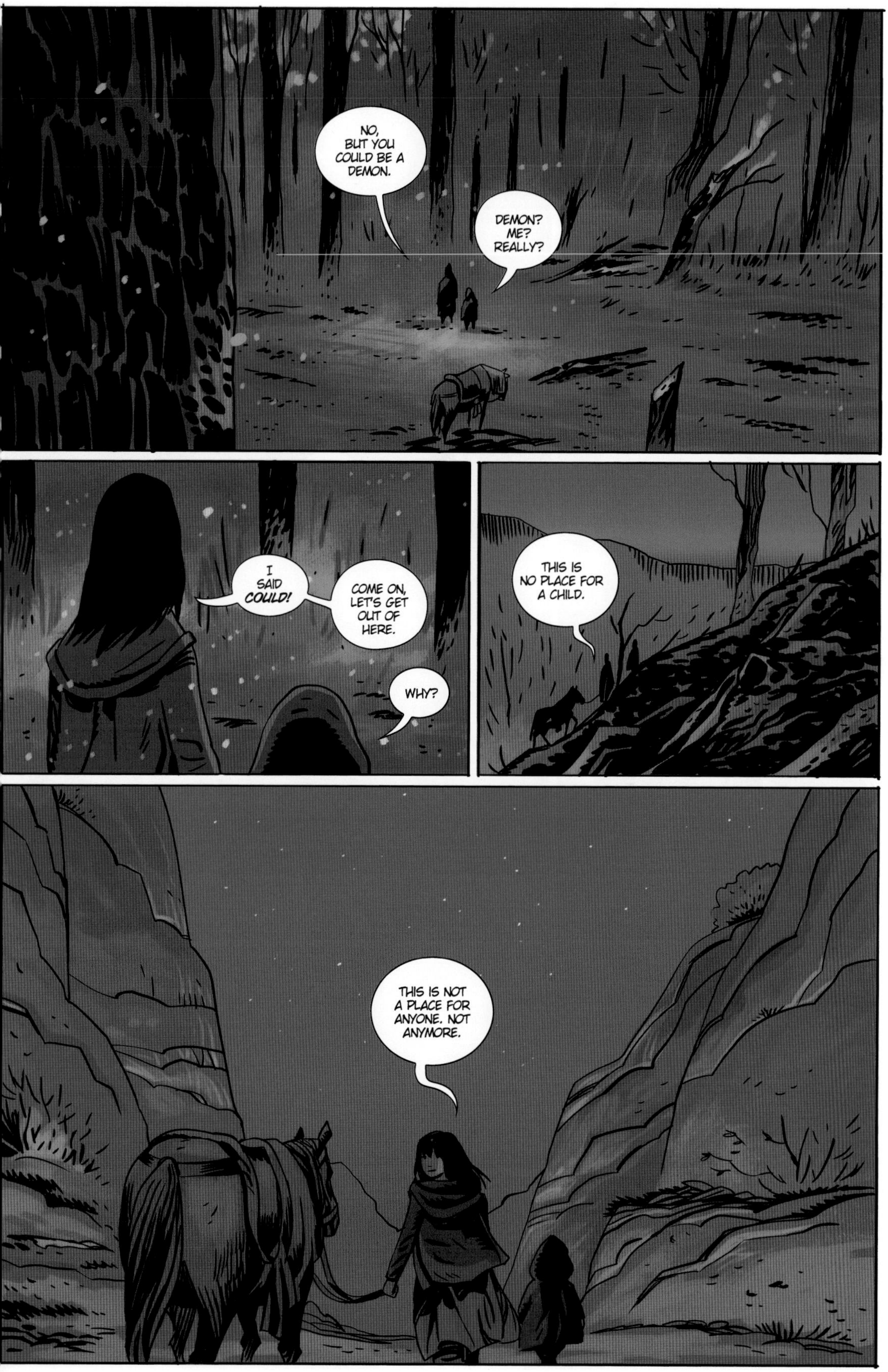

NO, BUT YOU COULD BE A DEMON.
DEMON? ME? REALLY?
I SAID ***COULD!***
COME ON, LET'S GET OUT OF HERE.
WHY?
THIS IS NO PLACE FOR A CHILD.
THIS IS NOT A PLACE FOR ANYONE. NOT ANYMORE.

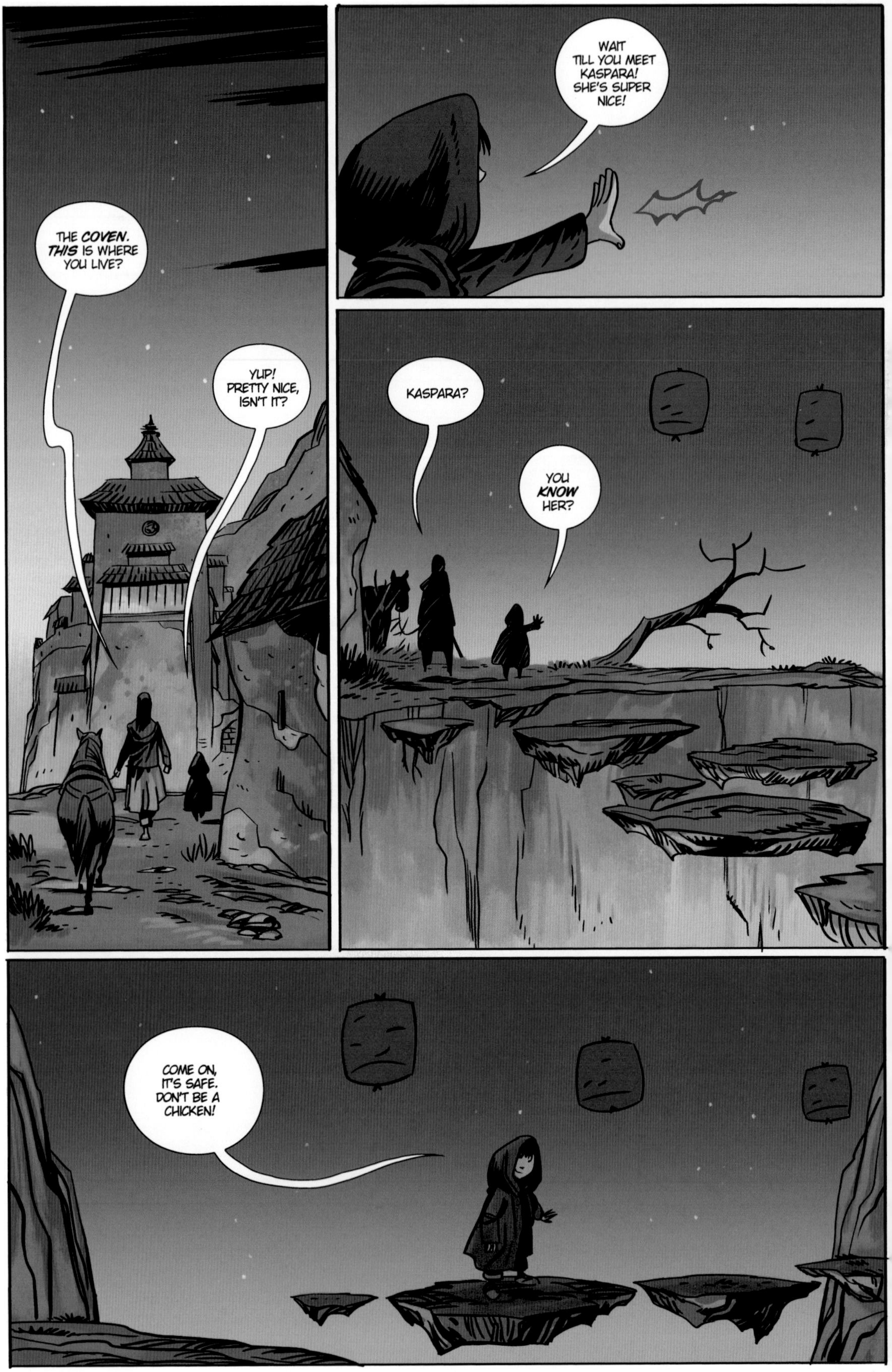
THE COVEN. THIS IS WHERE YOU LIVE?
YUP! PRETTY NICE, ISN'T IT?
WAIT TILL YOU MEET KASPARA! SHE'S SUPER NICE!
KASPARA?
YOU KNOW HER?
COME ON, IT'S SAFE. DON'T BE A CHICKEN!

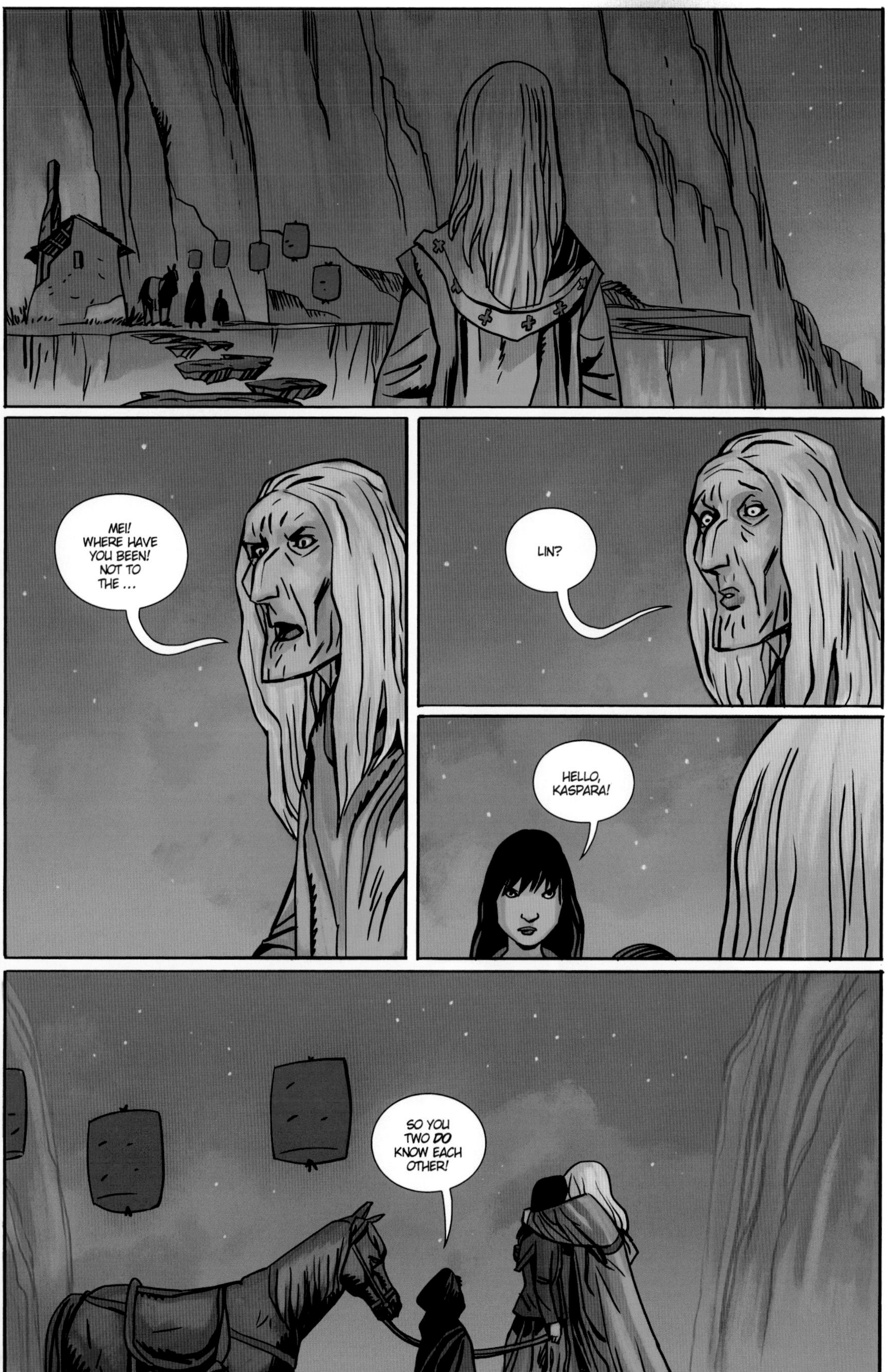
MEI! WHERE HAVE YOU BEEN! NOT TO THE . . .
LIN?
HELLO, KASPARA!
SO YOU TWO *DO* KNOW EACH OTHER!

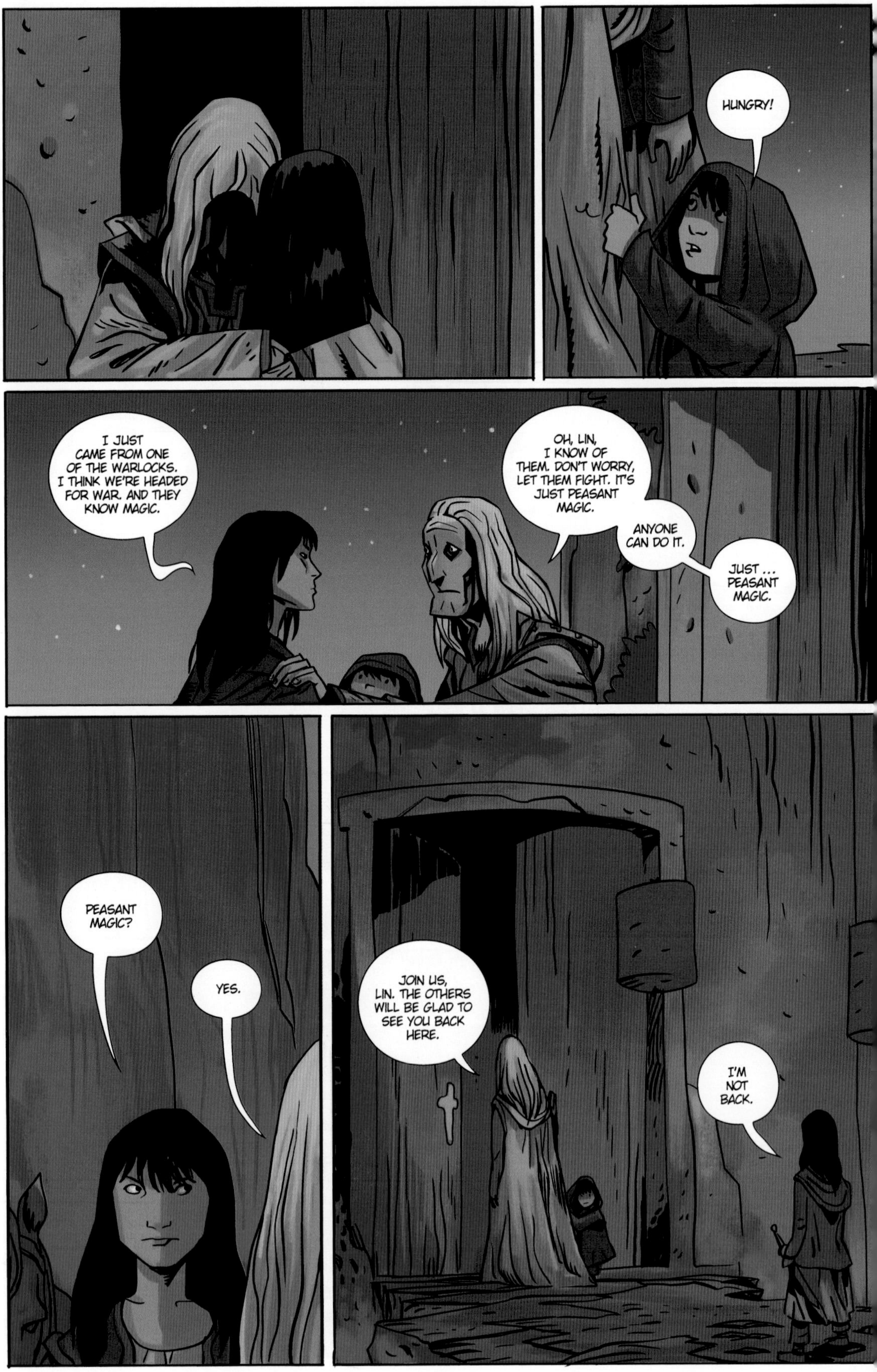
HUNGRY!
I JUST CAME FROM ONE OF THE WARLOCKS. I THINK WE'RE HEADED FOR WAR. AND THEY KNOW MAGIC.
OH, LIN, I KNOW OF THEM. DON'T WORRY, LET THEM FIGHT. IT'S JUST PEASANT MAGIC.
ANYONE CAN DO IT.
JUST ... PEASANT MAGIC.
PEASANT MAGIC?
YES.
JOIN US, LIN. THE OTHERS WILL BE GLAD TO SEE YOU BACK HERE.
I'M NOT BACK.

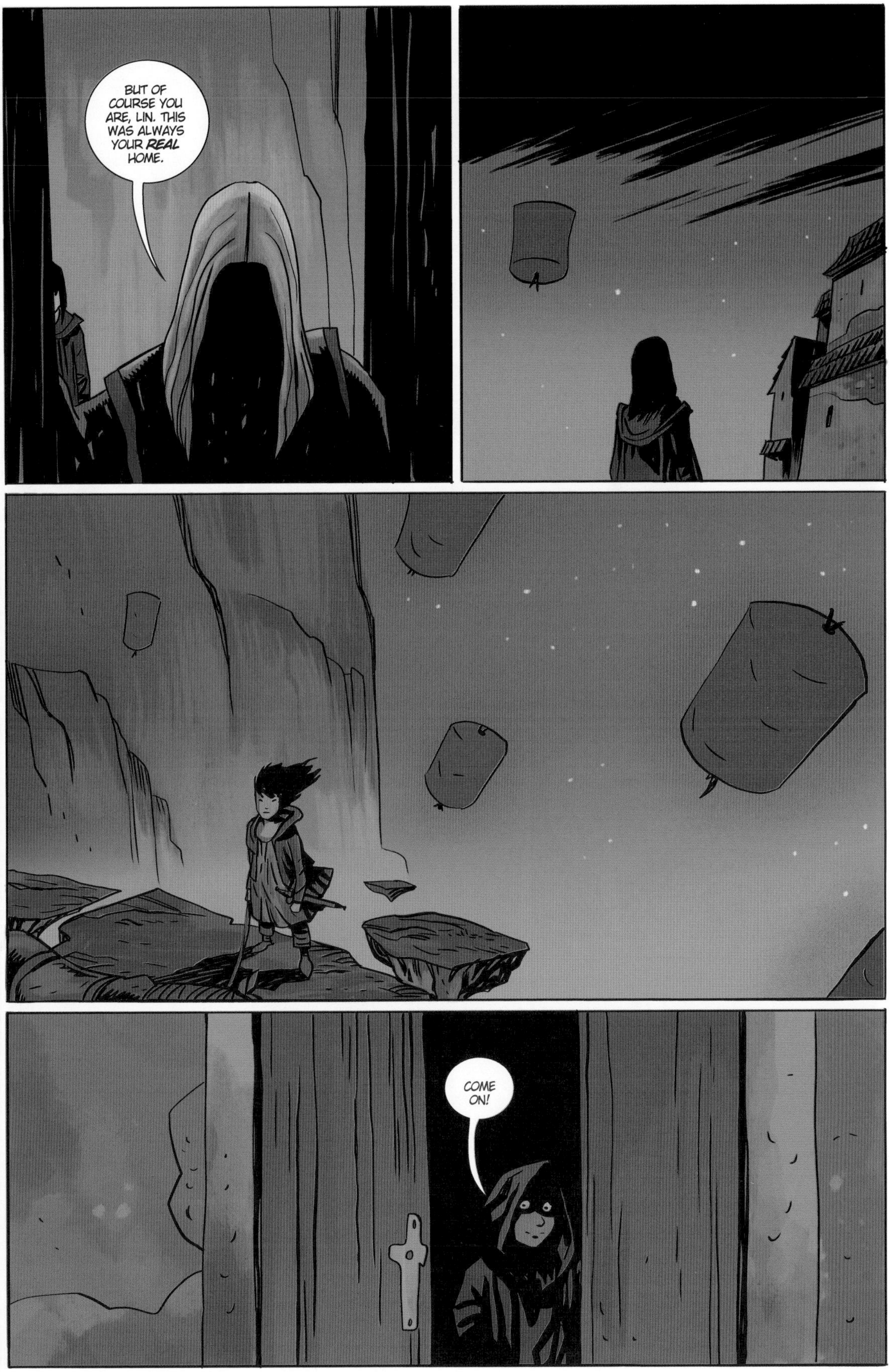
BUT OF COURSE YOU ARE, LIN. THIS WAS ALWAYS YOUR *REAL* HOME.
COME ON!

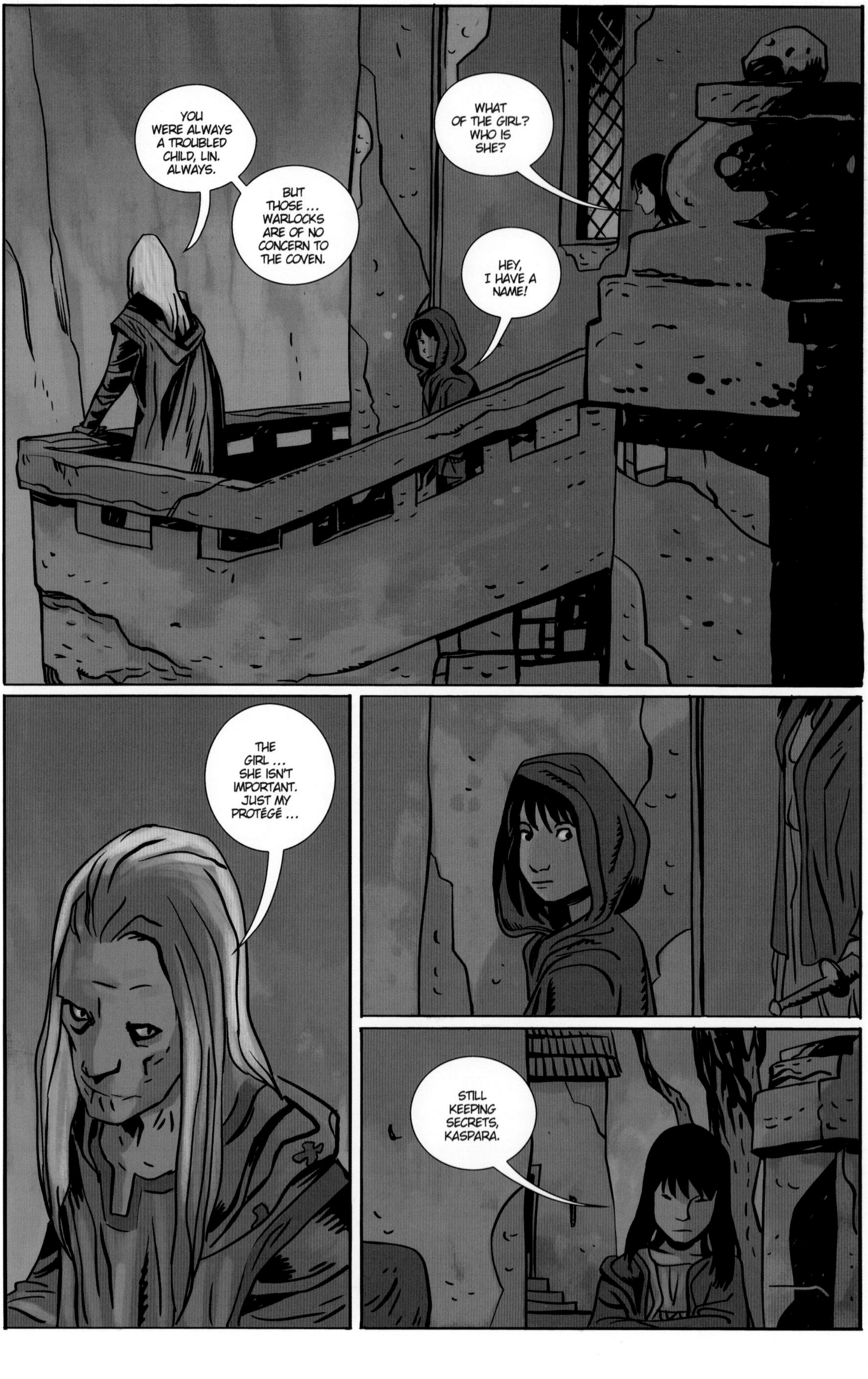
YOU WERE ALWAYS A TROUBLED CHILD, LIN. ALWAYS.
BUT THOSE ... WARLOCKS ARE OF NO CONCERN TO THE COVEN.
WHAT OF THE GIRL? WHO IS SHE?
HEY, I HAVE A NAME!
THE GIRL ... SHE ISN'T IMPORTANT. JUST MY PROTÉGÉ ...
STILL KEEPING SECRETS, KASPARA.

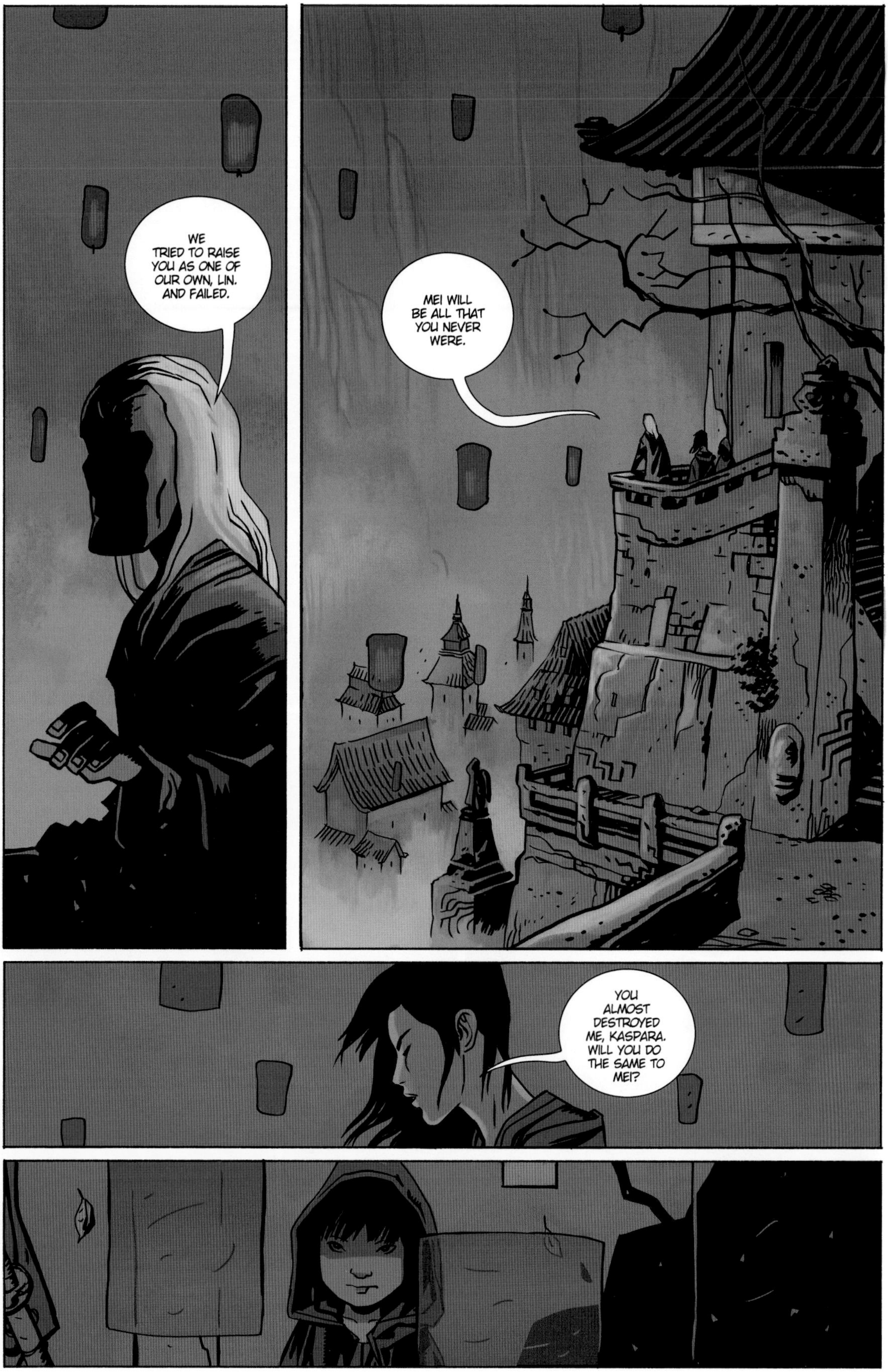
WE TRIED TO RAISE YOU AS ONE OF OUR OWN, LIN. AND FAILED.
MEI WILL BE ALL THAT YOU NEVER WERE.
YOU ALMOST DESTROYED ME, KASPARA. WILL YOU DO THE SAME TO MEI?

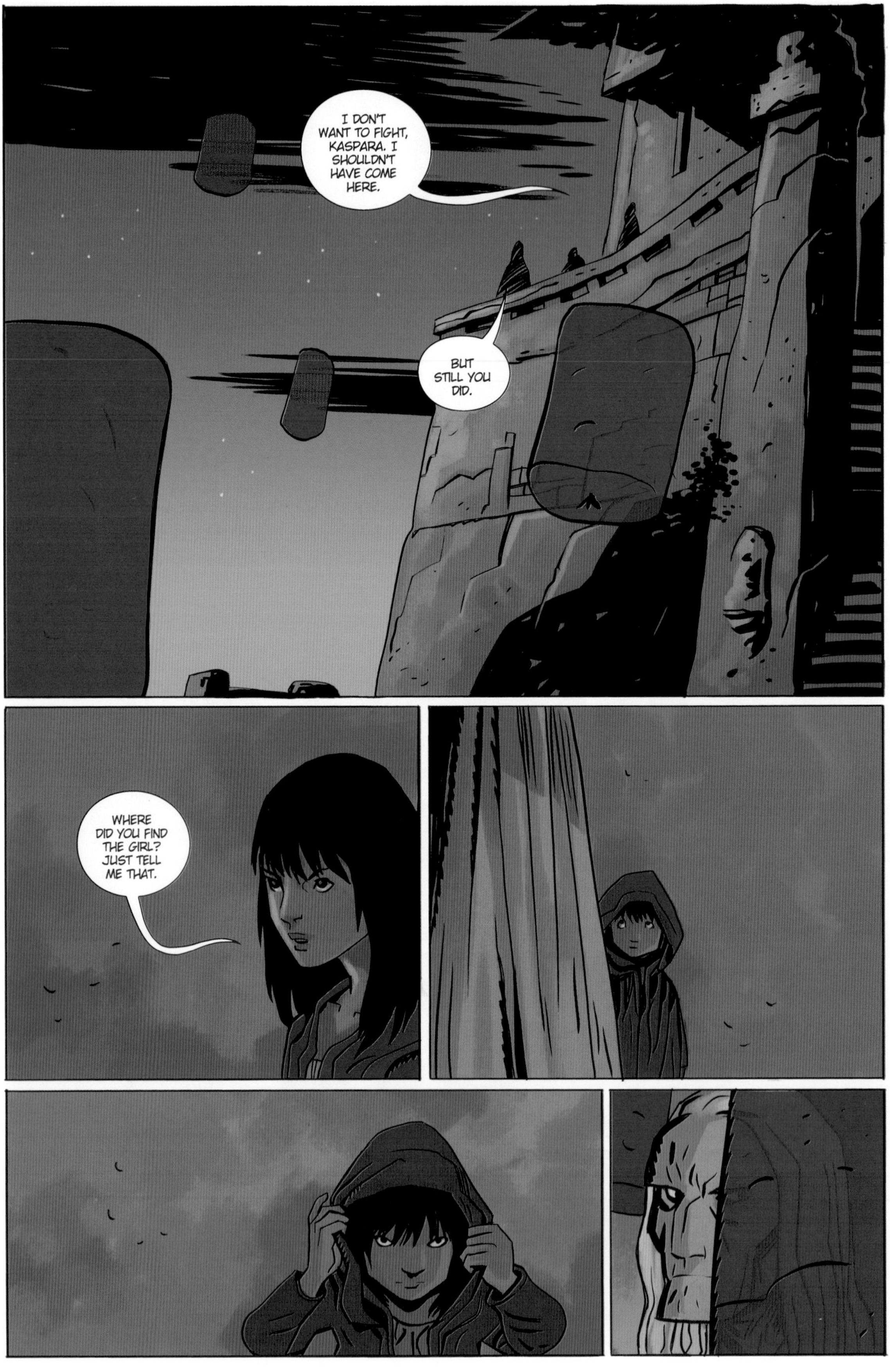
I DON'T WANT TO FIGHT, KASPARA. I SHOULDN'T HAVE COME HERE.
BUT STILL YOU DID.
WHERE DID YOU FIND THE GIRL? JUST TELL ME THAT.

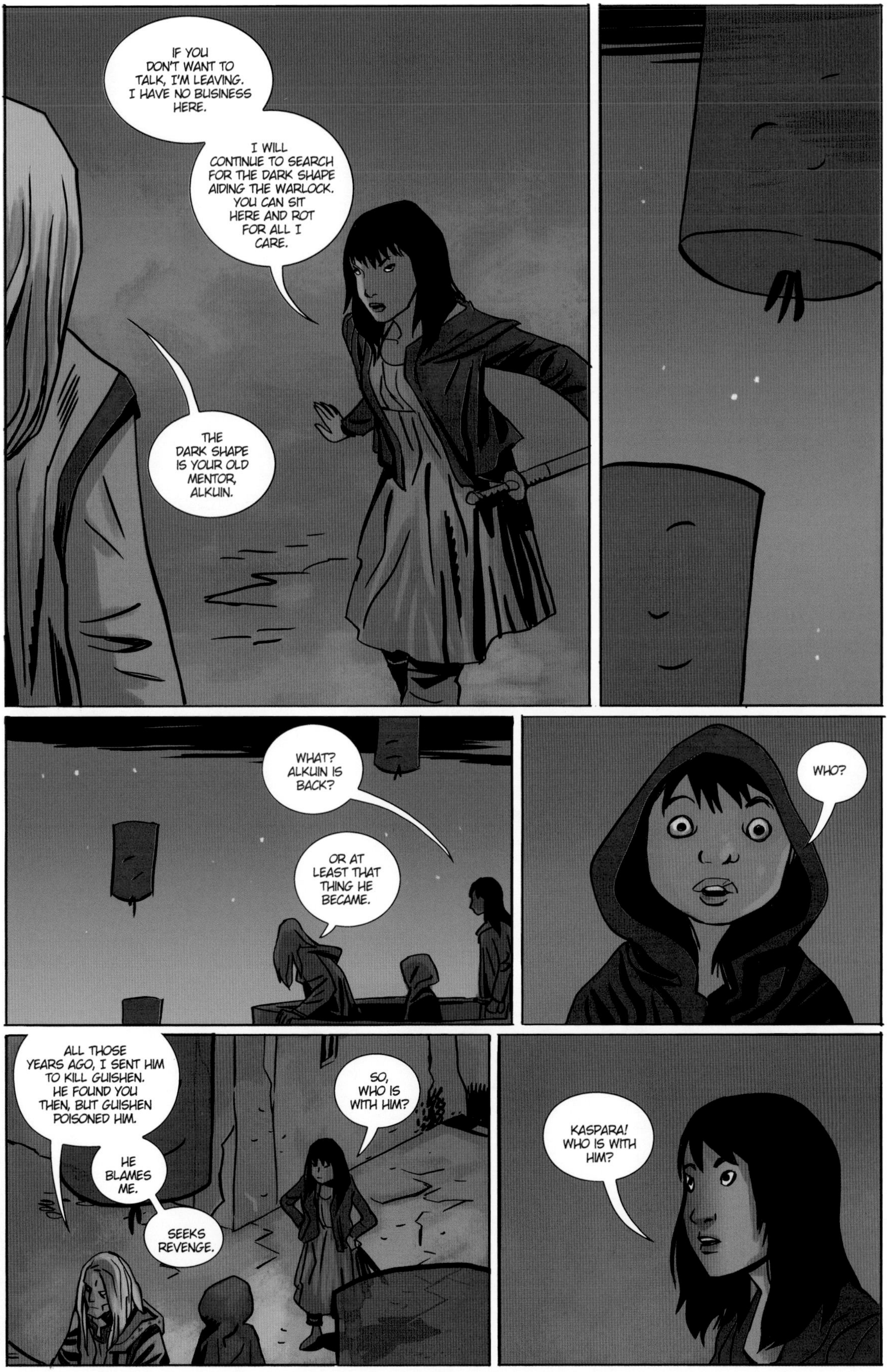
IF YOU DON'T WANT TO TALK, I'M LEAVING. I HAVE NO BUSINESS HERE.
I WILL CONTINUE TO SEARCH FOR THE DARK SHAPE AIDING THE WARLOCK. YOU CAN SIT HERE AND ROT FOR ALL I CARE.
THE DARK SHAPE IS YOUR OLD MENTOR, ALKUIN.
WHAT? ALKUIN IS BACK?
OR AT LEAST THAT THING HE BECAME.
WHO?
ALL THOSE YEARS AGO, I SENT HIM TO KILL GUISHEN. HE FOUND YOU THEN, BUT GUISHEN POISONED HIM.
HE BLAMES ME.
SEEKS REVENGE.
SO, WHO IS WITH HIM?
KASPARA! WHO IS WITH HIM?

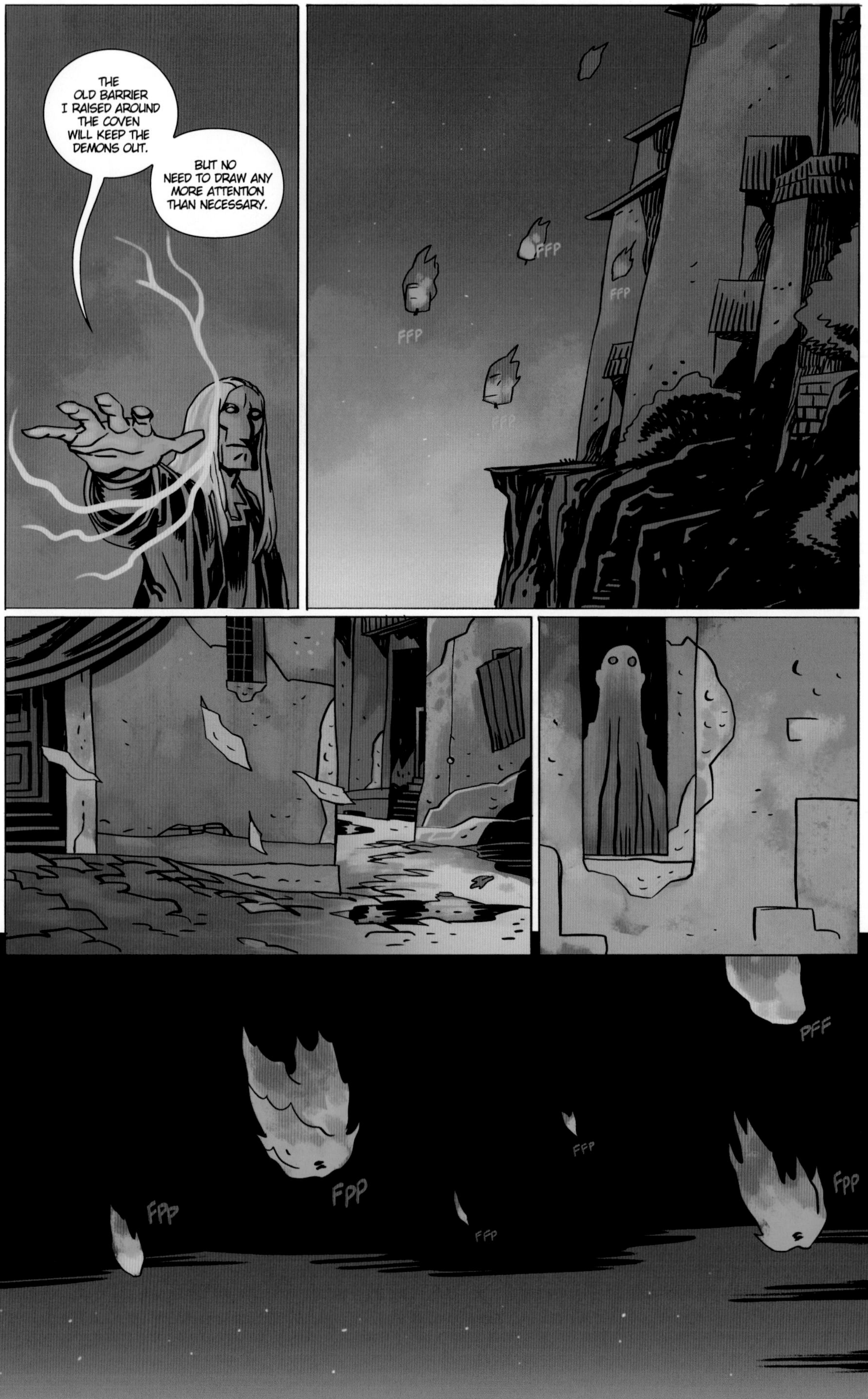
THE OLD BARRIER I RAISED AROUND THE COVEN WILL KEEP THE DEMONS OUT.
BUT NO NEED TO DRAW ANY MORE ATTENTION THAN NECESSARY.
FFP
FFP
FFP
FFP
PFF
FFP
FPP
FPP
FFP
FPP

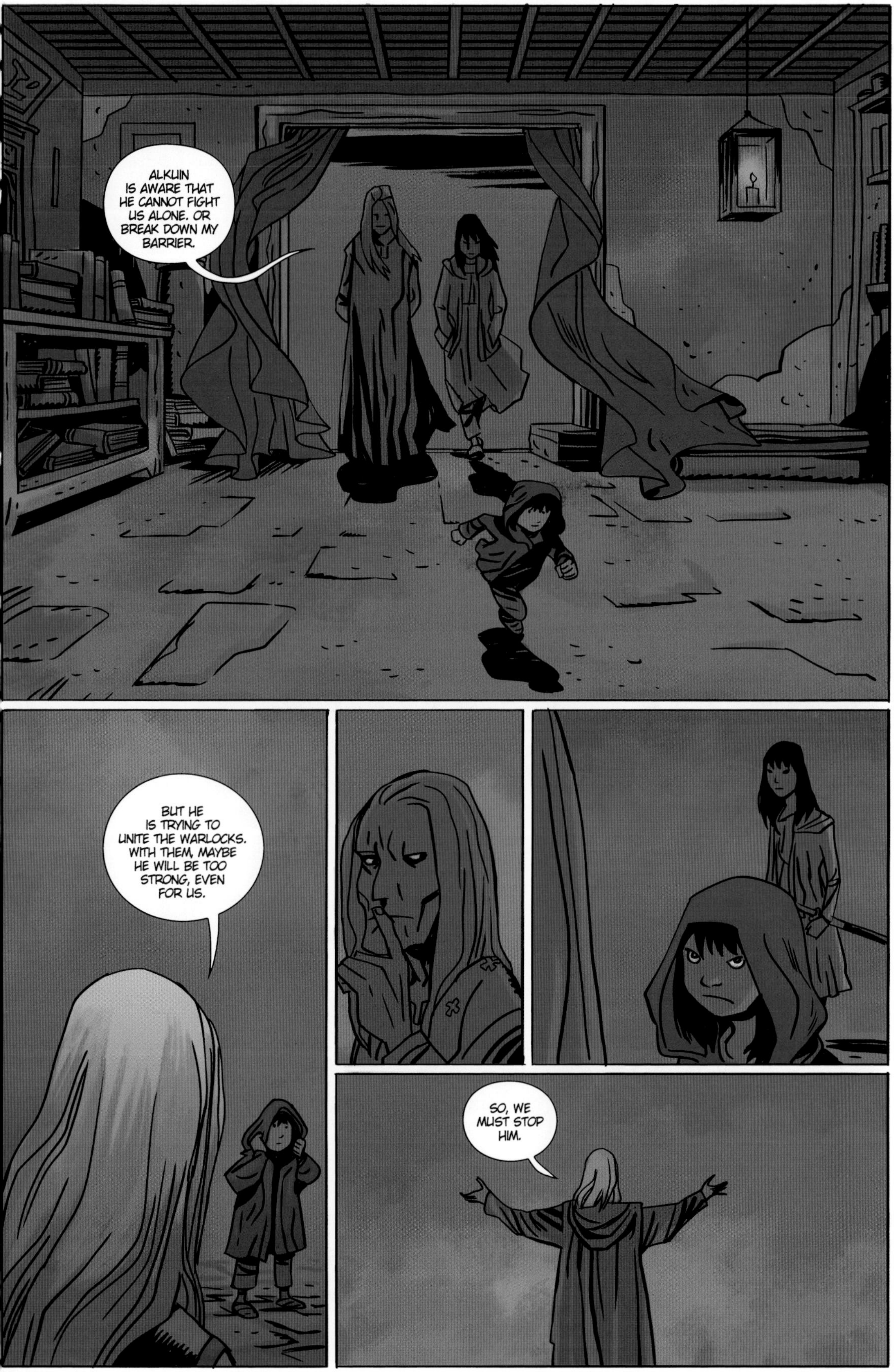
ALKUIN IS AWARE THAT HE CANNOT FIGHT US ALONE. OR BREAK DOWN MY BARRIER.
BUT HE IS TRYING TO UNITE THE WARLOCKS. WITH THEM, MAYBE HE WILL BE TOO STRONG, EVEN FOR US.
SO, WE MUST STOP HIM.

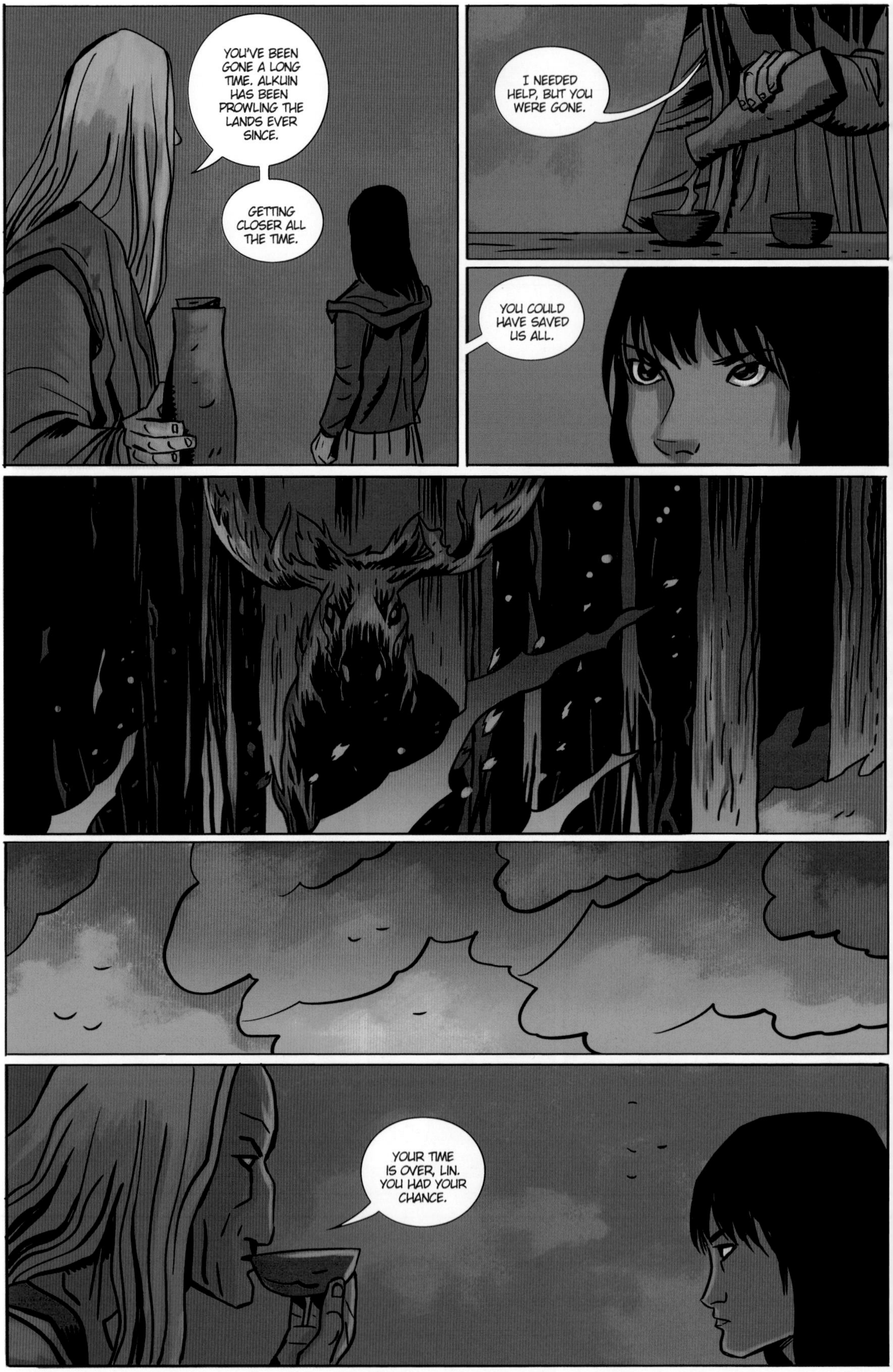
YOU'VE BEEN GONE A LONG TIME. ALKUIN HAS BEEN PROWLING THE LANDS EVER SINCE.
GETTING CLOSER ALL THE TIME.
I NEEDED HELP, BUT YOU WERE GONE.
YOU COULD HAVE SAVED US ALL.
YOUR TIME IS OVER, LIN. YOU HAD YOUR CHANCE.

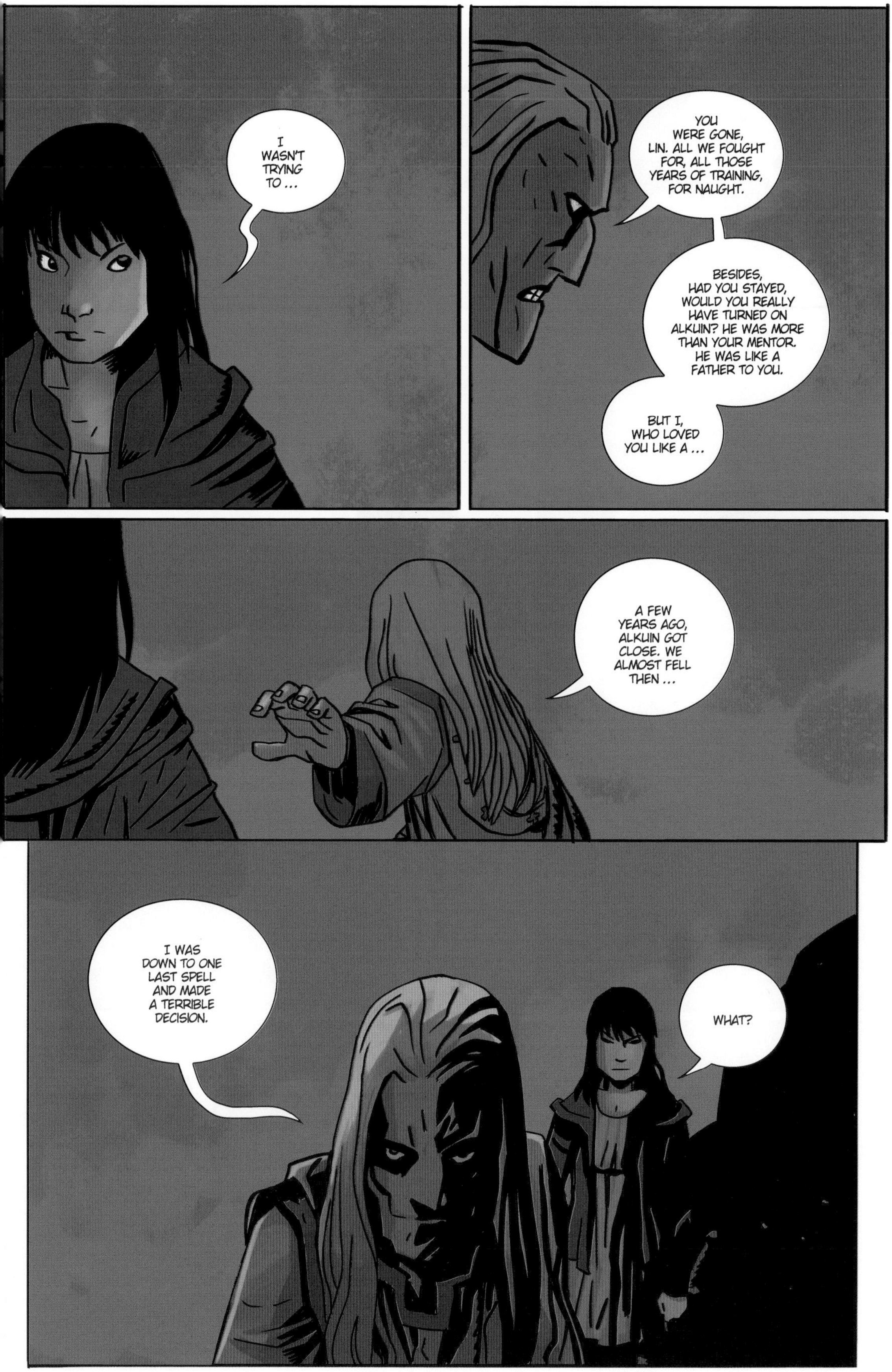
I WASN'T TRYING TO ...
YOU WERE GONE, LIN. ALL WE FOUGHT FOR, ALL THOSE YEARS OF TRAINING, FOR NAUGHT.
BESIDES, HAD YOU STAYED, WOULD YOU REALLY HAVE TURNED ON ALKUIN? HE WAS MORE THAN YOUR MENTOR. HE WAS LIKE A FATHER TO YOU.
BUT I, WHO LOVED YOU LIKE A ...
A FEW YEARS AGO, ALKUIN GOT CLOSE. WE ALMOST FELL THEN ...
I WAS DOWN TO ONE LAST SPELL AND MADE A TERRIBLE DECISION.
WHAT?

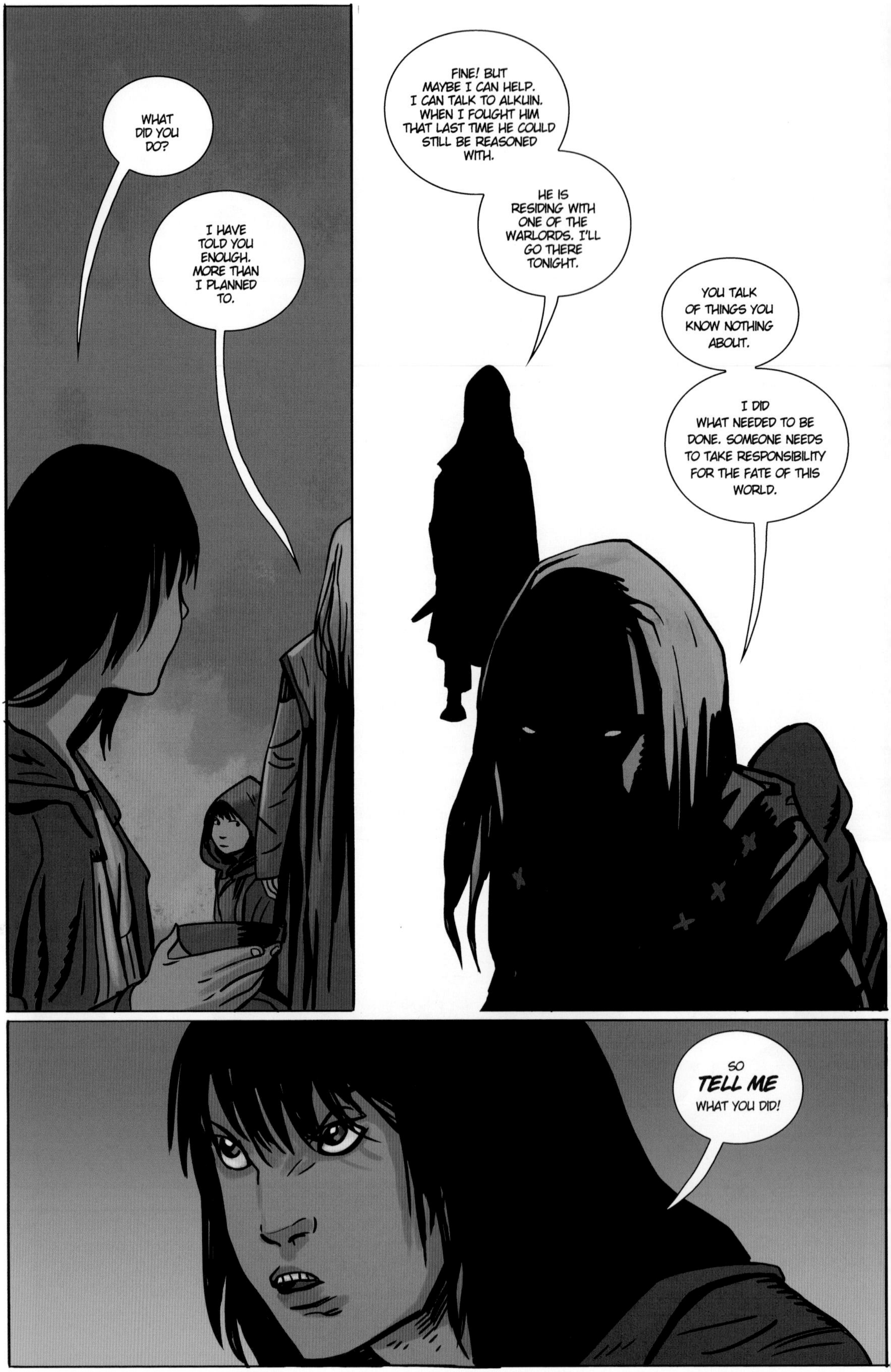
WHAT DID YOU DO?
I HAVE TOLD YOU ENOUGH. MORE THAN I PLANNED TO.
FINE! BUT MAYBE I CAN HELP. I CAN TALK TO ALKUIN. WHEN I FOUGHT HIM THAT LAST TIME HE COULD STILL BE REASONED WITH.
HE IS RESIDING WITH ONE OF THE WARLORDS. I'LL GO THERE TONIGHT.
YOU TALK OF THINGS YOU KNOW NOTHING ABOUT.
I DID WHAT NEEDED TO BE DONE. SOMEONE NEEDS TO TAKE RESPONSIBILITY FOR THE FATE OF THIS WORLD.
SO TELL ME WHAT YOU DID!

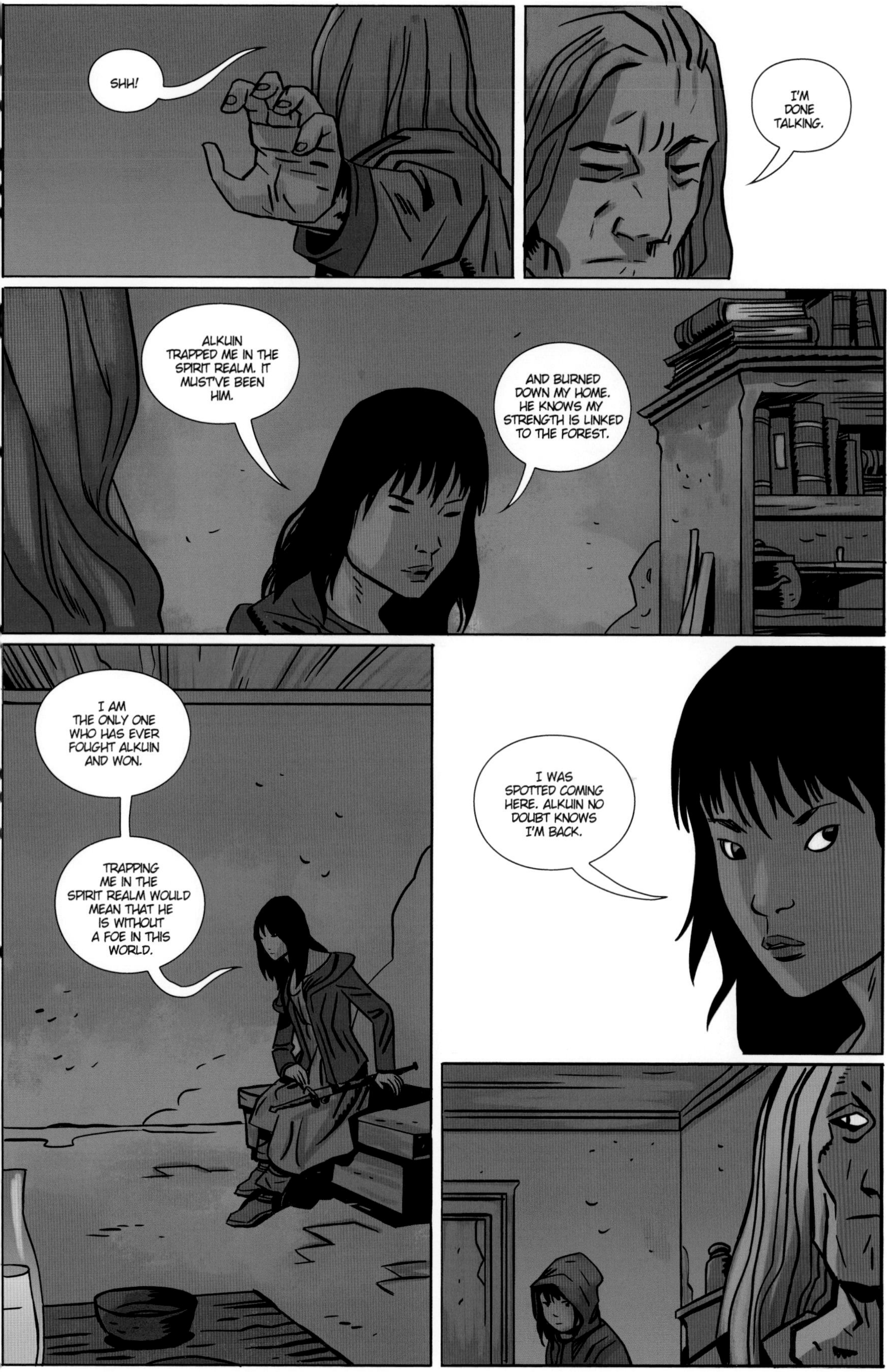
SHH!
I'M DONE TALKING.
ALKUIN TRAPPED ME IN THE SPIRIT REALM. IT MUST'VE BEEN HIM.
AND BURNED DOWN MY HOME. HE KNOWS MY STRENGTH IS LINKED TO THE FOREST.
I AM THE ONLY ONE WHO HAS EVER FOUGHT ALKUIN AND WON.
TRAPPING ME IN THE SPIRIT REALM WOULD MEAN THAT HE IS WITHOUT A FOE IN THIS WORLD.
I WAS SPOTTED COMING HERE. ALKUIN NO DOUBT KNOWS I'M BACK.

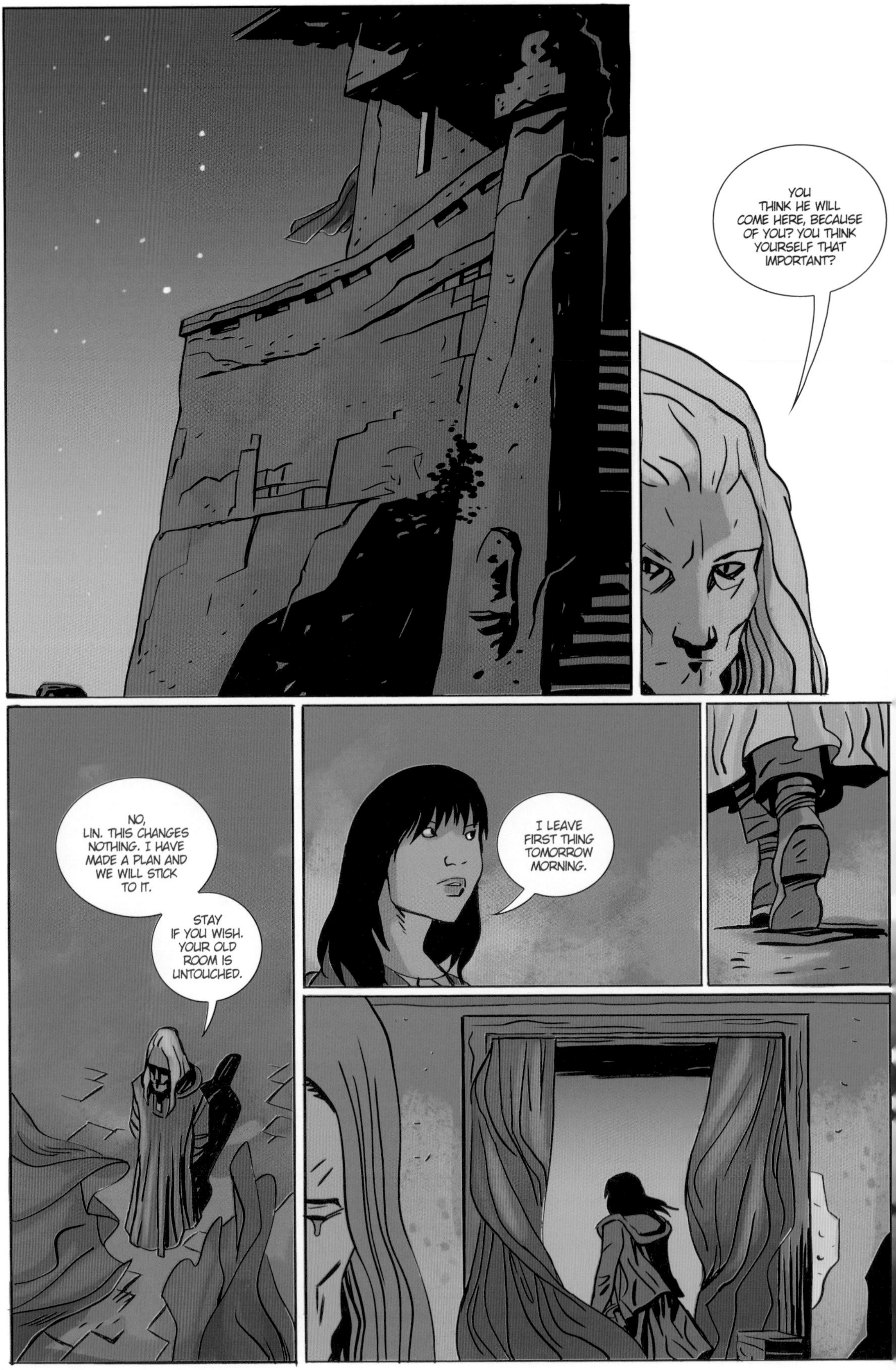
YOU THINK HE WILL COME HERE, BECAUSE OF YOU? YOU THINK YOURSELF THAT IMPORTANT?
NO, LIN. THIS CHANGES NOTHING. I HAVE MADE A PLAN AND WE WILL STICK TO IT.
STAY IF YOU WISH. YOUR OLD ROOM IS UNTOUCHED.
I LEAVE FIRST THING TOMORROW MORNING.

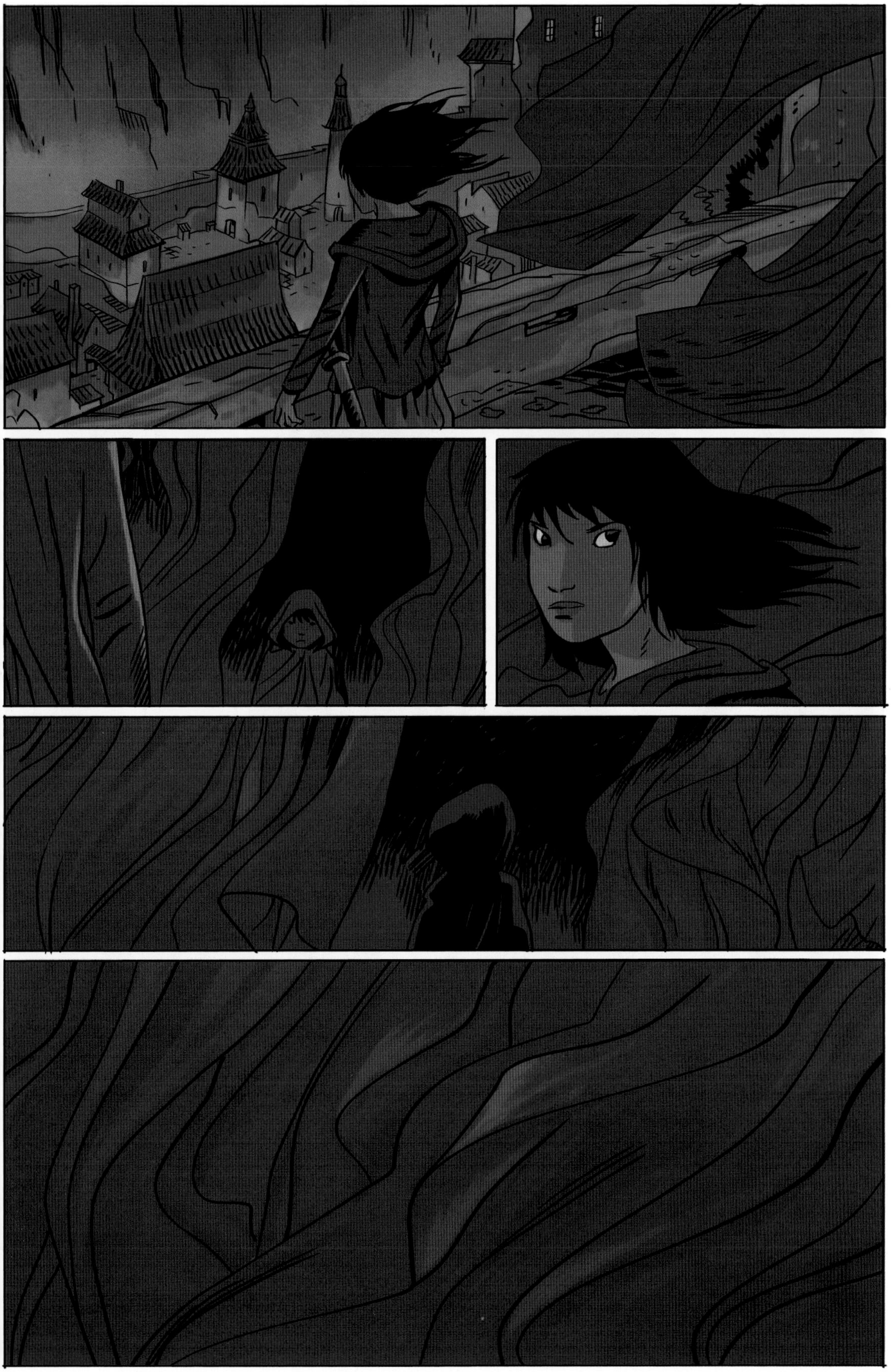

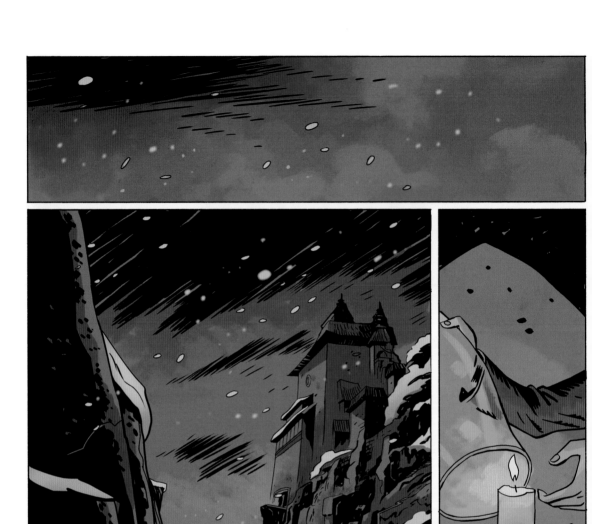

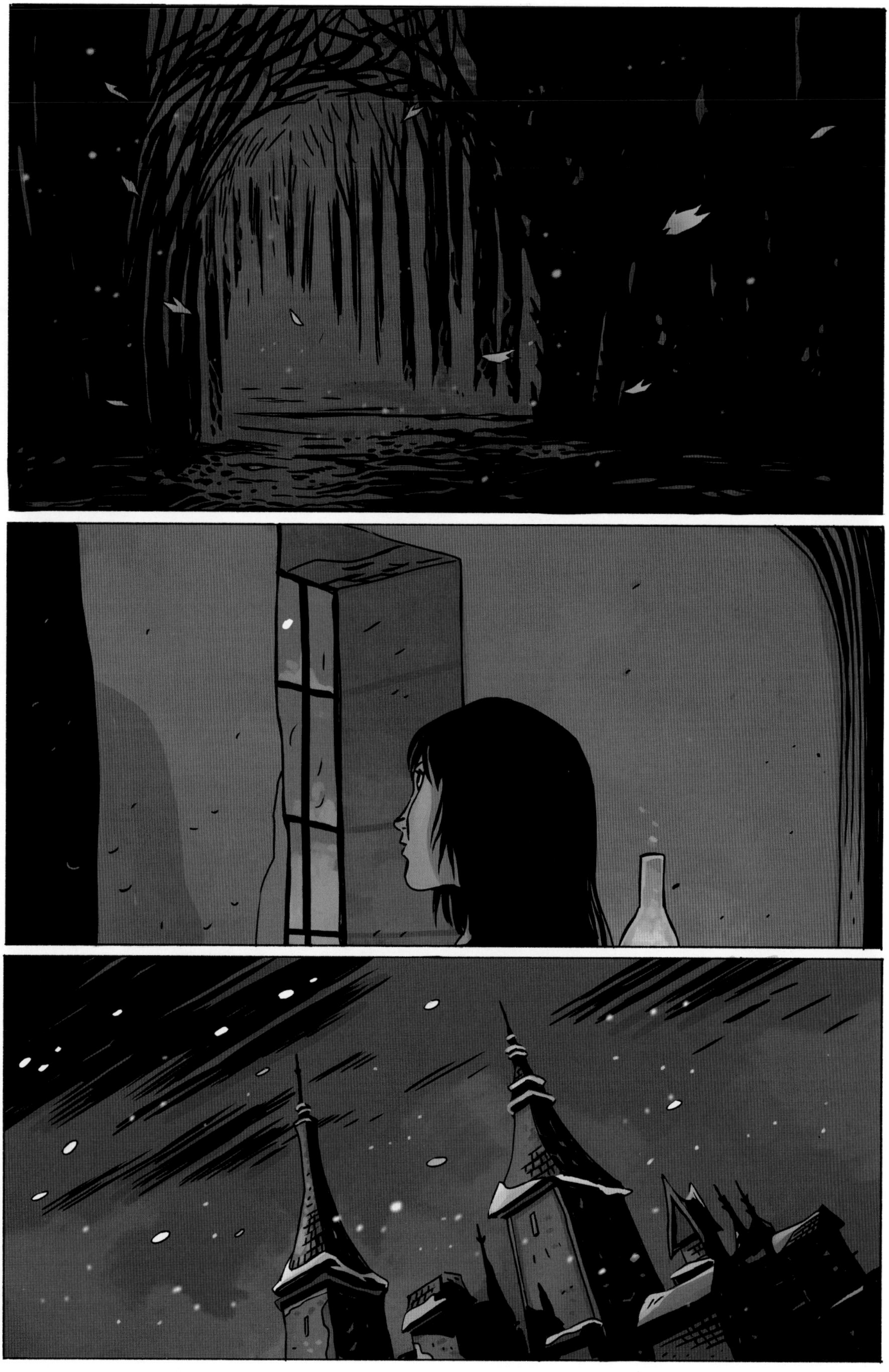

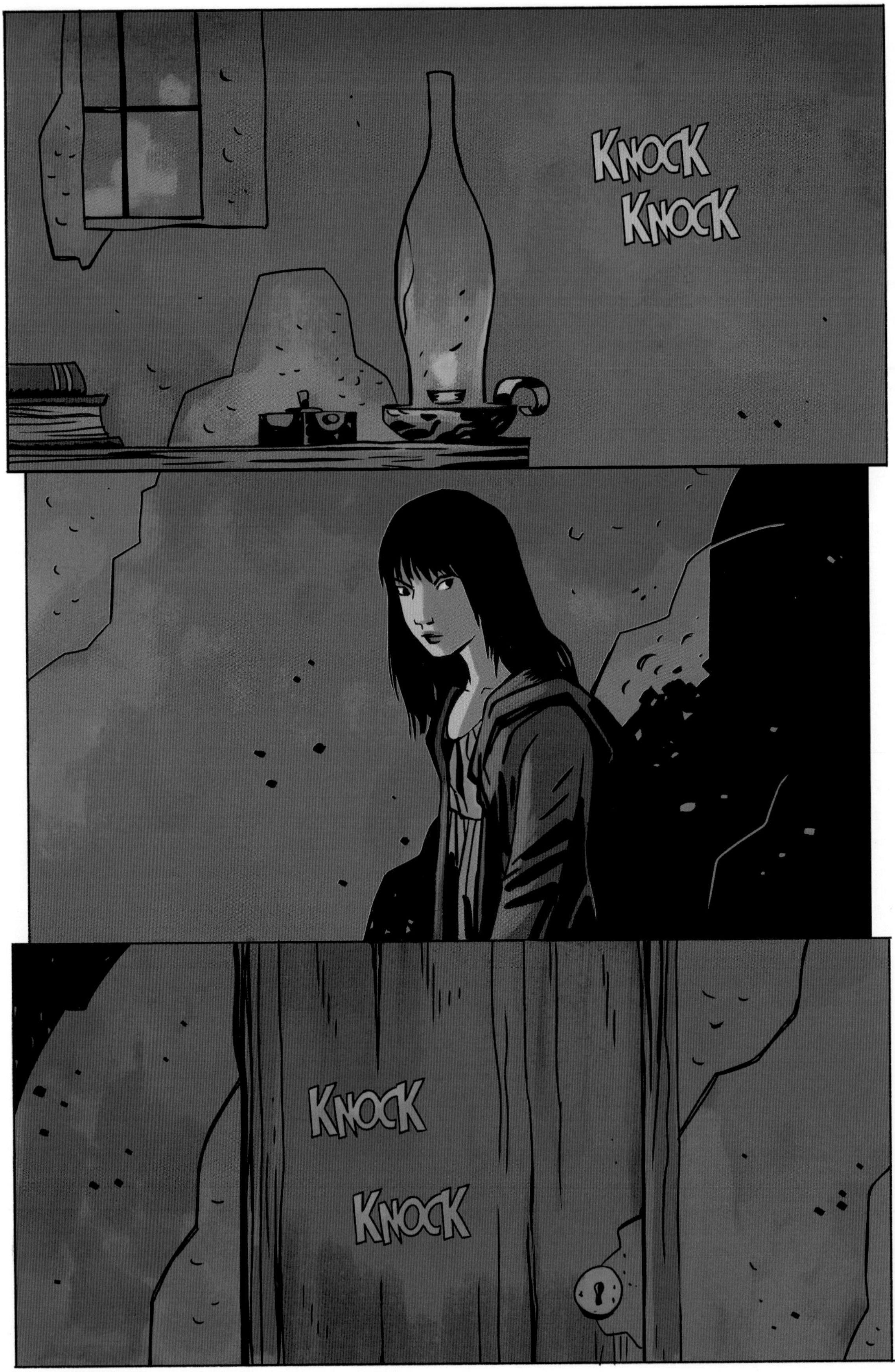
KNOCK
KNOCK
KNOCK
KNOCK

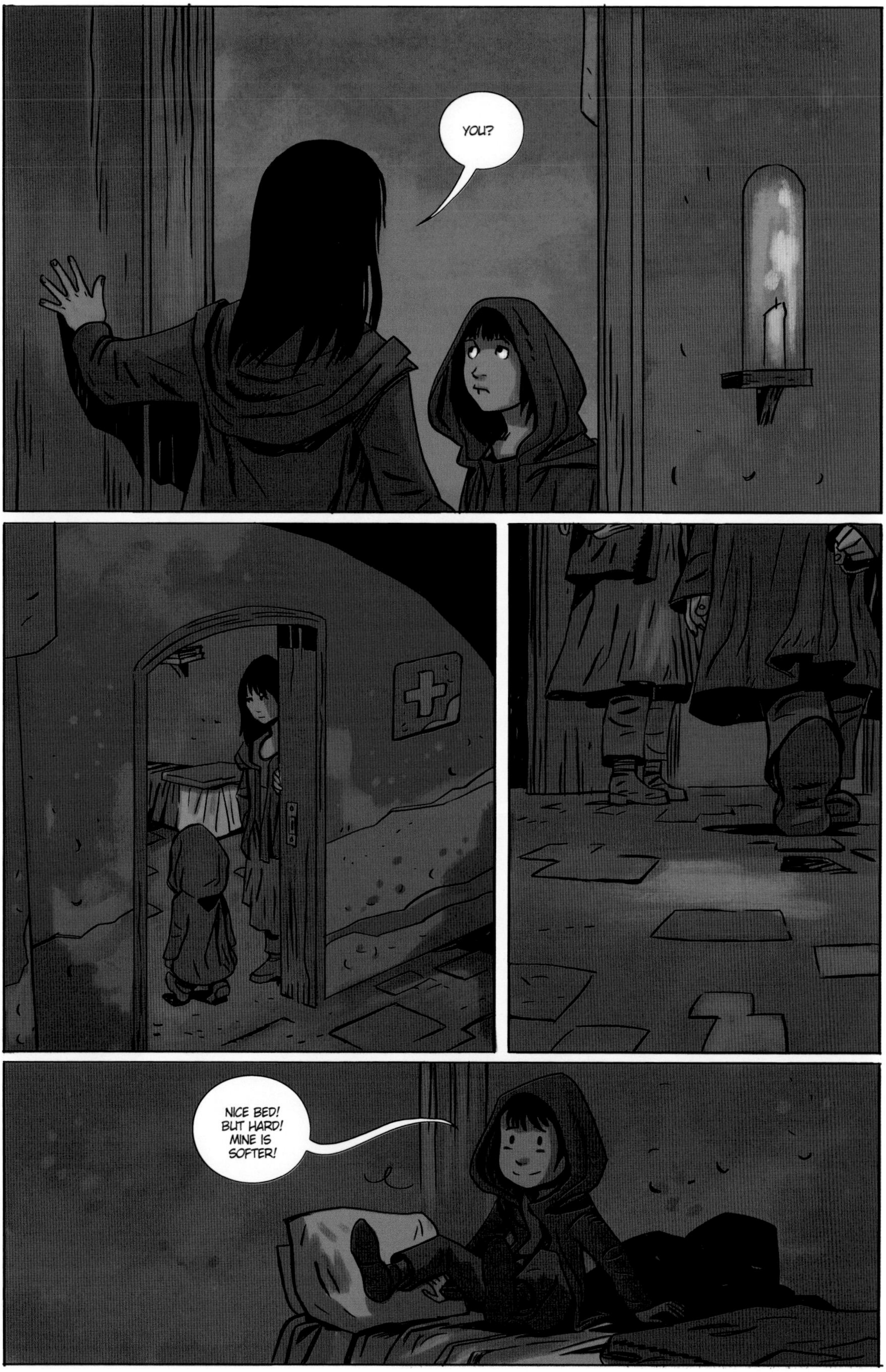

YOU?
NICE BED! BUT HARD! MINE IS SOFTER!

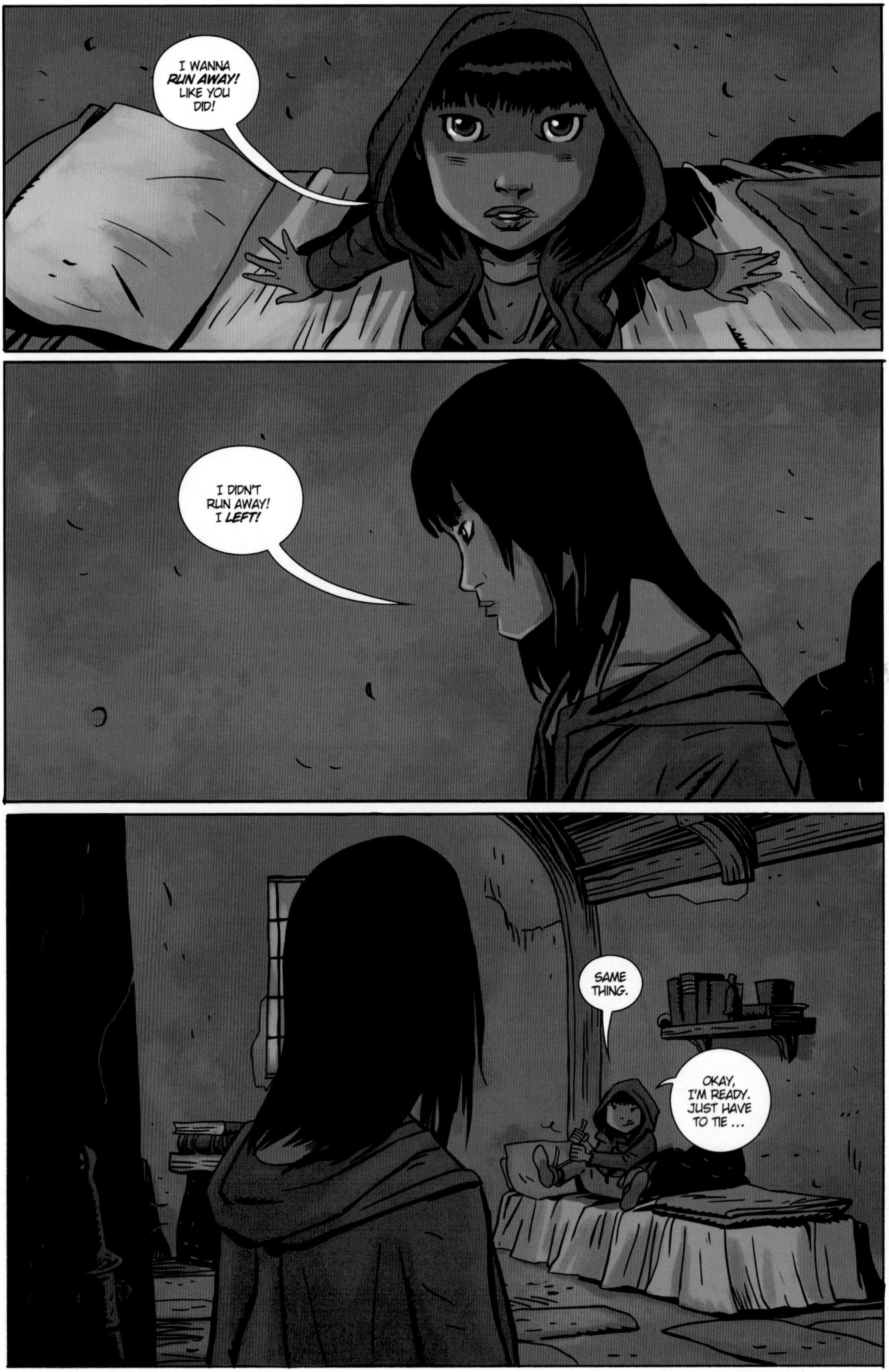
I WANNA RUN AWAY! LIKE YOU DID!
I DIDN'T RUN AWAY! I LEFT!
SAME THING.
OKAY, I'M READY. JUST HAVE TO TIE ...

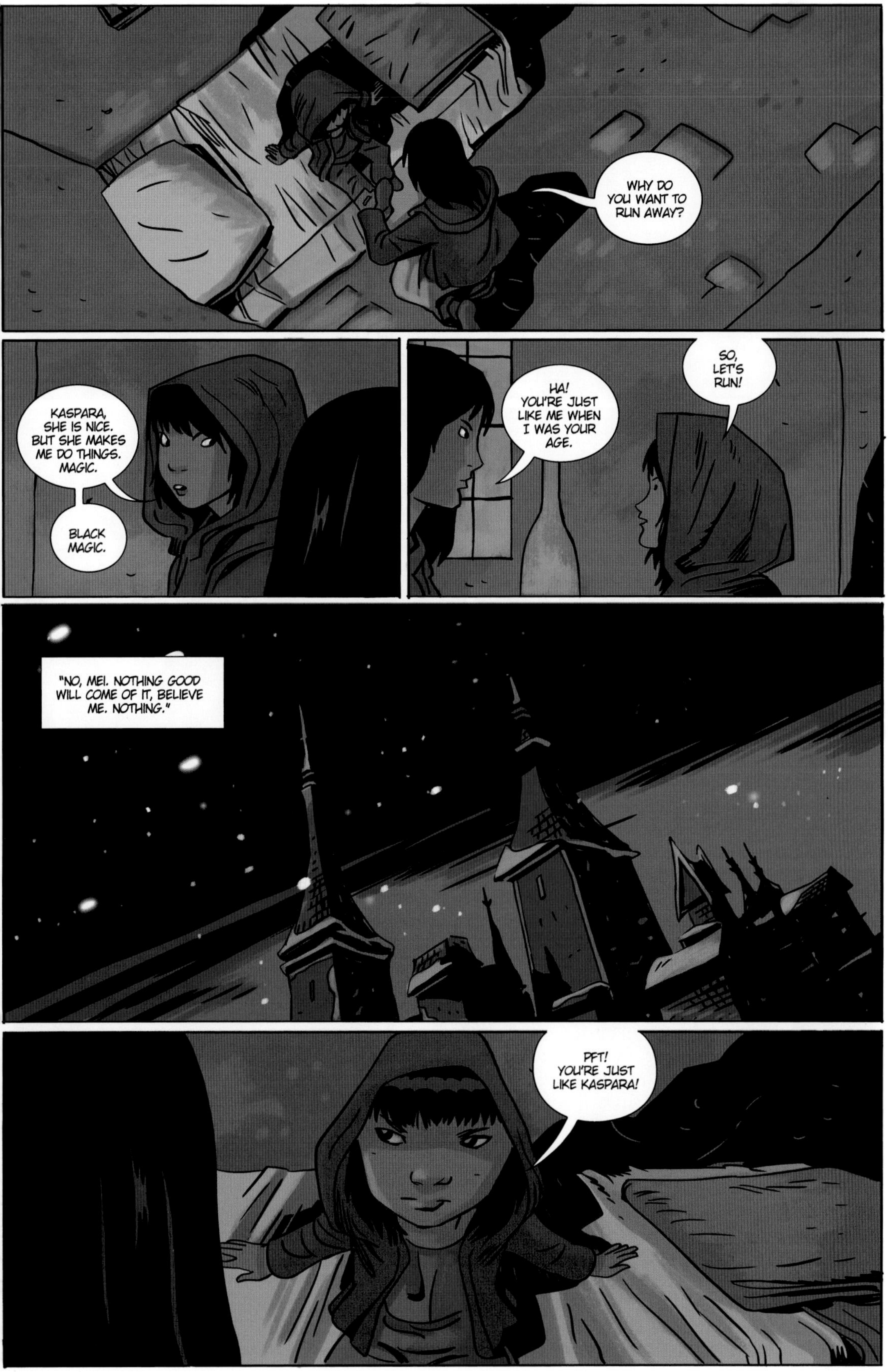
WHY DO YOU WANT TO RUN AWAY?
KASPARA, SHE IS NICE. BUT SHE MAKES ME DO THINGS. MAGIC.
BLACK MAGIC.
HA! YOU'RE JUST LIKE ME WHEN I WAS YOUR AGE.
SO, LET'S RUN!
"NO, MEI. NOTHING GOOD WILL COME OF IT, BELIEVE ME. NOTHING."
PFT! YOU'RE JUST LIKE KASPARA!

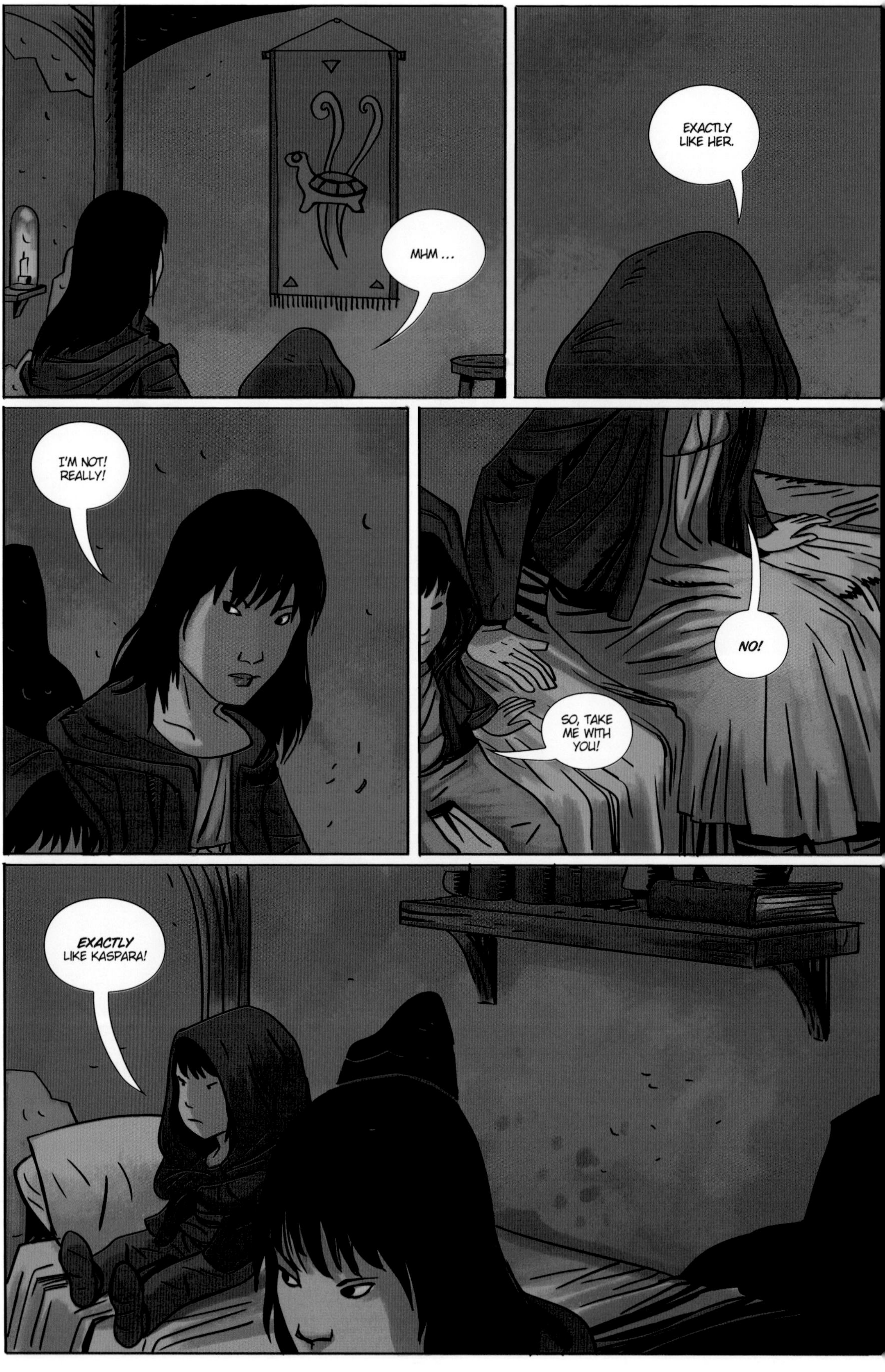
MHM ...
EXACTLY LIKE HER.
I'M NOT! REALLY!
NO!
SO, TAKE ME WITH YOU!
EXACTLY LIKE KASPARA!

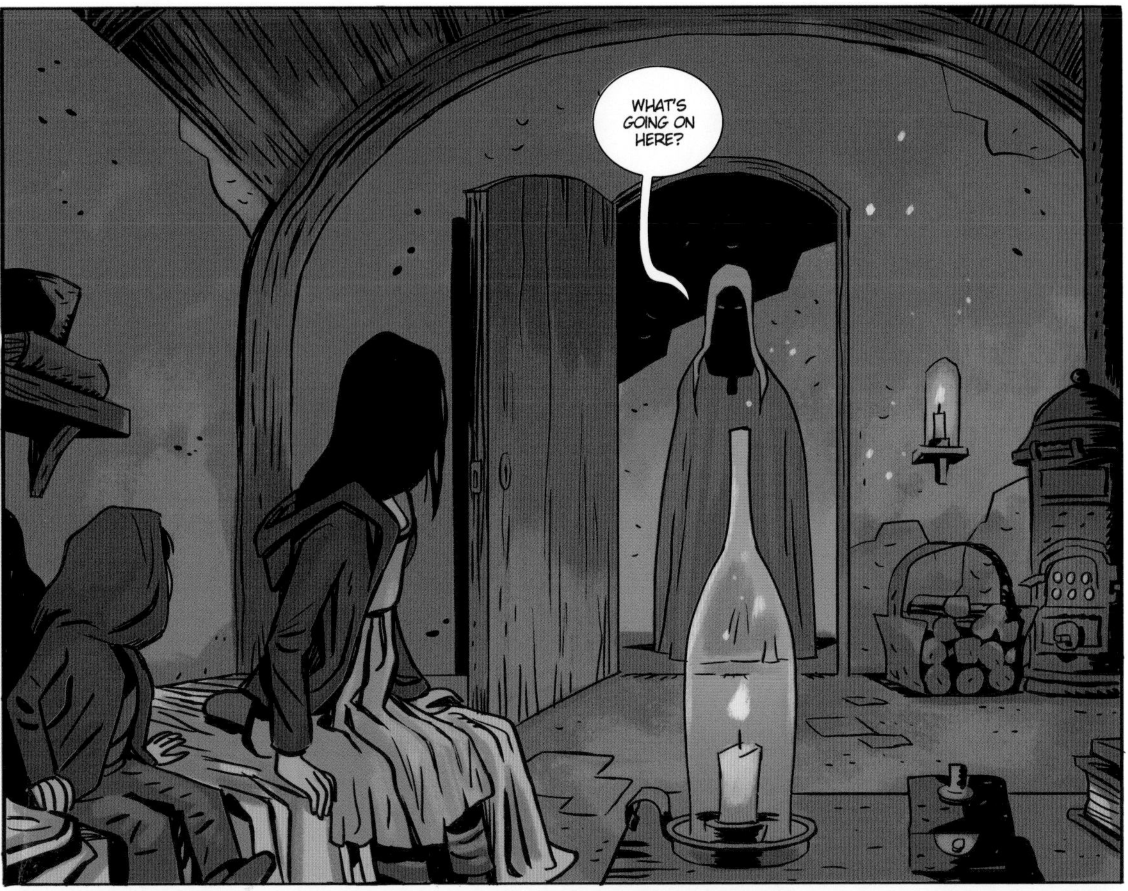
WHAT'S GOING ON HERE?

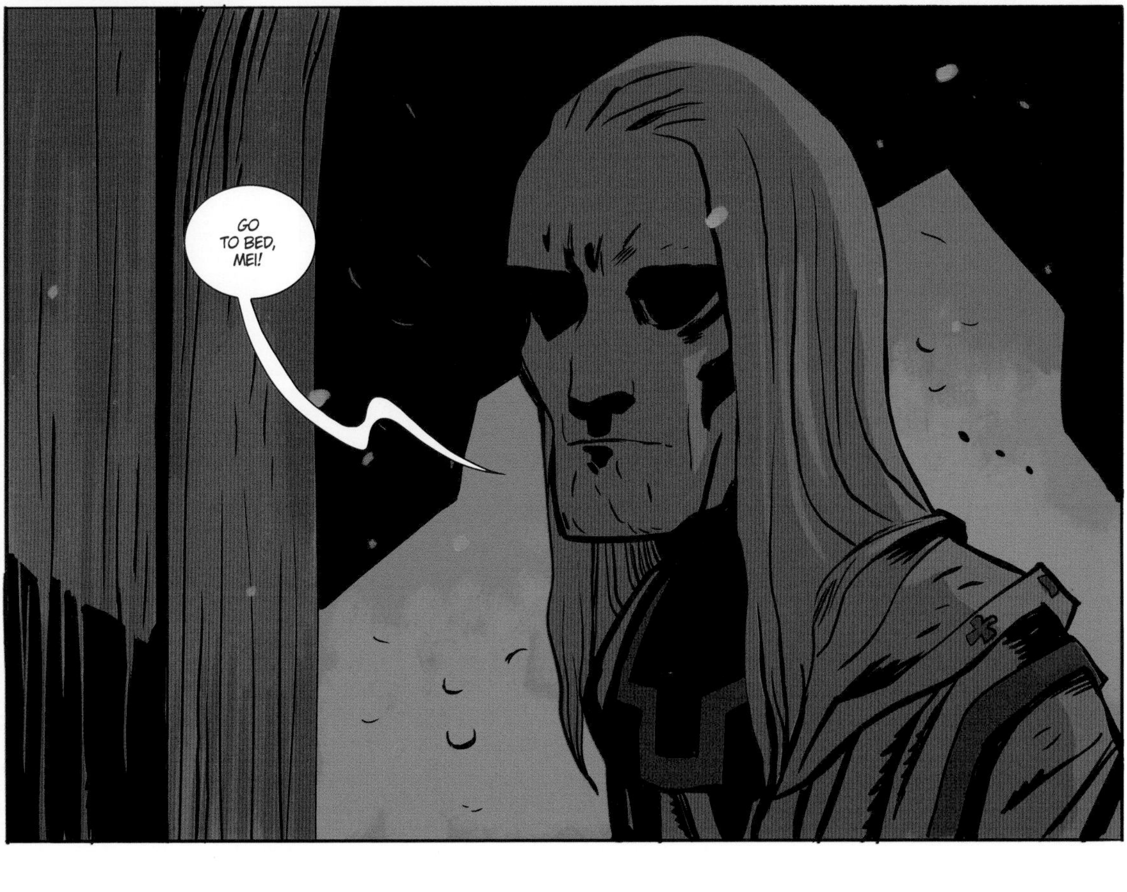
GO TO BED, MEI!

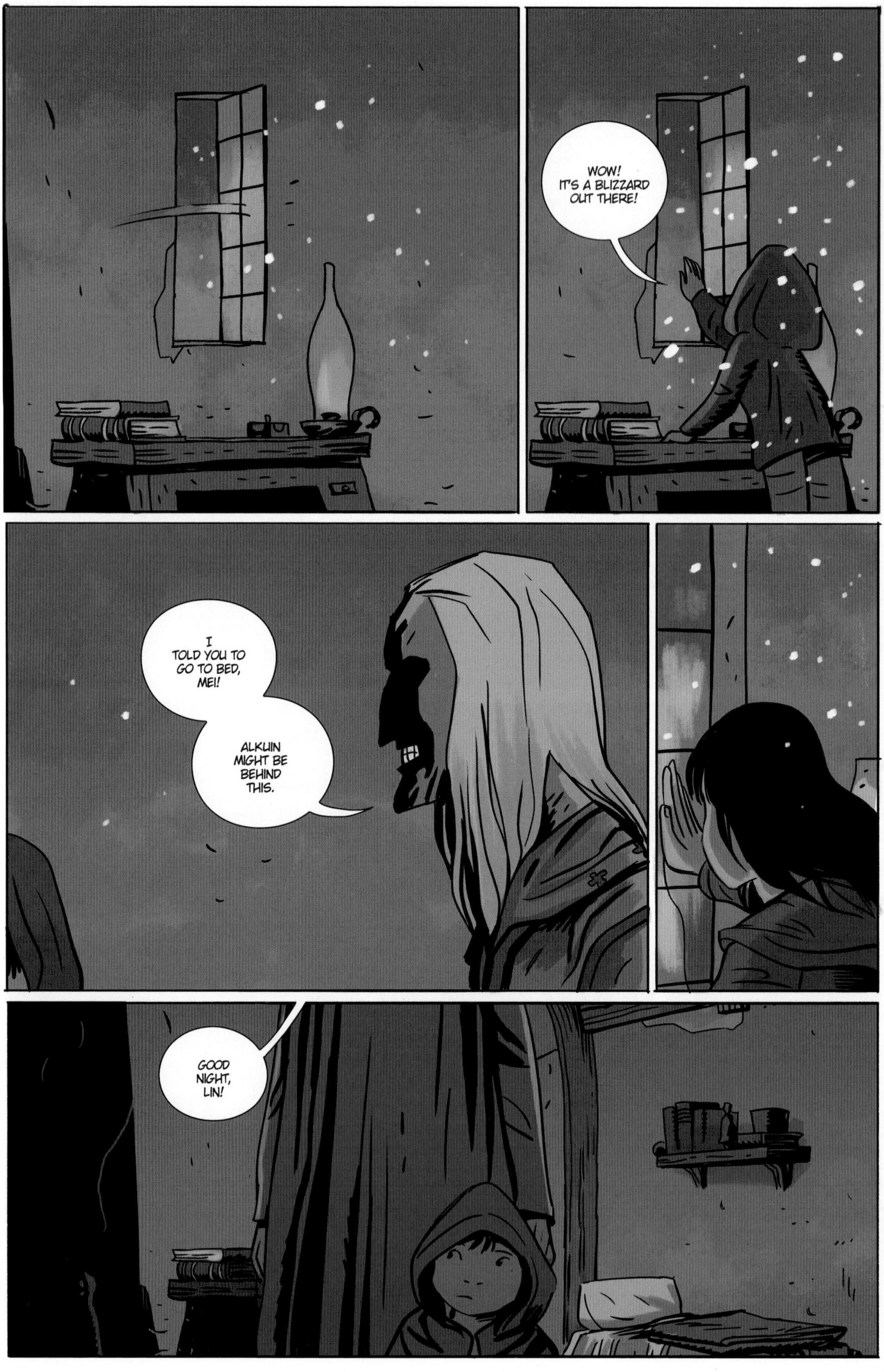
WOW! IT'S A BLIZZARD OUT THERE!
I TOLD YOU TO GO TO BED, MEI!
ALKUIN MIGHT BE BEHIND THIS.
GOOD NIGHT, LIN!

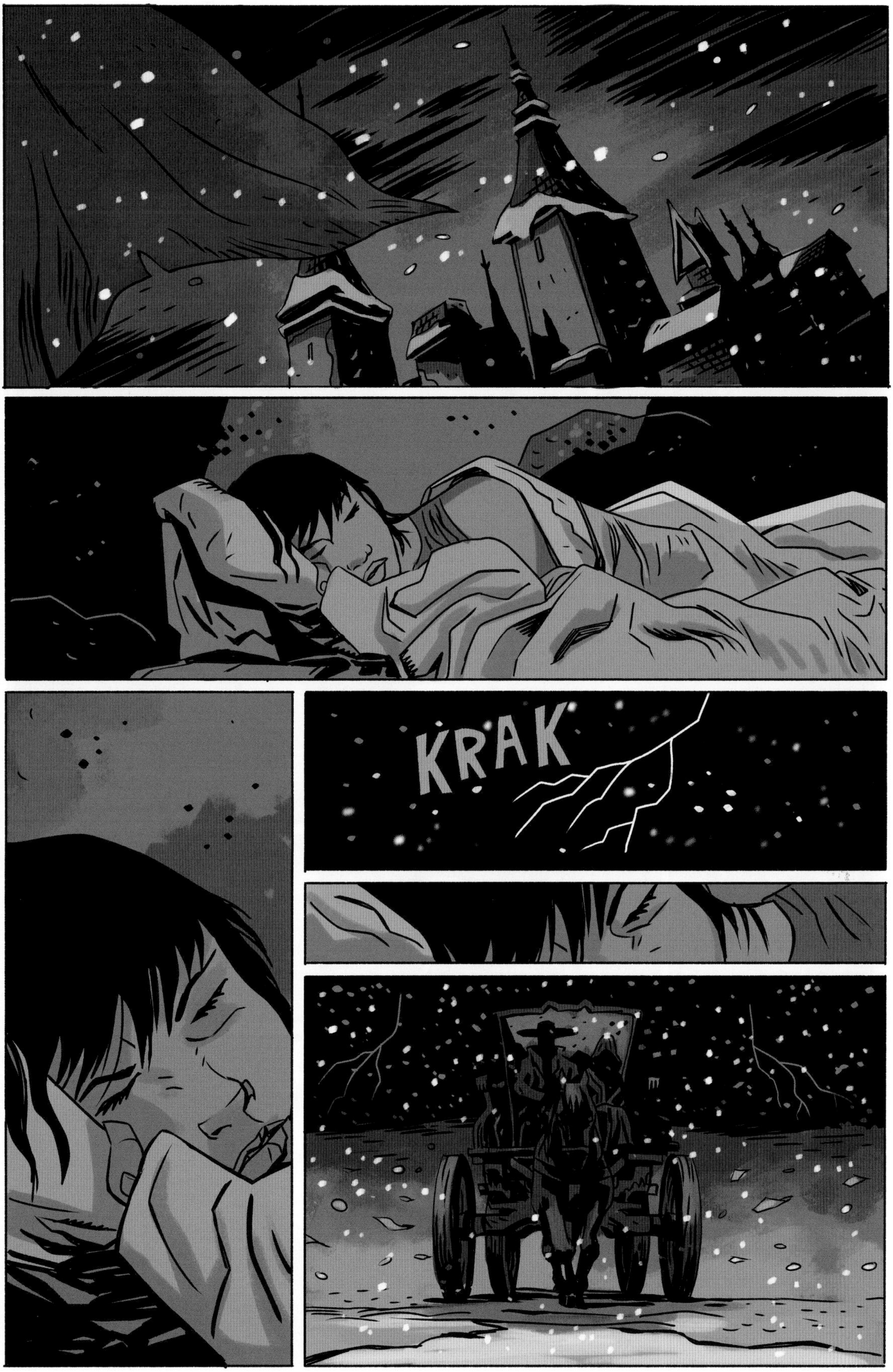
KRAK

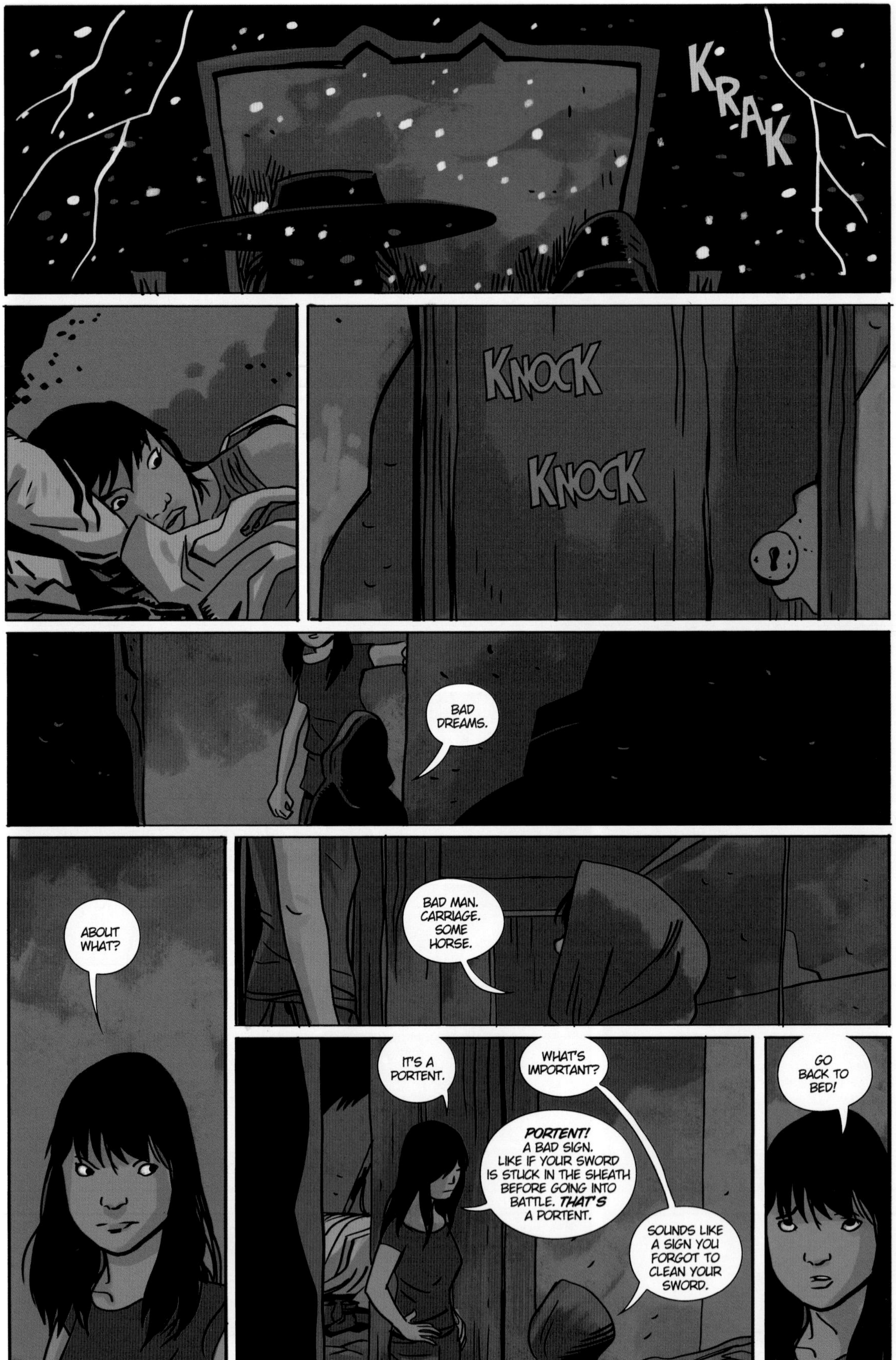
KRAK
KNOCK
KNOCK
BAD DREAMS.
ABOUT WHAT?
BAD MAN. CARRIAGE. SOME HORSE.
IT'S A PORTENT.
WHAT'S IMPORTANT?
PORTENT! A BAD SIGN. LIKE IF YOUR SWORD IS STUCK IN THE SHEATH BEFORE GOING INTO BATTLE. THAT'S A PORTENT.
SOUNDS LIKE A SIGN YOU FORGOT TO CLEAN YOUR SWORD.
GO BACK TO BED!

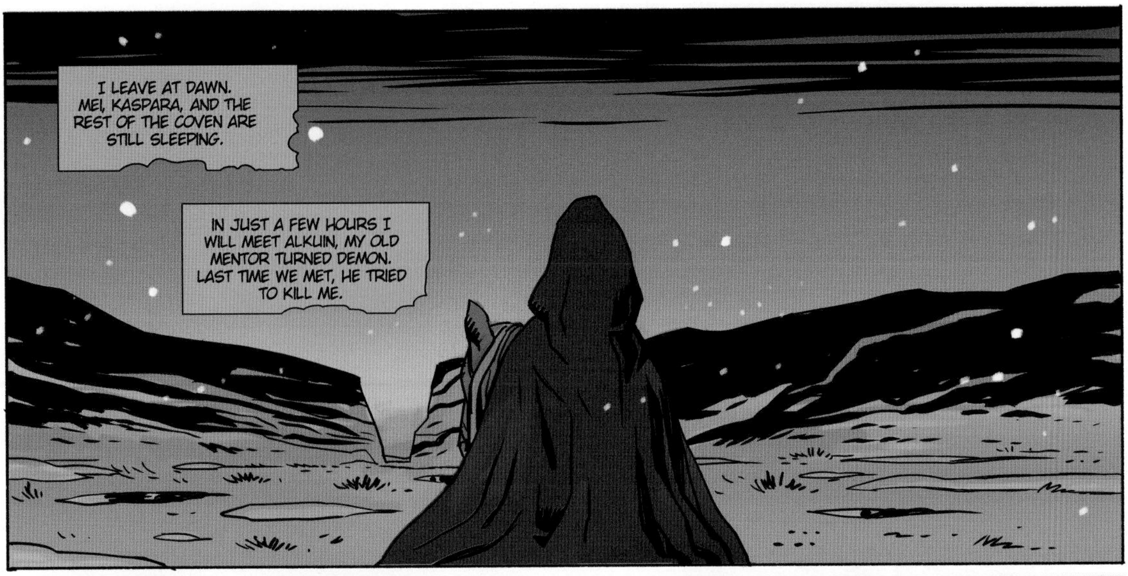
I LEAVE AT DAWN. MEI, KASPARA, AND THE REST OF THE COVEN ARE STILL SLEEPING.
IN JUST A FEW HOURS I WILL MEET ALKUIN, MY OLD MENTOR TURNED DEMON. LAST TIME WE MET, HE TRIED TO KILL ME.

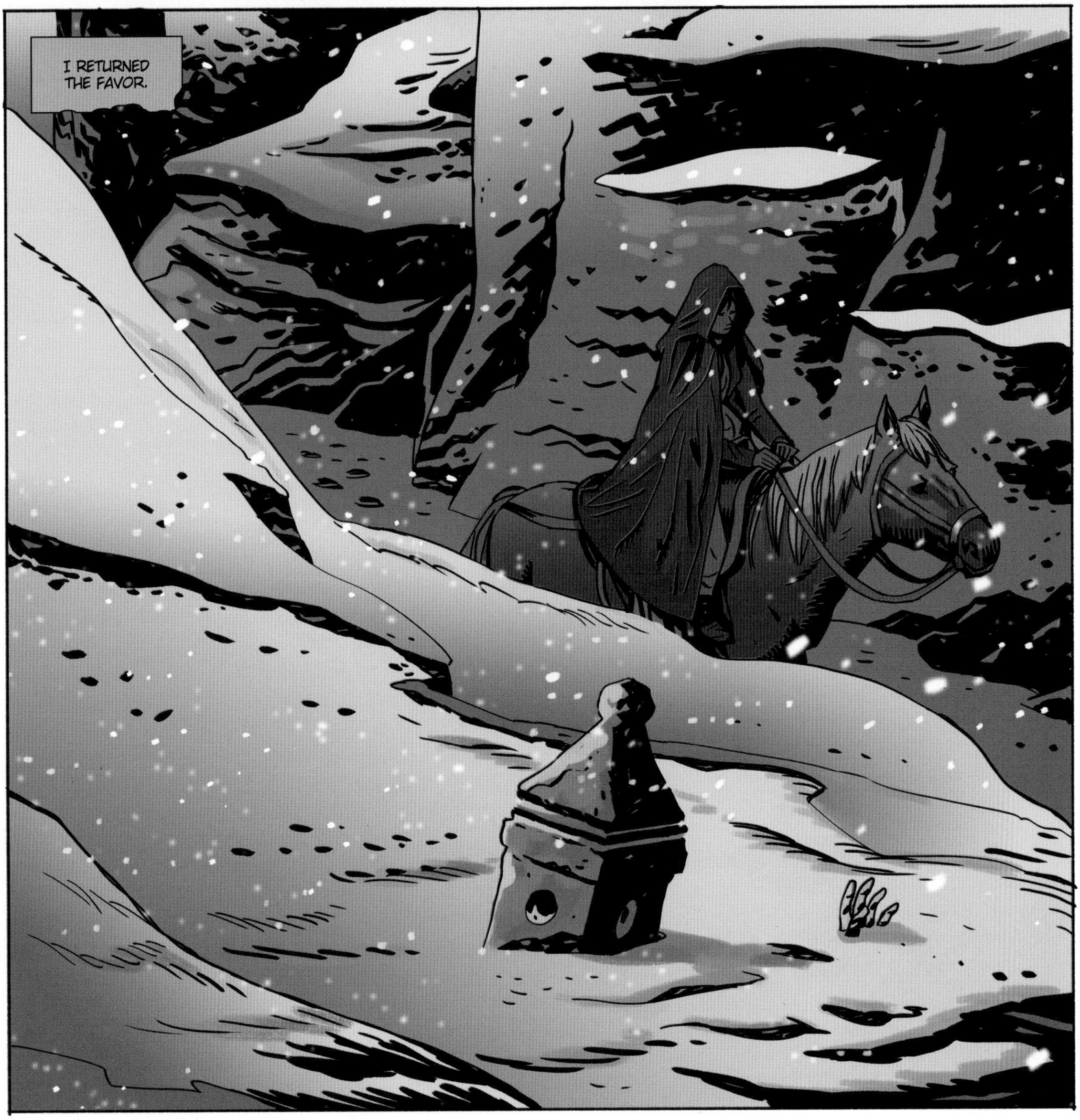
I RETURNED THE FAVOR.

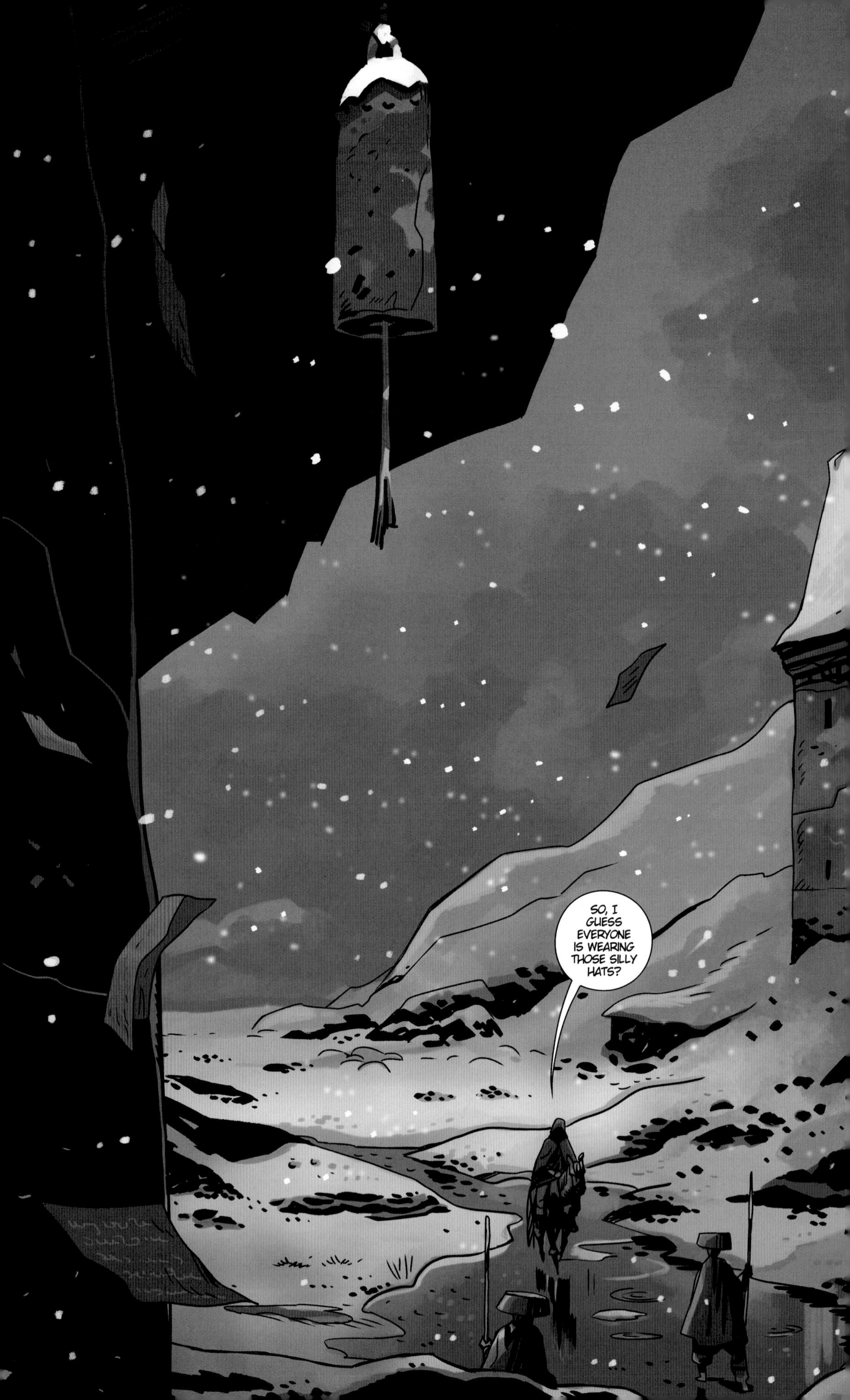
SO, I GUESS EVERYONE IS WEARING THOSE SILLY HATS?

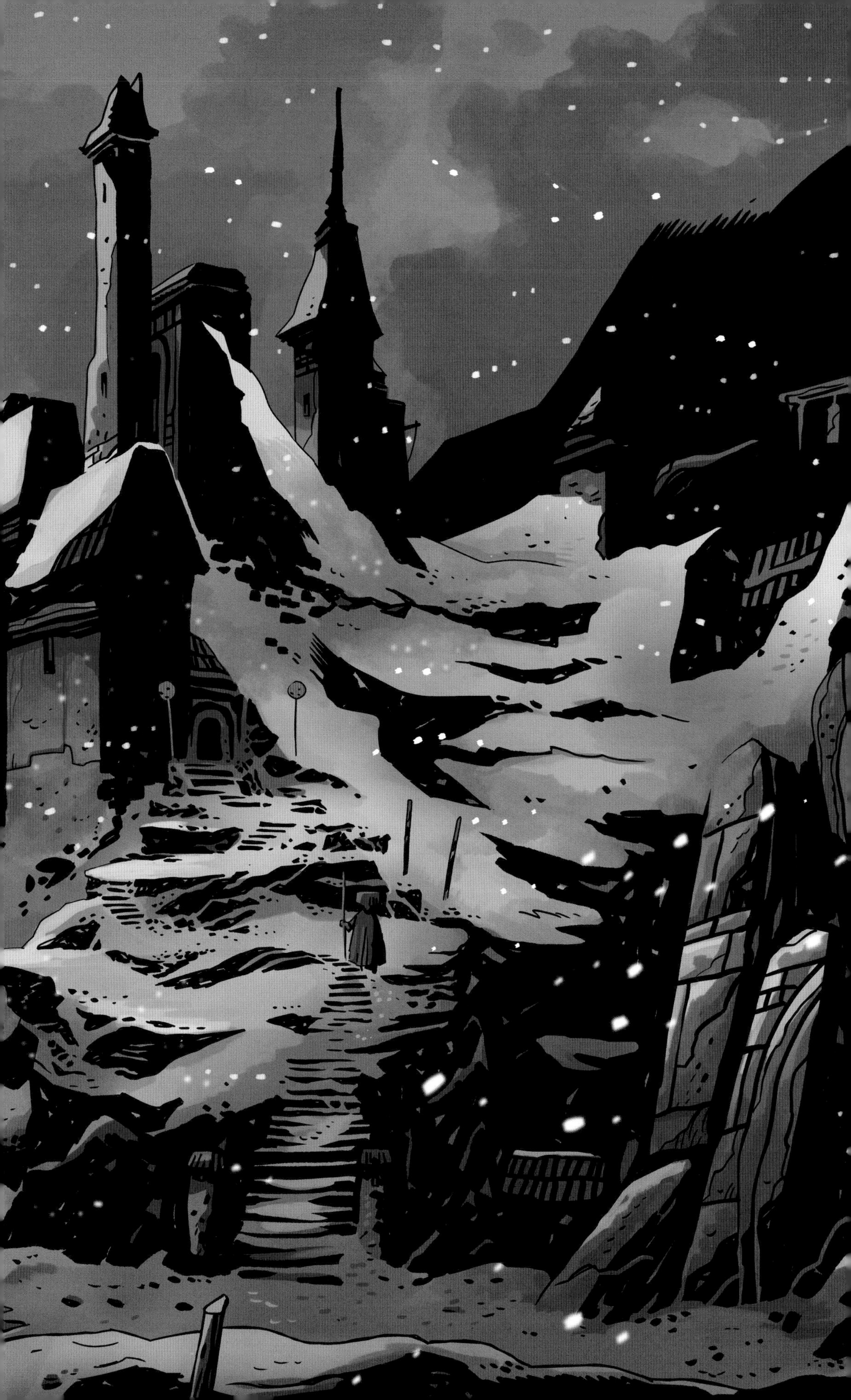

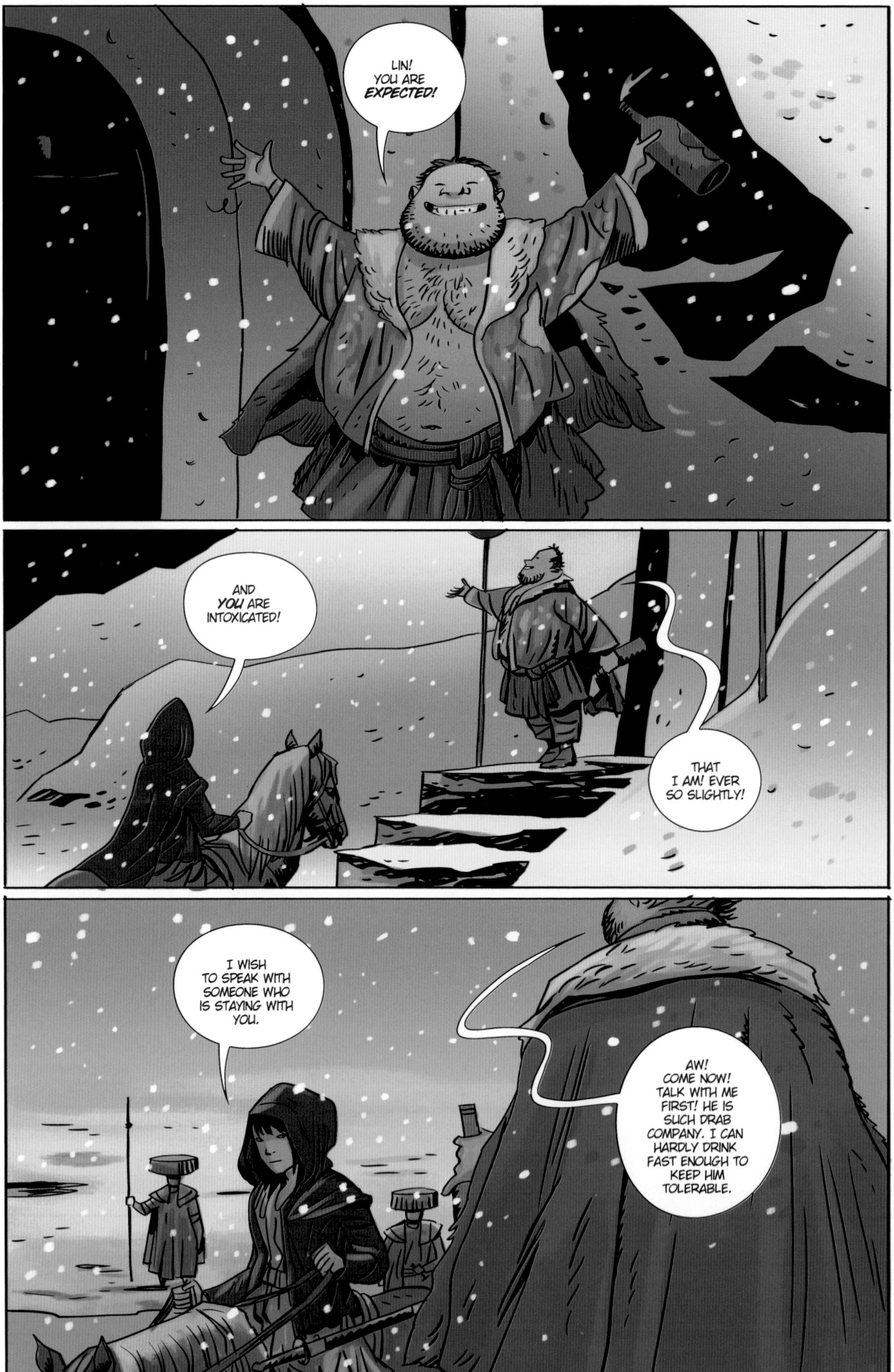
LIN! YOU ARE *EXPECTED!*
AND *YOU* ARE INTOXICATED!
THAT I AM! EVER SO SLIGHTLY!
I WISH TO SPEAK WITH SOMEONE WHO IS STAYING WITH YOU.
AW! COME NOW! TALK WITH ME FIRST! HE IS SUCH DRAB COMPANY. I CAN HARDLY DRINK FAST ENOUGH TO KEEP HIM TOLERABLE.

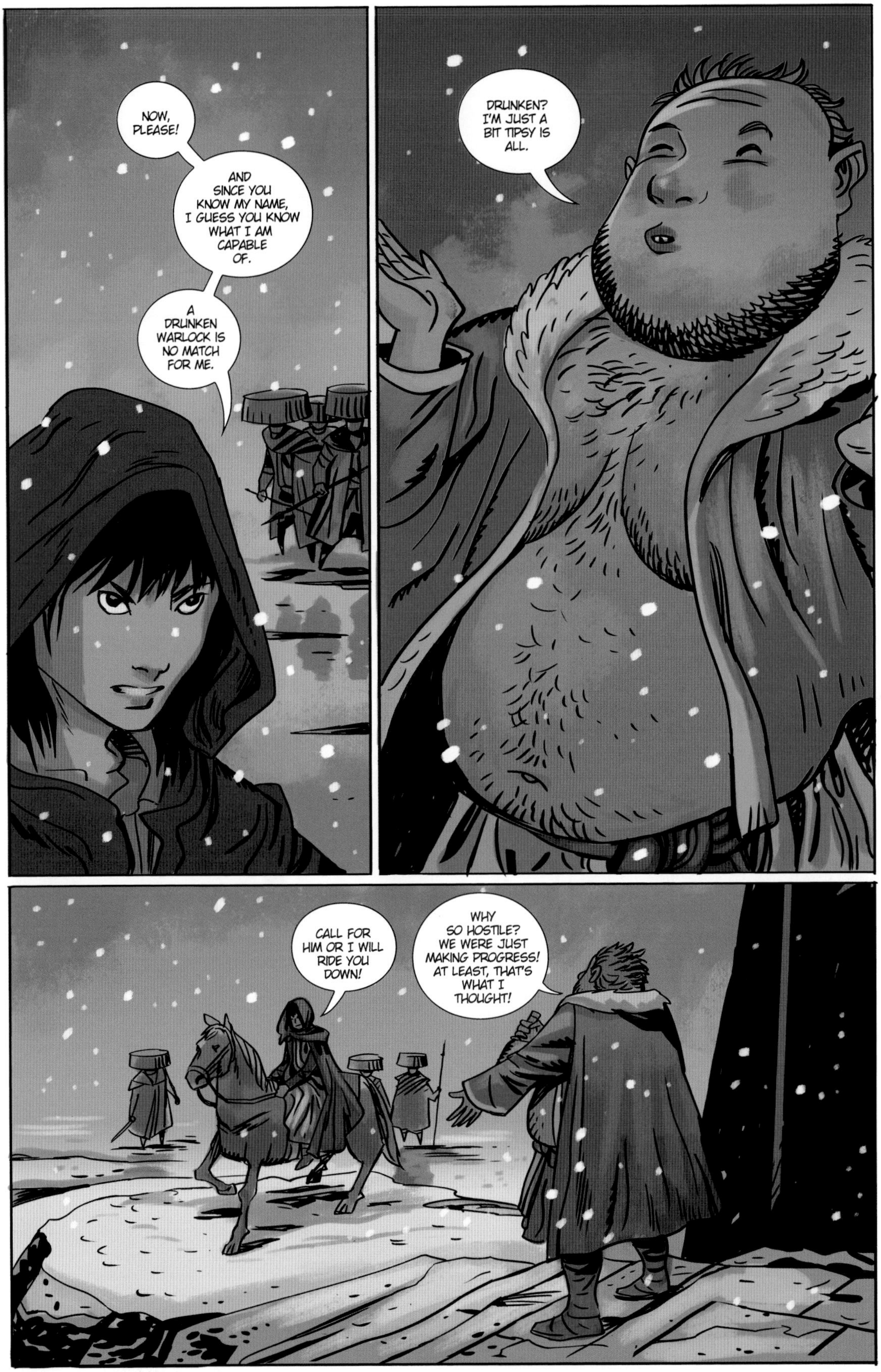
NOW, PLEASE!
AND SINCE YOU KNOW MY NAME, I GUESS YOU KNOW WHAT I AM CAPABLE OF.
A DRUNKEN WARLOCK IS NO MATCH FOR ME.
DRUNKEN? I'M JUST A BIT TIPSY IS ALL.
CALL FOR HIM OR I WILL RIDE YOU DOWN!
WHY SO HOSTILE? WE WERE JUST MAKING PROGRESS! AT LEAST, THAT'S WHAT I THOUGHT!

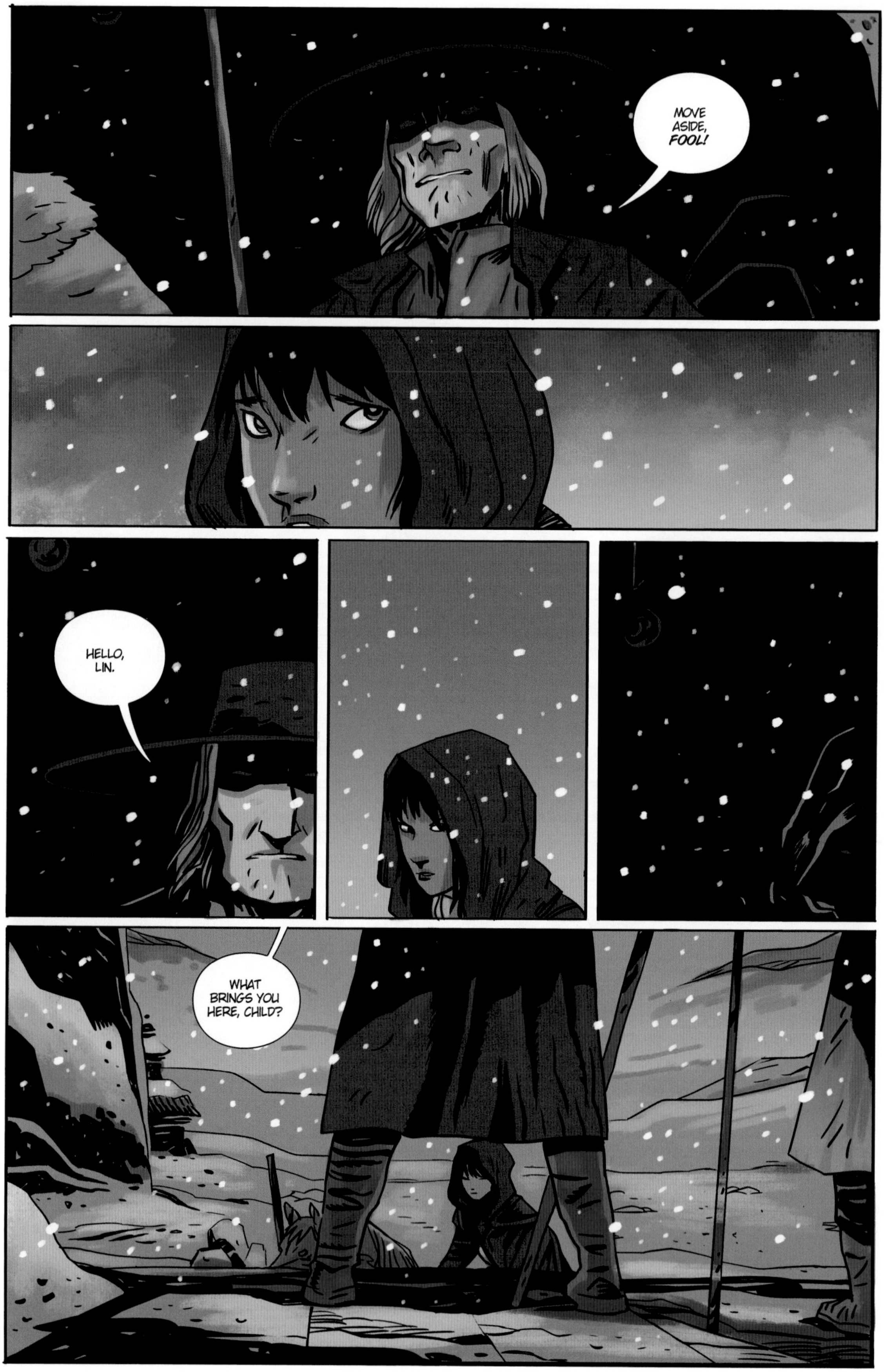

MOVE ASIDE, FOOL!
HELLO, LIN.
WHAT BRINGS YOU HERE, CHILD?

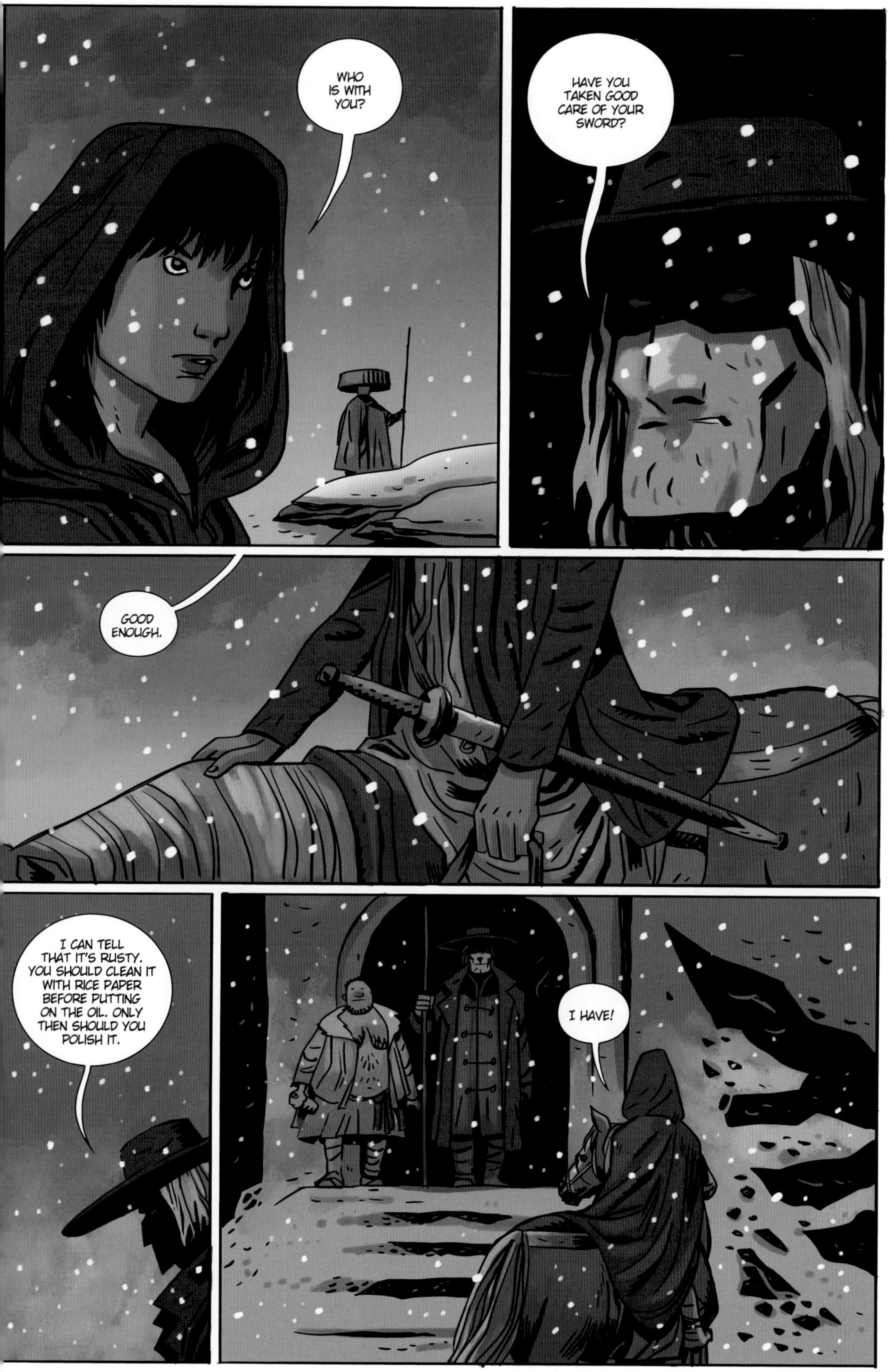
WHO IS WITH YOU?
HAVE YOU TAKEN GOOD CARE OF YOUR SWORD?
GOOD ENOUGH.
I CAN TELL THAT IT'S RUSTY. YOU SHOULD CLEAN IT WITH RICE PAPER BEFORE PUTTING ON THE OIL. ONLY THEN SHOULD YOU POLISH IT.
I HAVE!

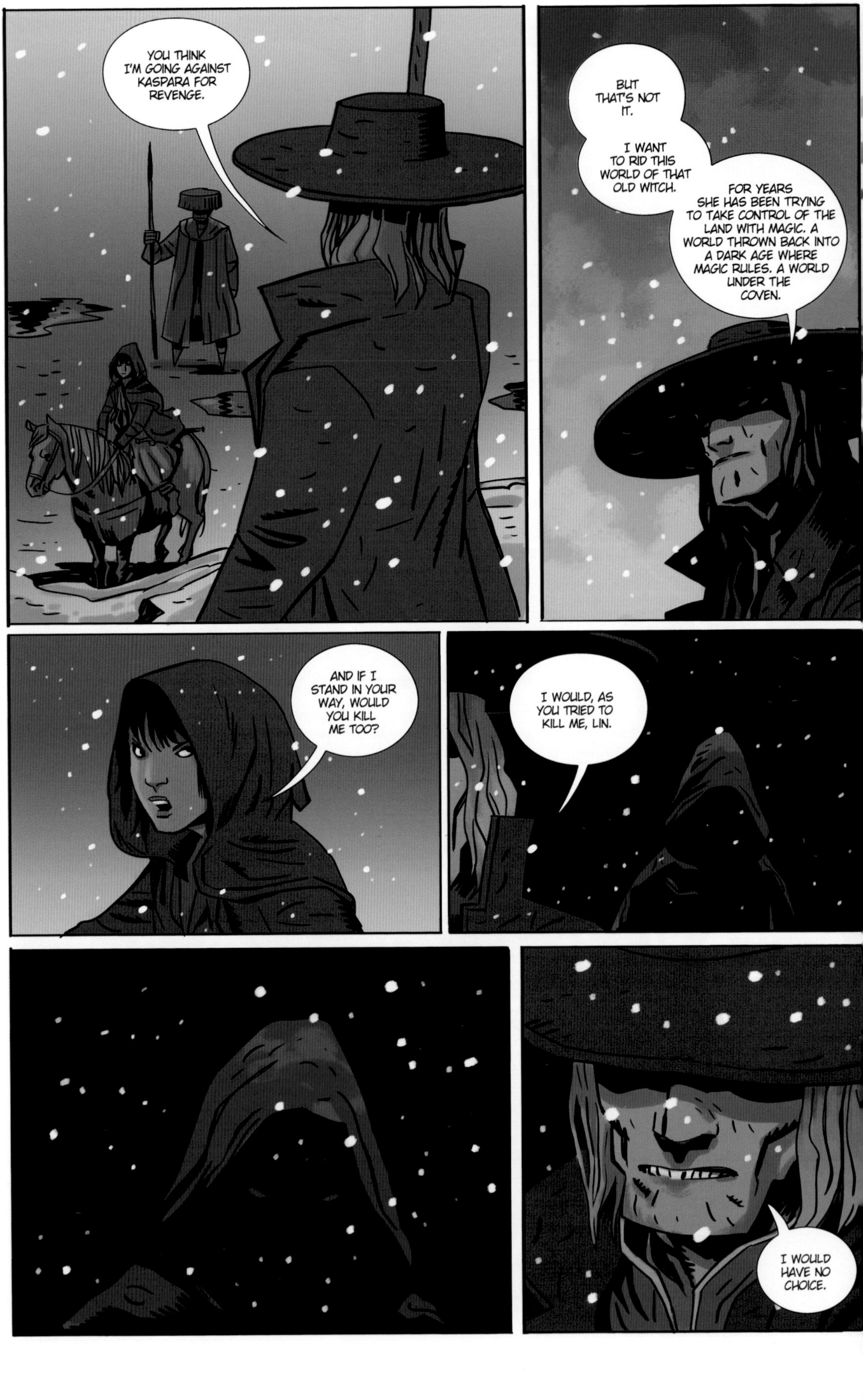
YOU THINK I'M GOING AGAINST KASPARA FOR REVENGE.
BUT THAT'S NOT IT.
I WANT TO RID THIS WORLD OF THAT OLD WITCH.
FOR YEARS SHE HAS BEEN TRYING TO TAKE CONTROL OF THE LAND WITH MAGIC. A WORLD THROWN BACK INTO A DARK AGE WHERE MAGIC RULES. A WORLD UNDER THE COVEN.
AND IF I STAND IN YOUR WAY, WOULD YOU KILL ME TOO?
I WOULD, AS YOU TRIED TO KILL ME, LIN.
I WOULD HAVE NO CHOICE.

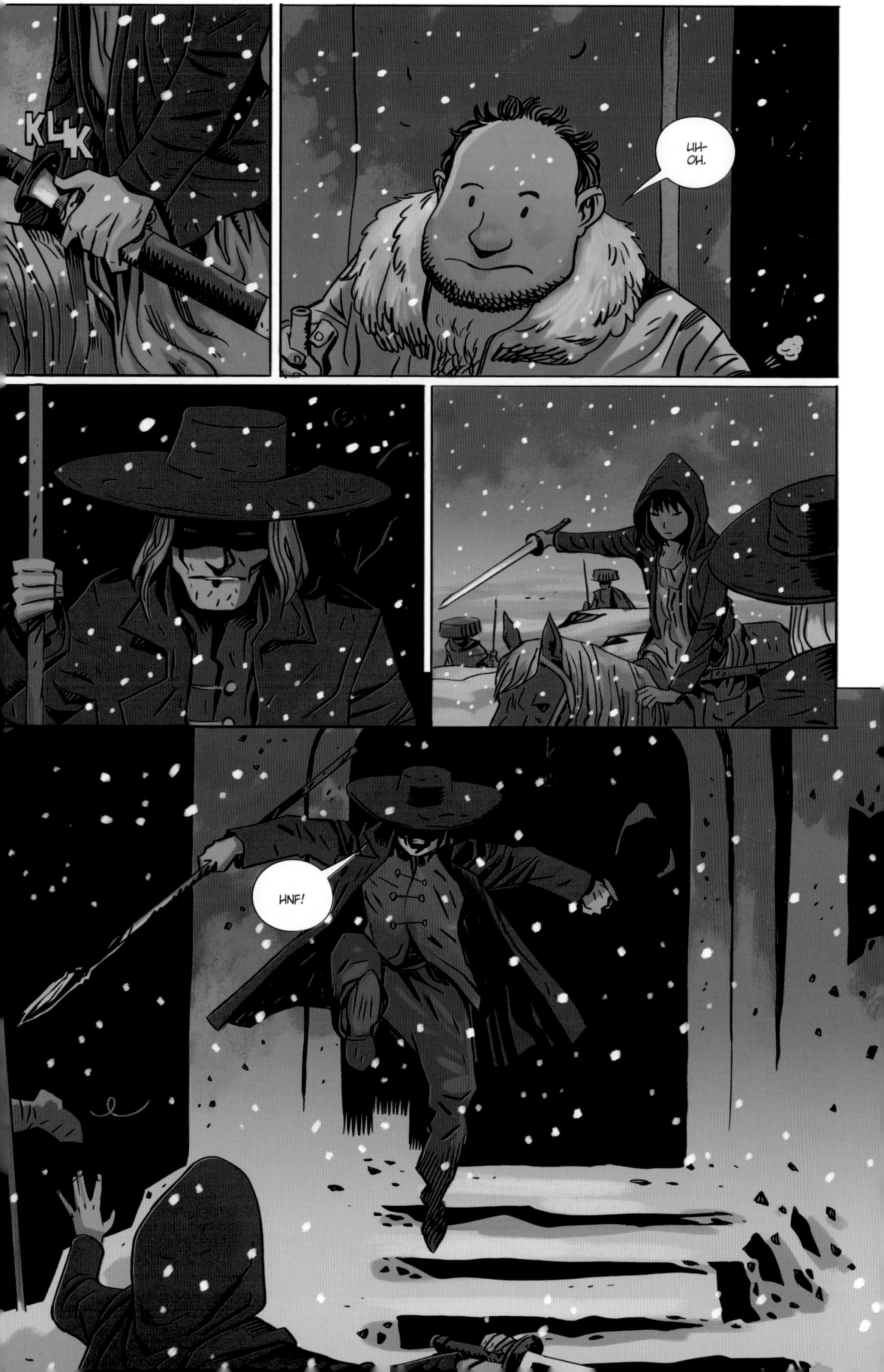
KLIK
UH-OH.
HNF!

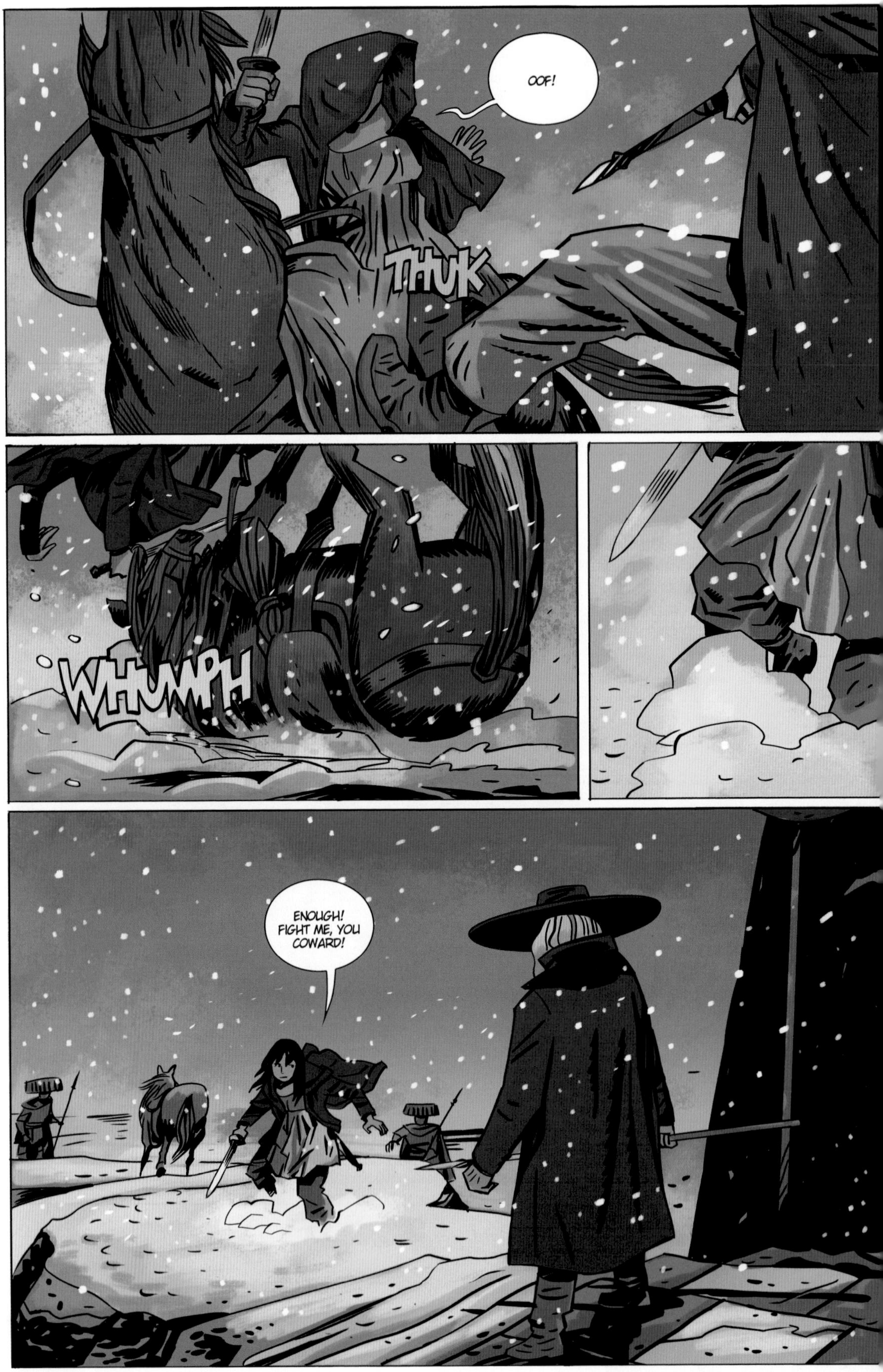
OOF!
THUK
WHUMPH
ENOUGH! FIGHT ME, YOU COWARD!

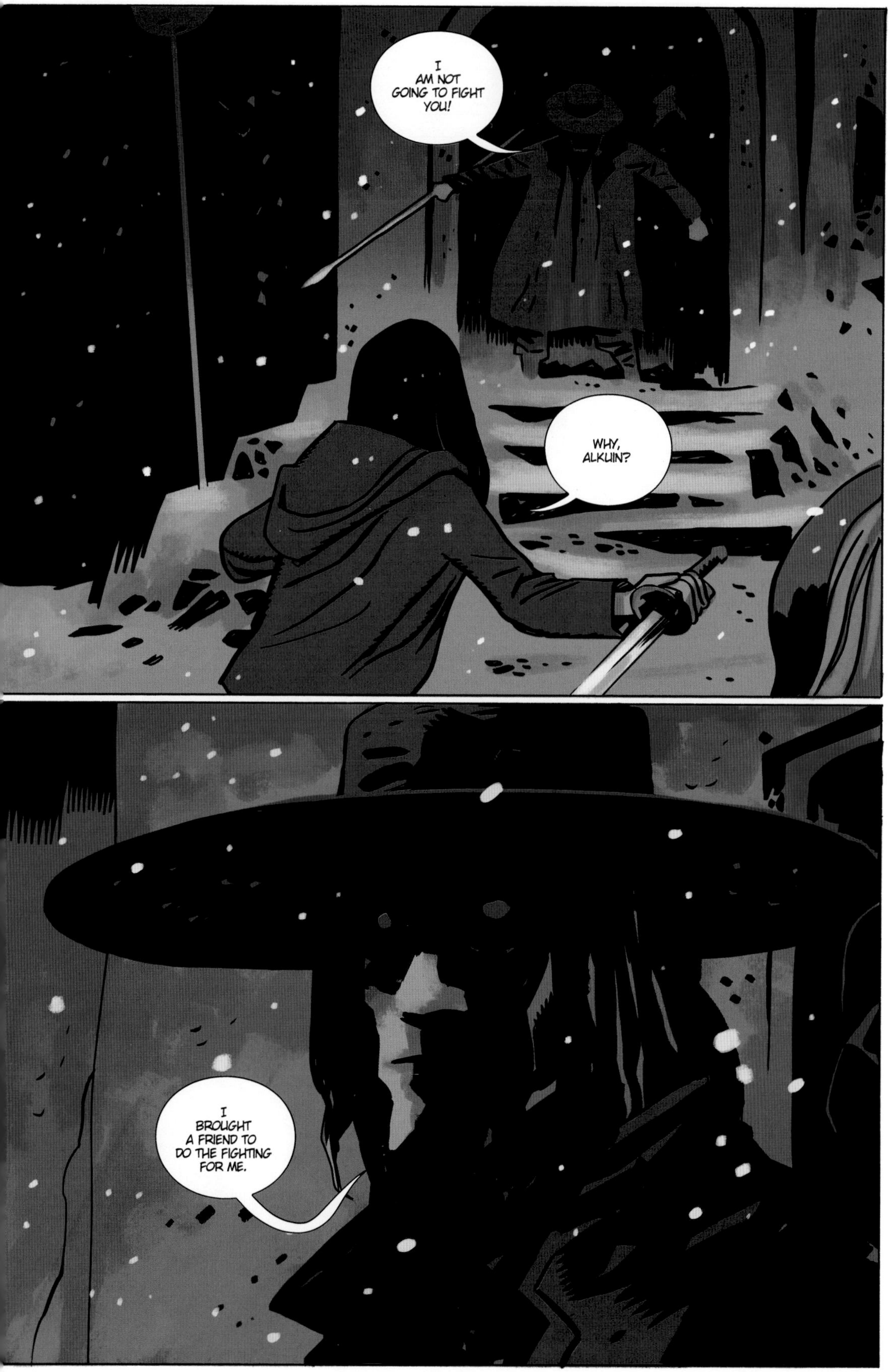
I AM NOT GOING TO FIGHT YOU!
WHY, ALKUIN?
I BROUGHT A FRIEND TO DO THE FIGHTING FOR ME.

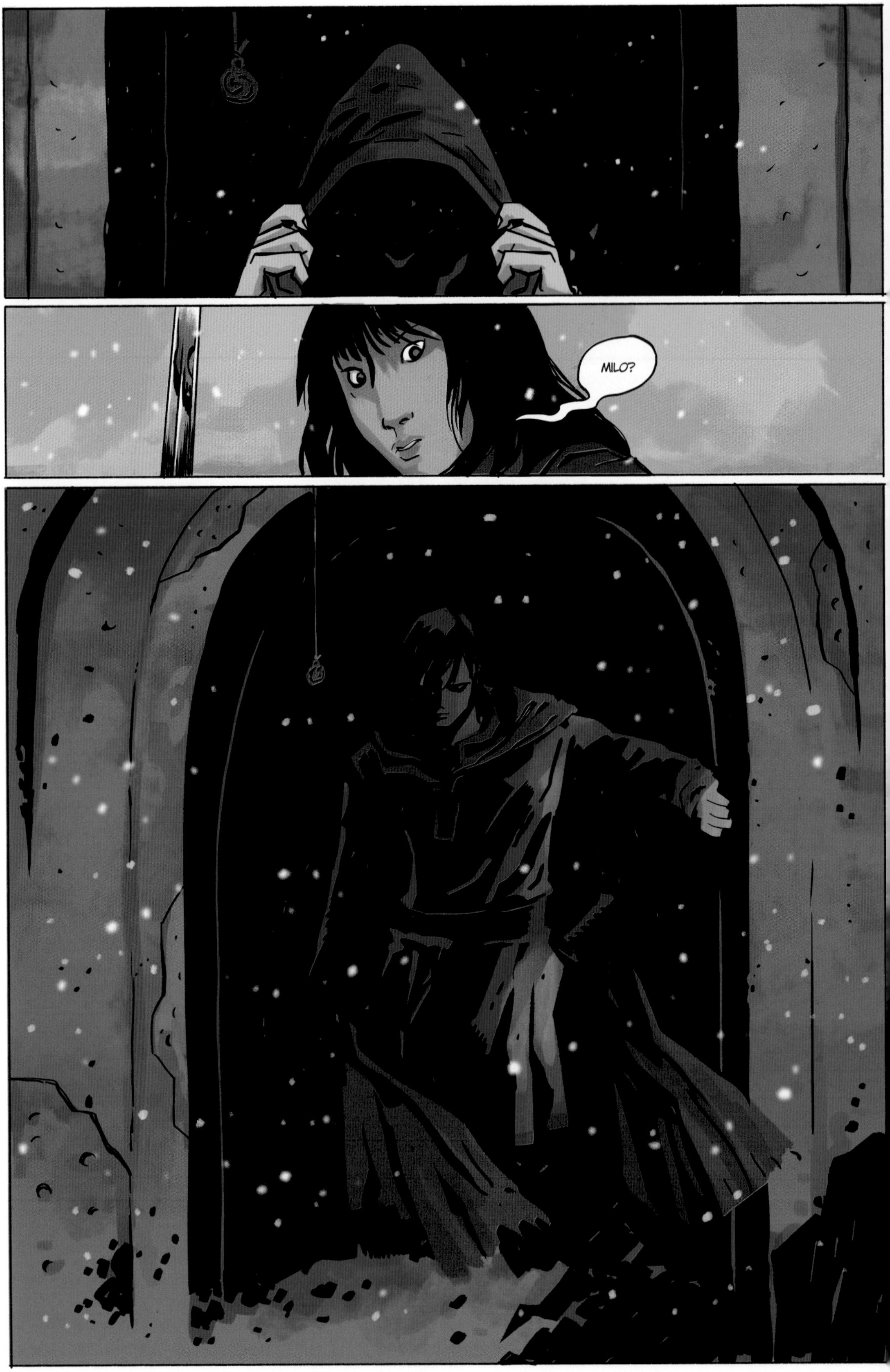
MILO?

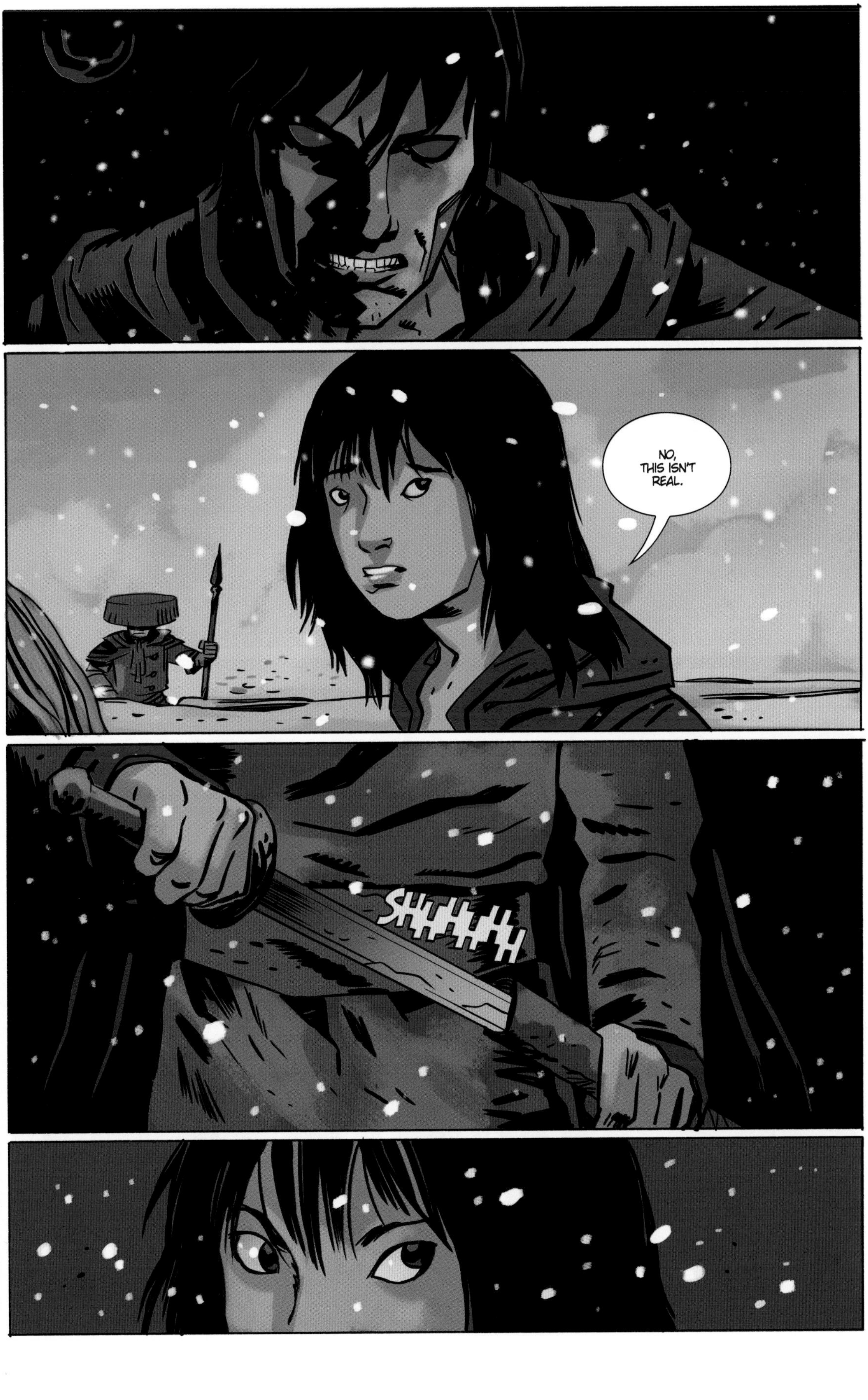
NO, THIS ISN'T REAL.
SHHHHH

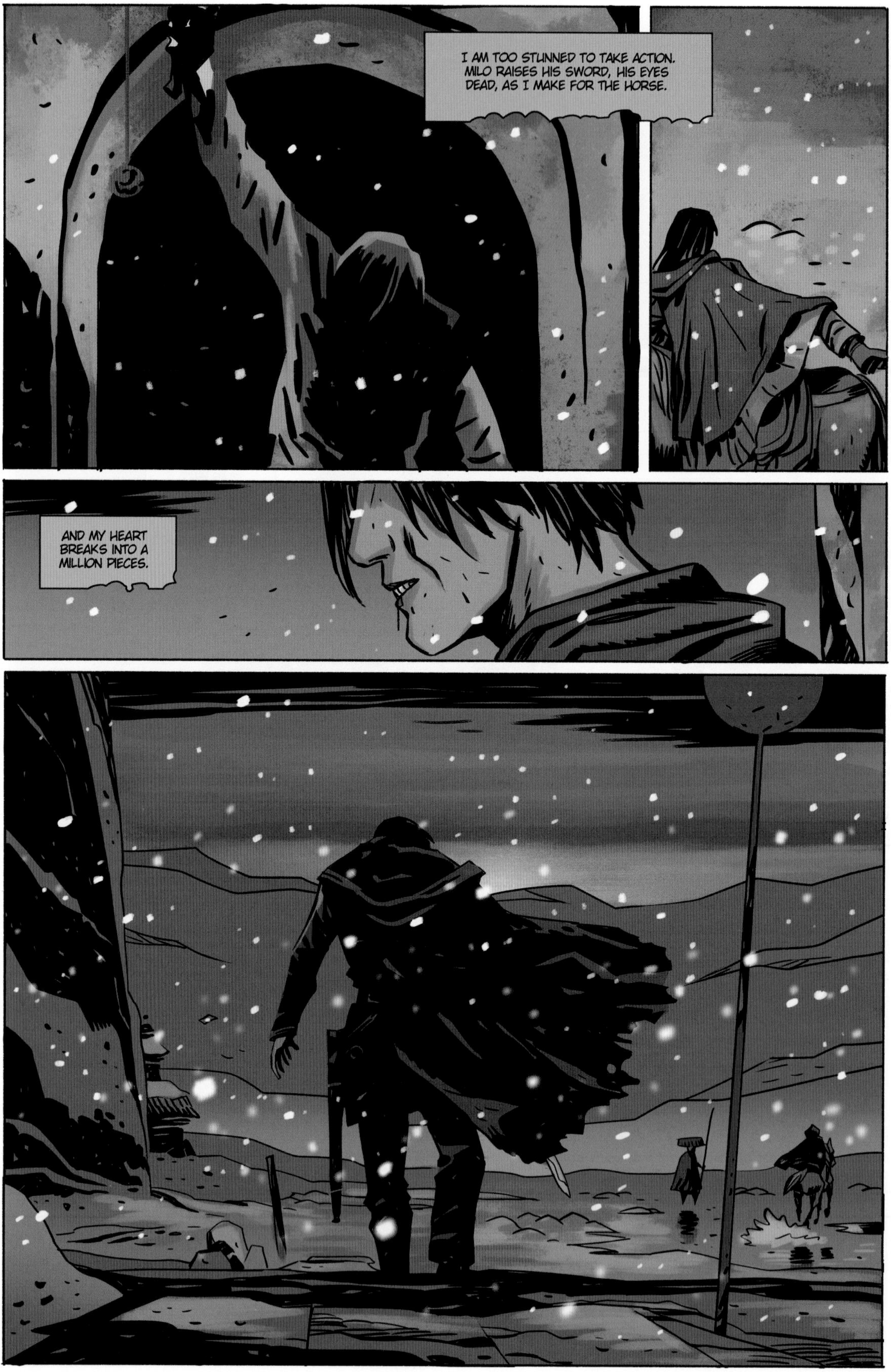
I AM TOO STUNNED TO TAKE ACTION. MILO RAISES HIS SWORD, HIS EYES DEAD, AS I MAKE FOR THE HORSE.
AND MY HEART BREAKS INTO A MILLION PIECES.

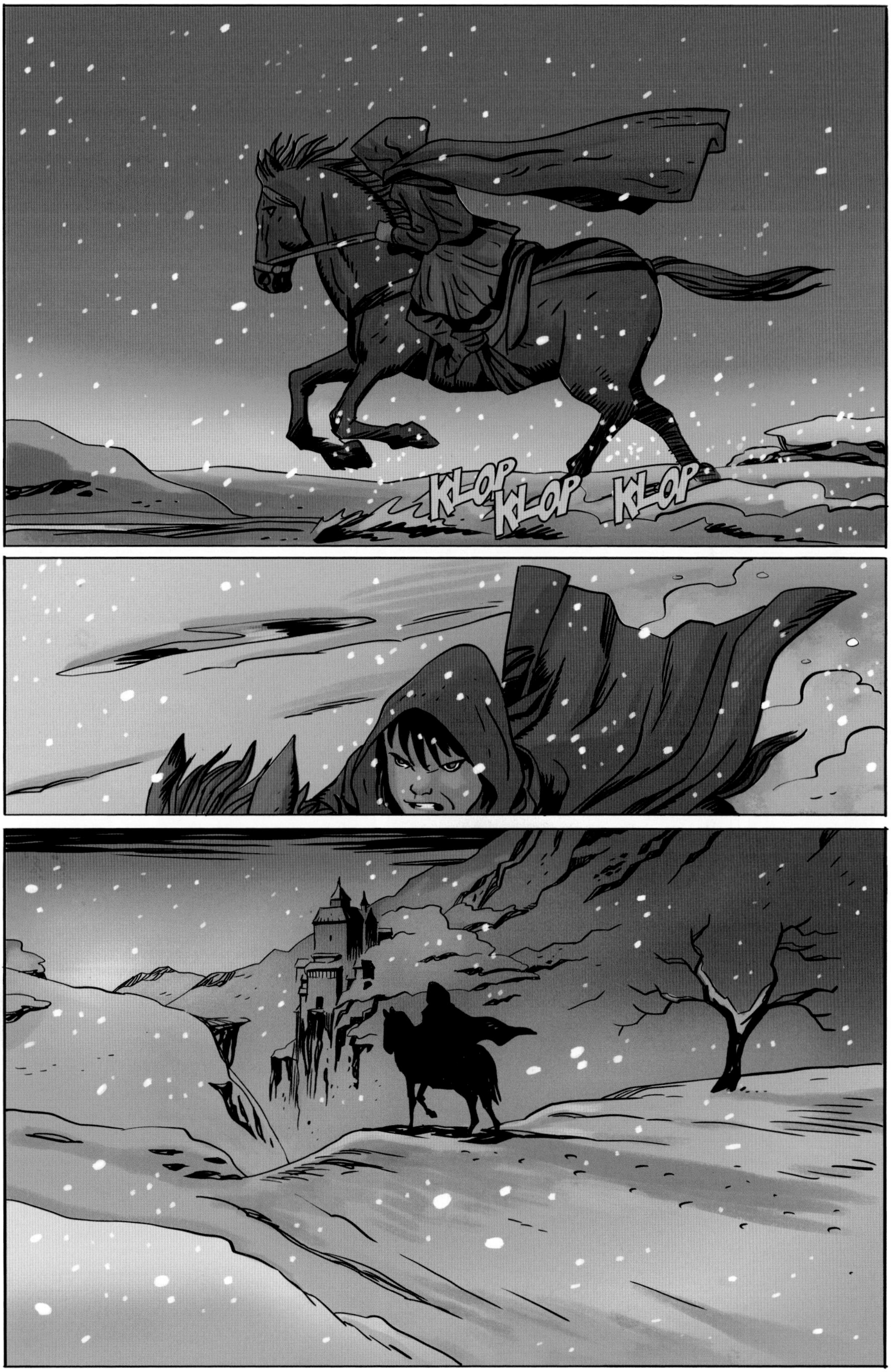
KLOP
KLOP
KLOP

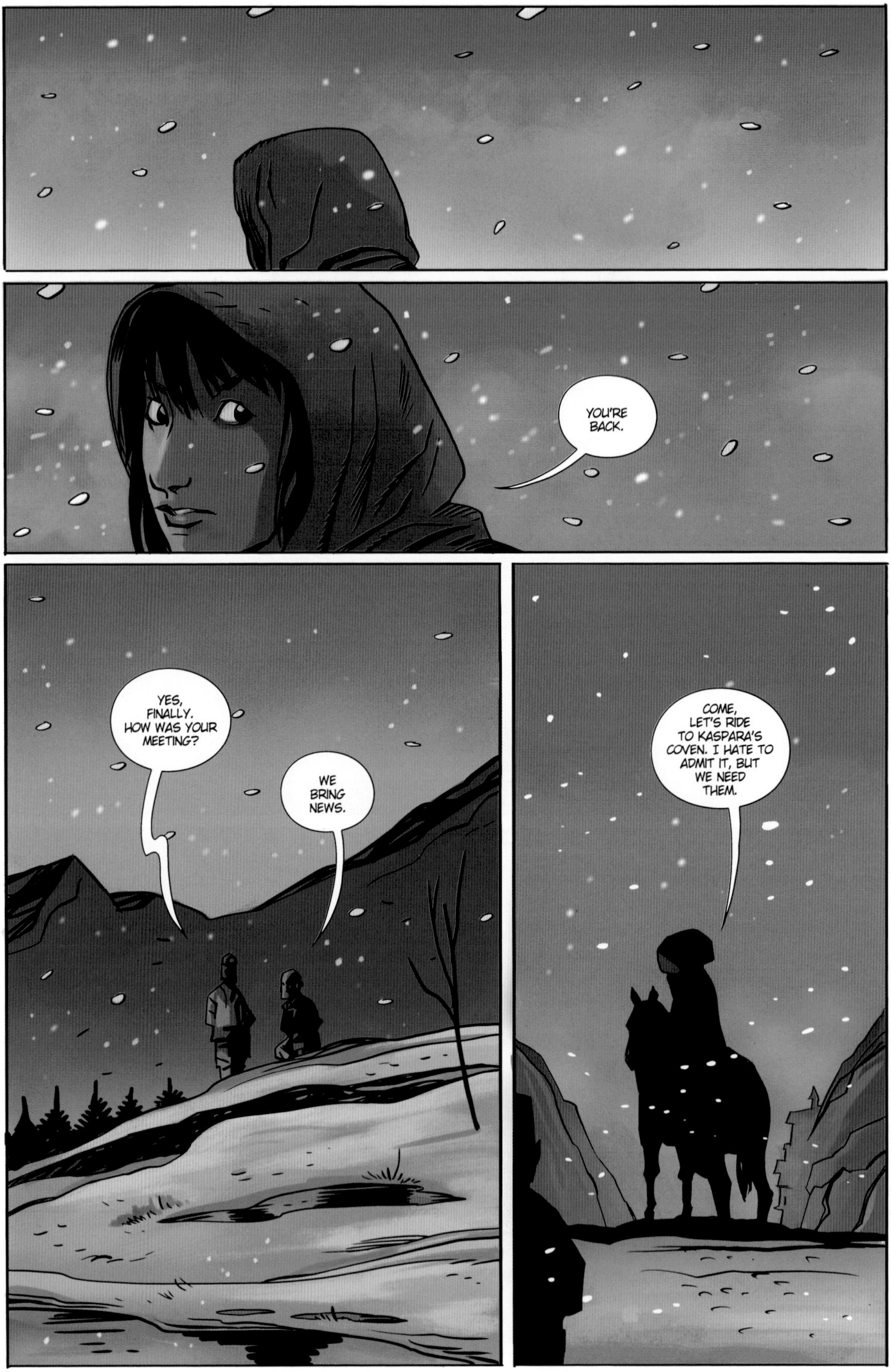
YOU'RE BACK.
YES, FINALLY. HOW WAS YOUR MEETING?
WE BRING NEWS.
COME, LET'S RIDE TO KASPARA'S COVEN. I HATE TO ADMIT IT, BUT WE NEED THEM.

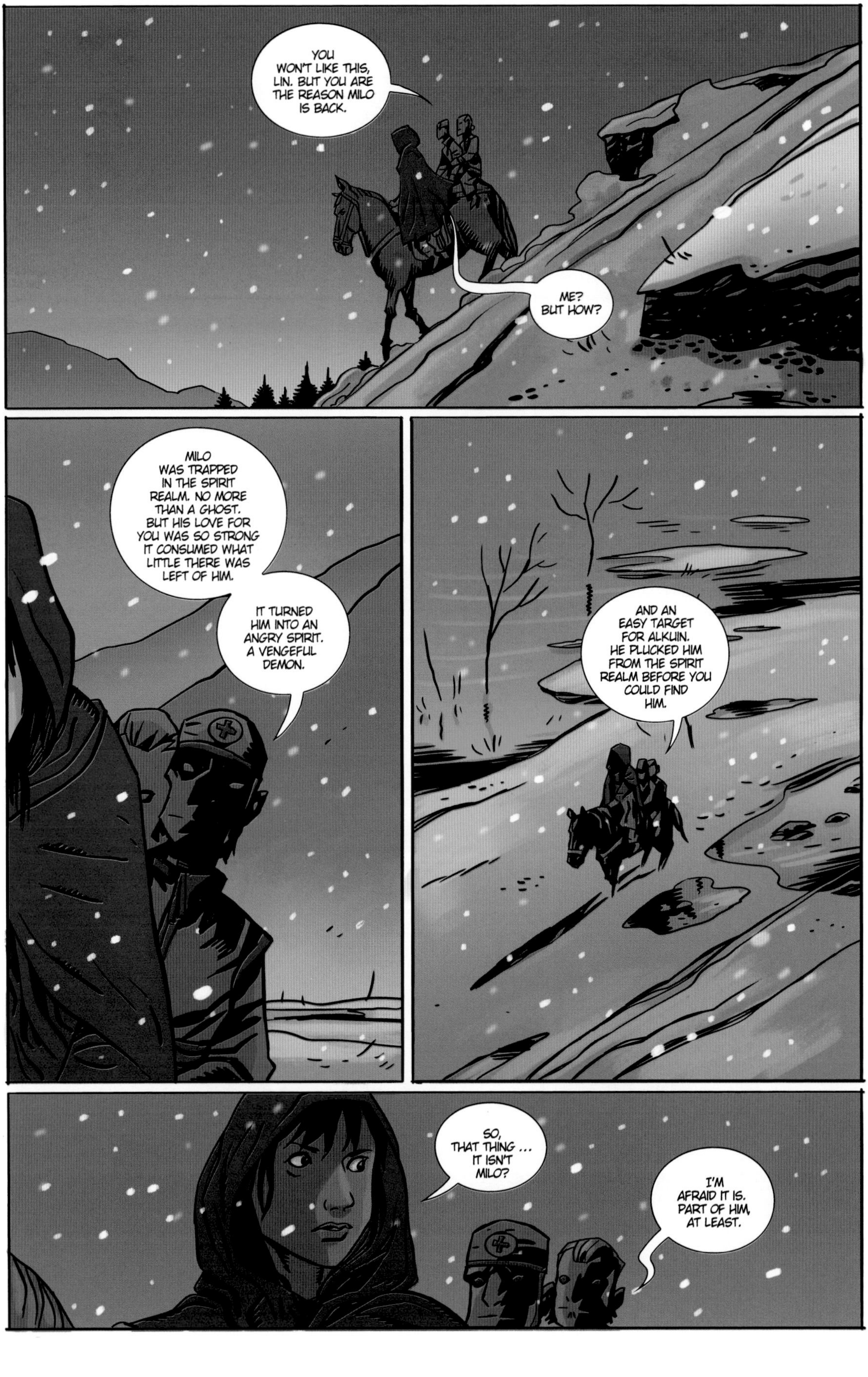
YOU WON'T LIKE THIS, LIN. BUT YOU ARE THE REASON MILO IS BACK.
ME? BUT HOW?
MILO WAS TRAPPED IN THE SPIRIT REALM. NO MORE THAN A GHOST. BUT HIS LOVE FOR YOU WAS SO STRONG IT CONSUMED WHAT LITTLE THERE WAS LEFT OF HIM.
IT TURNED HIM INTO AN ANGRY SPIRIT. A VENGEFUL DEMON.
AND AN EASY TARGET FOR ALKUIN. HE PLUCKED HIM FROM THE SPIRIT REALM BEFORE YOU COULD FIND HIM.
SO, THAT THING ... IT ISN'T MILO?
I'M AFRAID IT IS. PART OF HIM, AT LEAST.

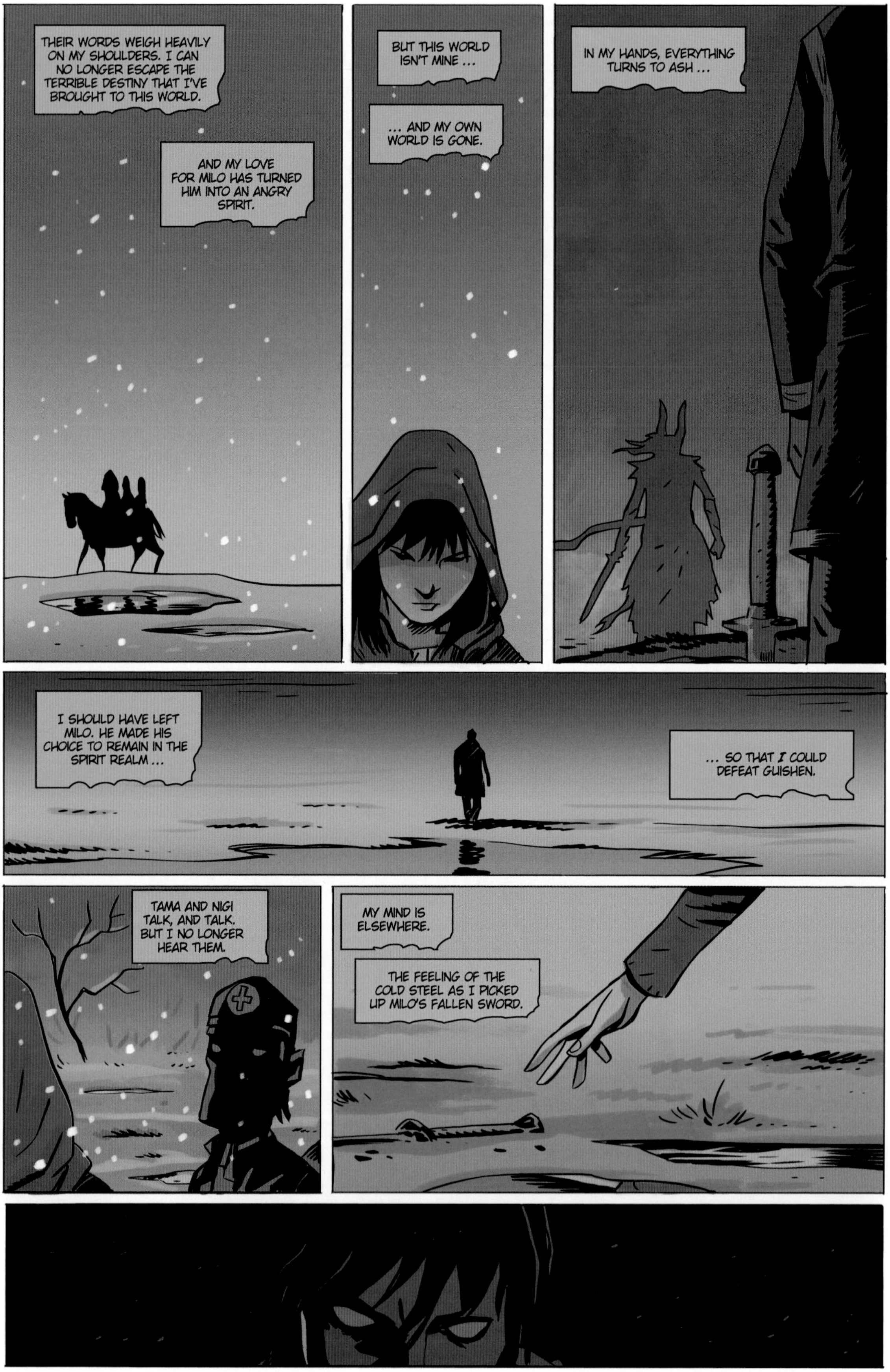
THEIR WORDS WEIGH HEAVILY ON MY SHOULDERS. I CAN NO LONGER ESCAPE THE TERRIBLE DESTINY THAT I'VE BROUGHT TO THIS WORLD.
AND MY LOVE FOR MILO HAS TURNED HIM INTO AN ANGRY SPIRIT.
BUT THIS WORLD ISN'T MINE ...
... AND MY OWN WORLD IS GONE.
IN MY HANDS, EVERYTHING TURNS TO ASH ...
I SHOULD HAVE LEFT MILO. HE MADE HIS CHOICE TO REMAIN IN THE SPIRIT REALM ...
... SO THAT I COULD DEFEAT GUISHEN.
TAMA AND NIGI TALK, AND TALK. BUT I NO LONGER HEAR THEM.
MY MIND IS ELSEWHERE.
THE FEELING OF THE COLD STEEL AS I PICKED UP MILO'S FALLEN SWORD.

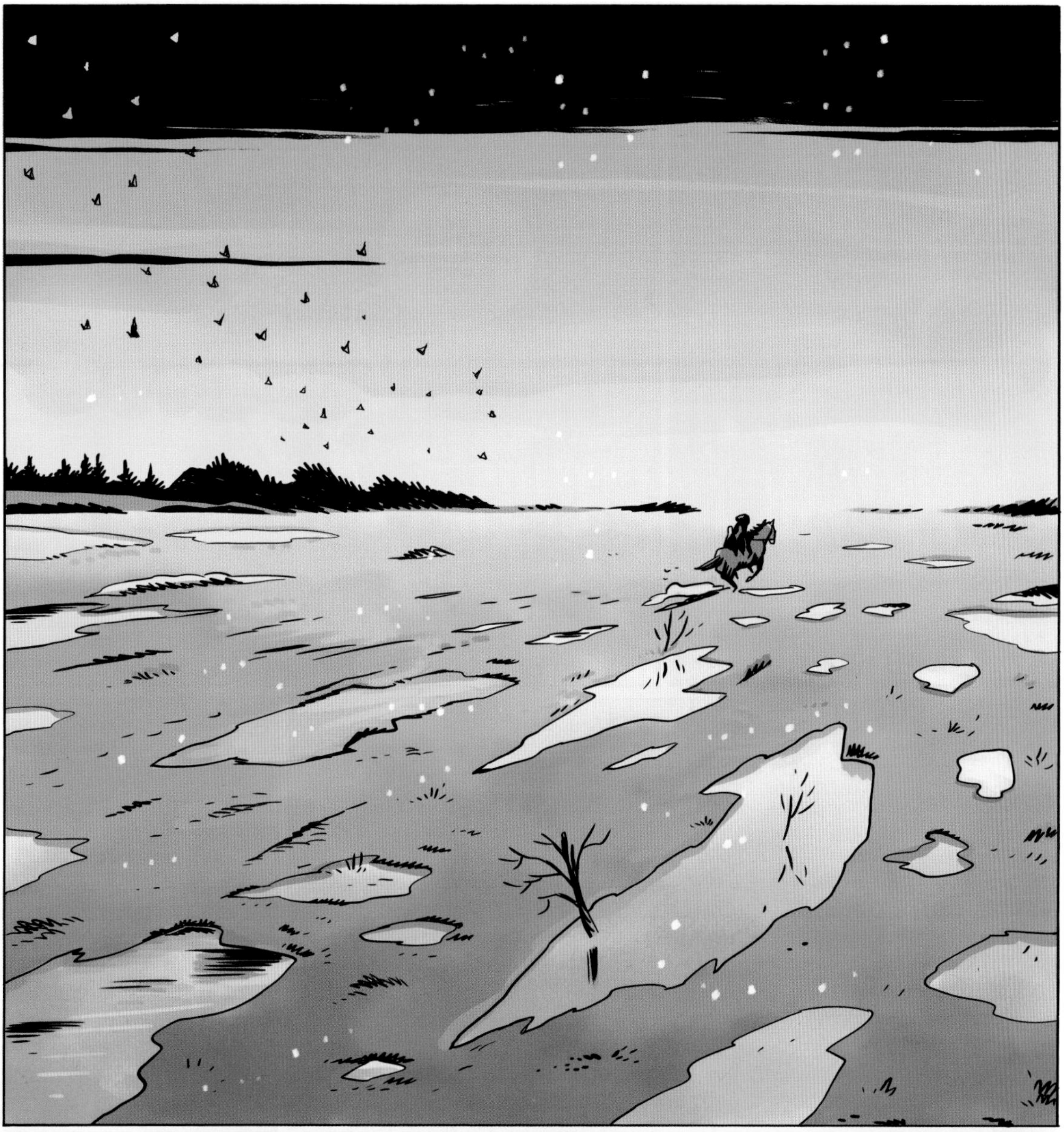
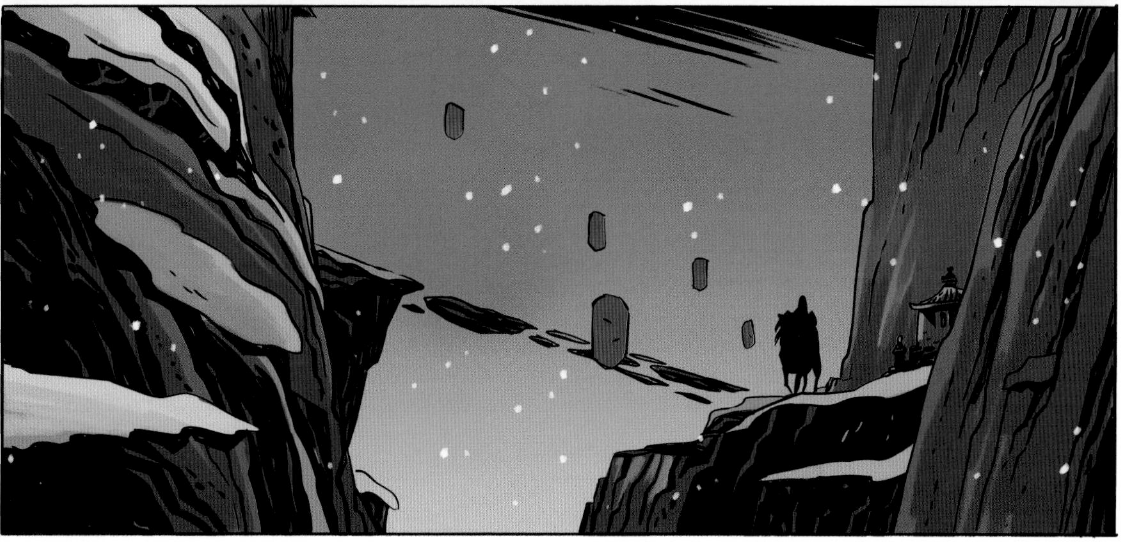

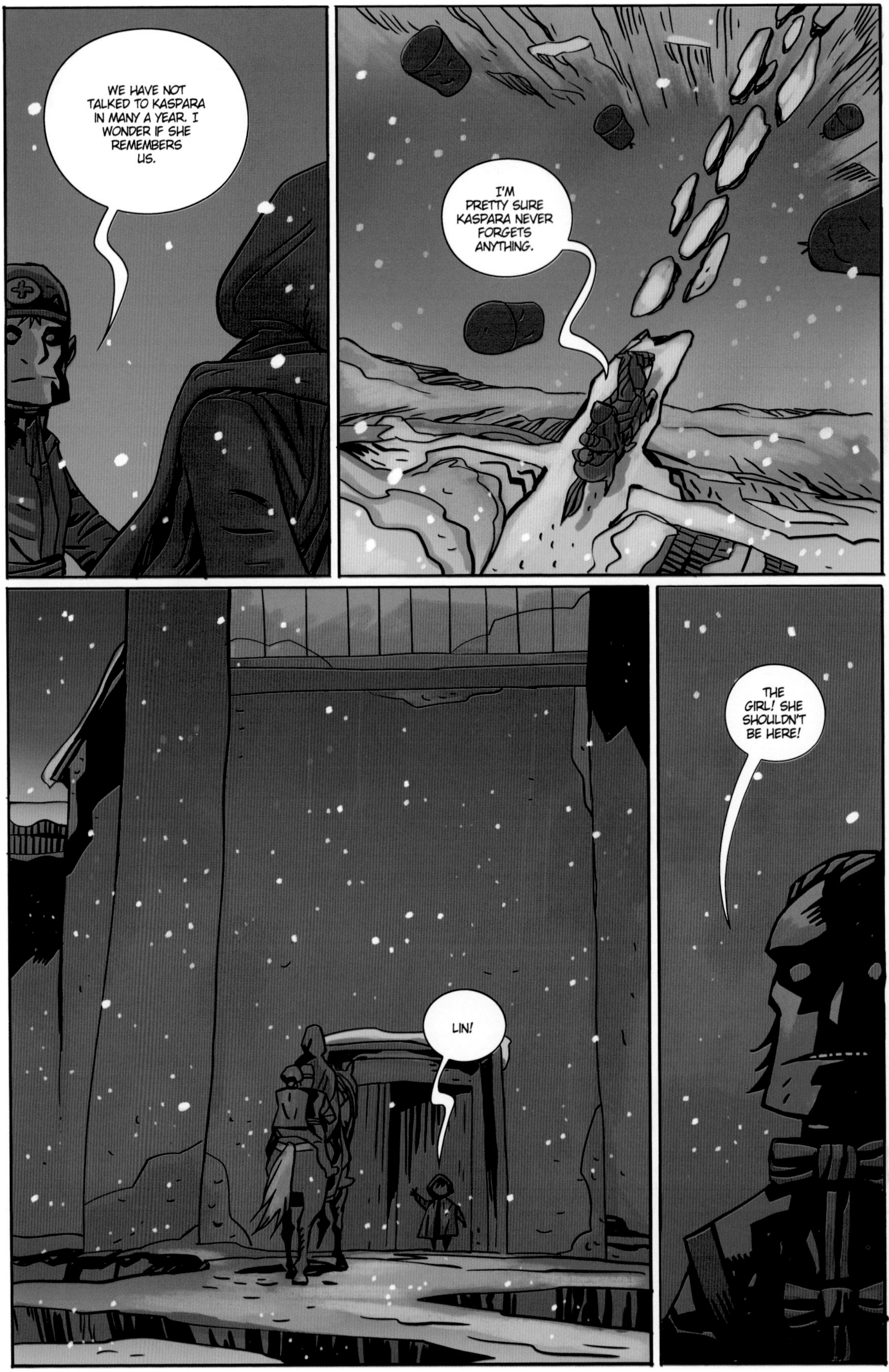
WE HAVE NOT TALKED TO KASPARA IN MANY A YEAR. I WONDER IF SHE REMEMBERS US.
I'M PRETTY SURE KASPARA NEVER FORGETS ANYTHING.
LIN!
THE GIRL! SHE SHOULDN'T BE HERE!

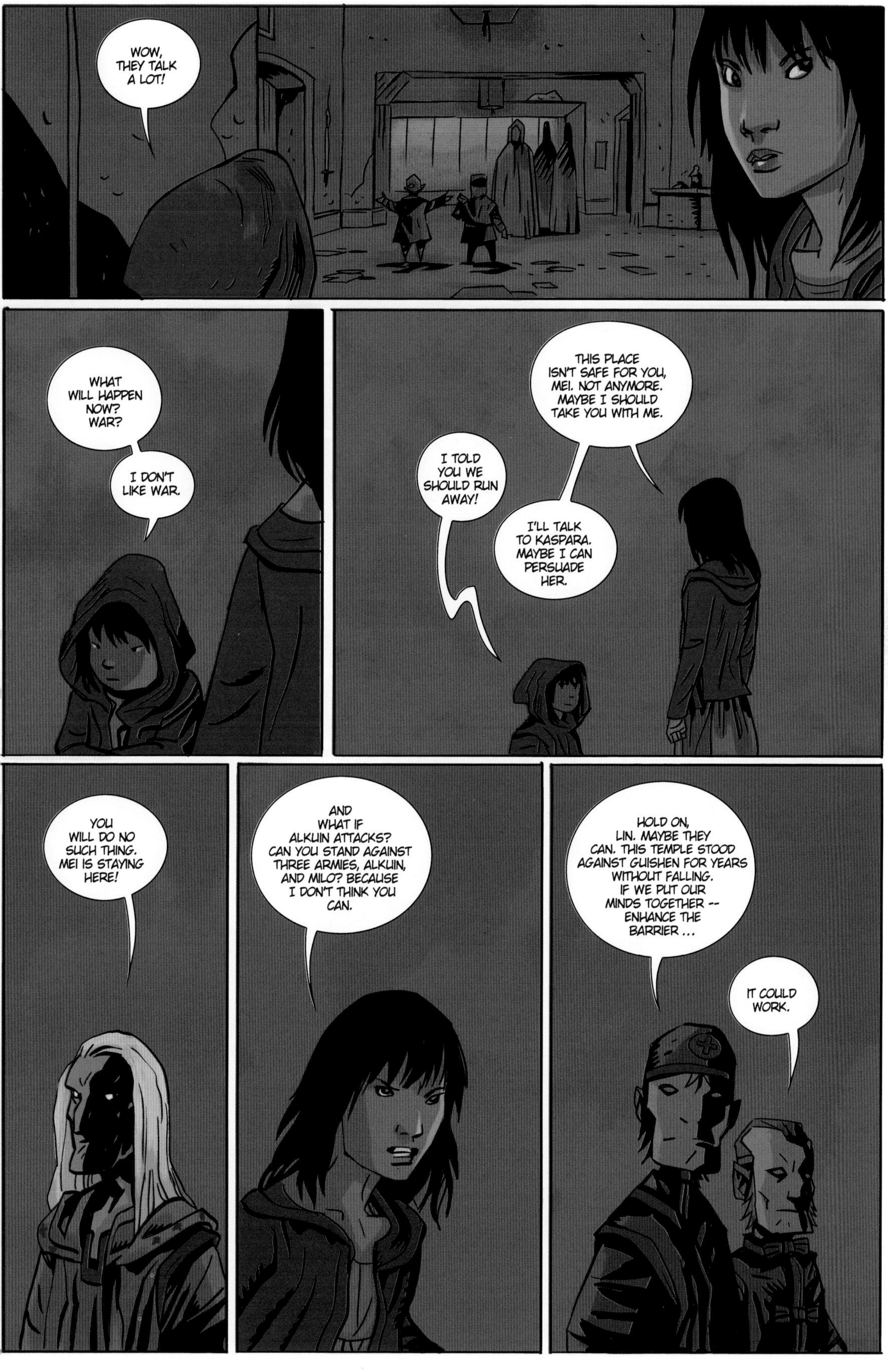
WOW, THEY TALK A LOT!
WHAT WILL HAPPEN NOW? WAR?
I DON'T LIKE WAR.
THIS PLACE ISN'T SAFE FOR YOU, MEI. NOT ANYMORE. MAYBE I SHOULD TAKE YOU WITH ME.
I TOLD YOU WE SHOULD RUN AWAY!
I'LL TALK TO KASPARA. MAYBE I CAN PERSUADE HER.
YOU WILL DO NO SUCH THING. MEI IS STAYING HERE!
AND WHAT IF ALKUIN ATTACKS? CAN YOU STAND AGAINST THREE ARMIES, ALKUIN, AND MILO? BECAUSE I DON'T THINK YOU CAN.
HOLD ON, LIN. MAYBE THEY CAN. THIS TEMPLE STOOD AGAINST GUISHEN FOR YEARS WITHOUT FALLING. IF WE PUT OUR MINDS TOGETHER -- ENHANCE THE BARRIER ...
IT COULD WORK.

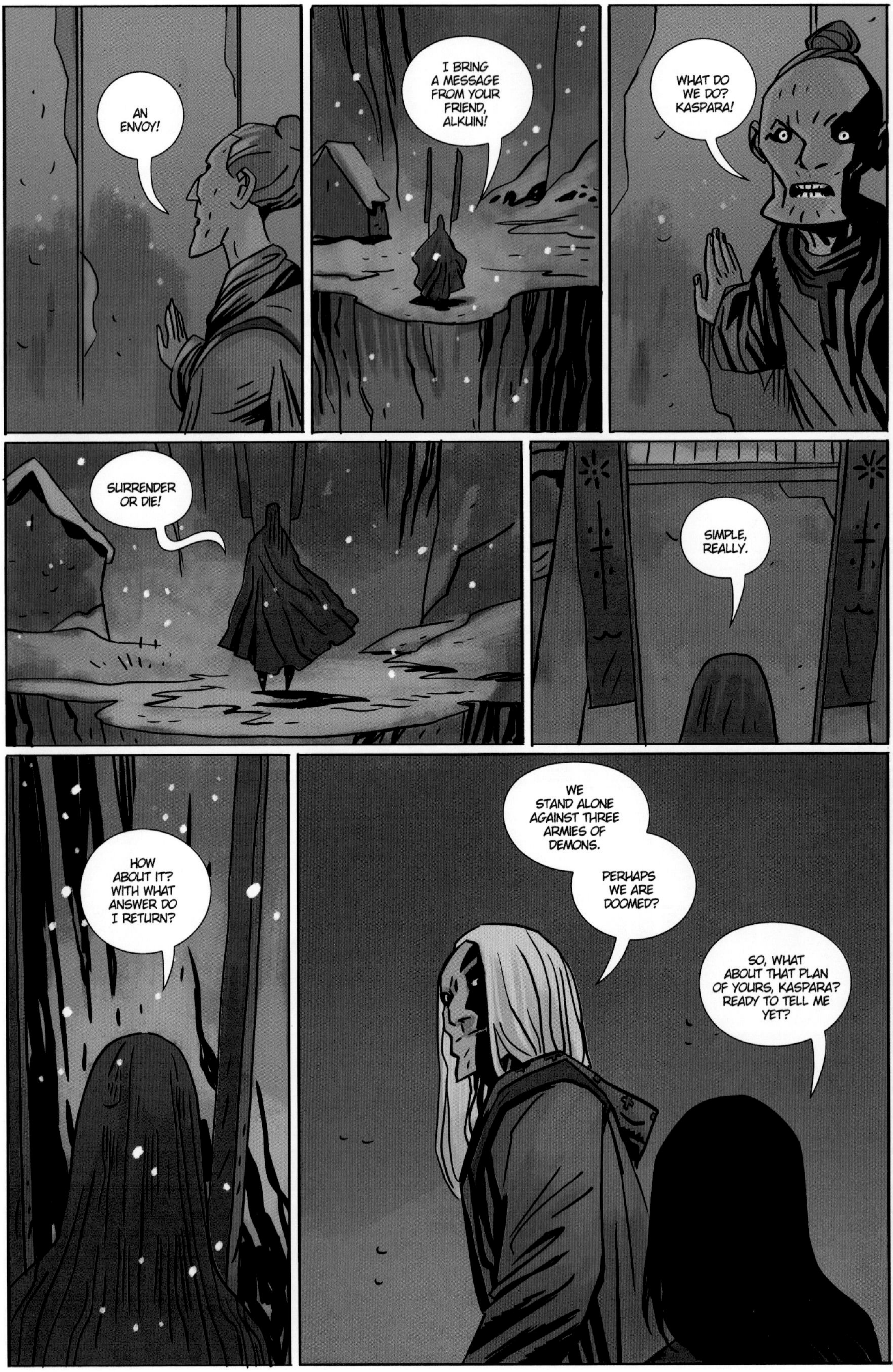
AN ENVOY!
I BRING A MESSAGE FROM YOUR FRIEND, ALKUIN!
WHAT DO WE DO? KASPARA!
SURRENDER OR DIE!
SIMPLE, REALLY.
HOW ABOUT IT? WITH WHAT ANSWER DO I RETURN?
WE STAND ALONE AGAINST THREE ARMIES OF DEMONS.
PERHAPS WE ARE DOOMED?
SO, WHAT ABOUT THAT PLAN OF YOURS, KASPARA? READY TO TELL ME YET?

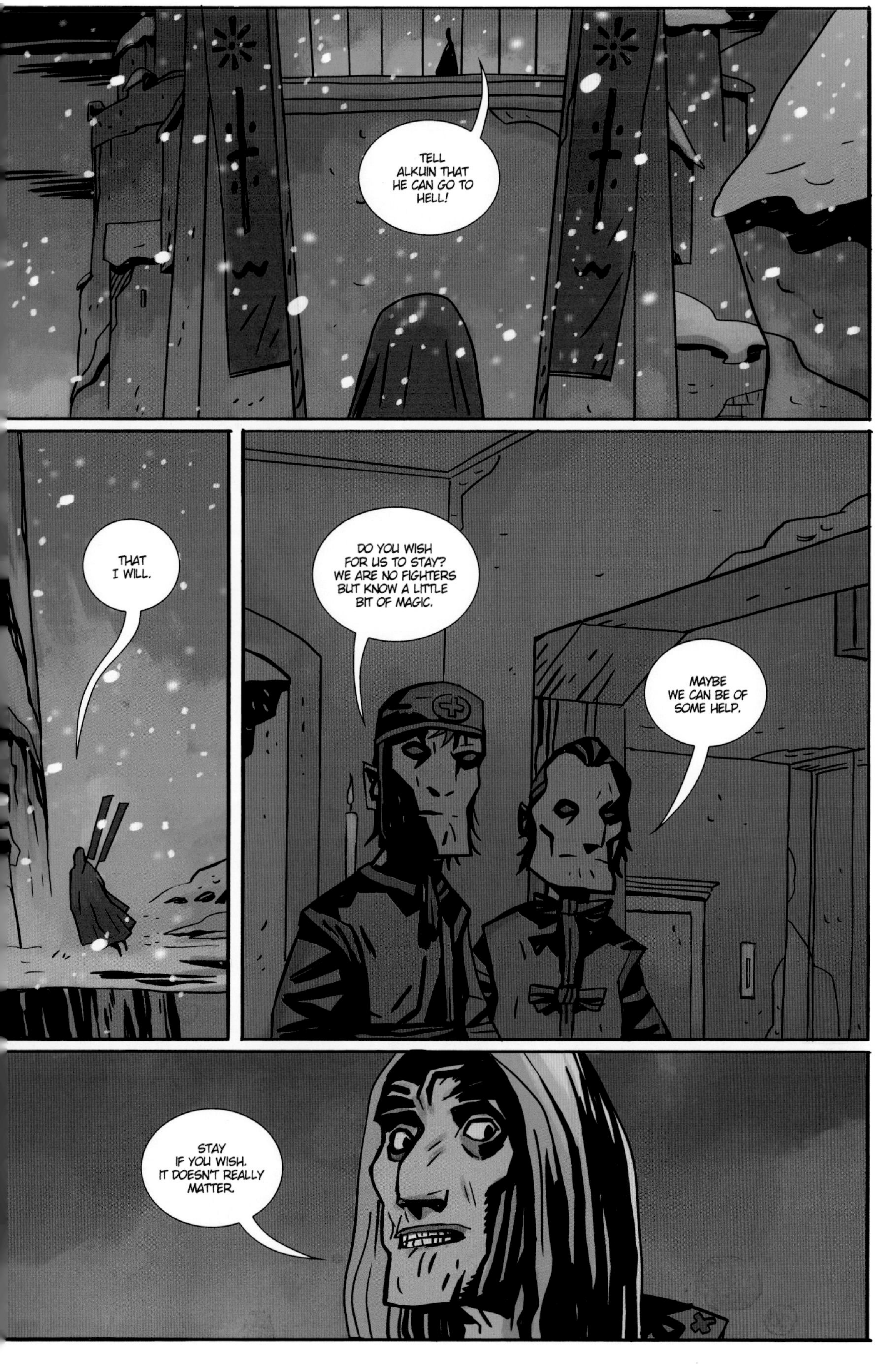
TELL ALKUIN THAT HE CAN GO TO HELL!
THAT I WILL.
DO YOU WISH FOR US TO STAY? WE ARE NO FIGHTERS BUT KNOW A LITTLE BIT OF MAGIC.
MAYBE WE CAN BE OF SOME HELP.
STAY IF YOU WISH. IT DOESN'T REALLY MATTER.

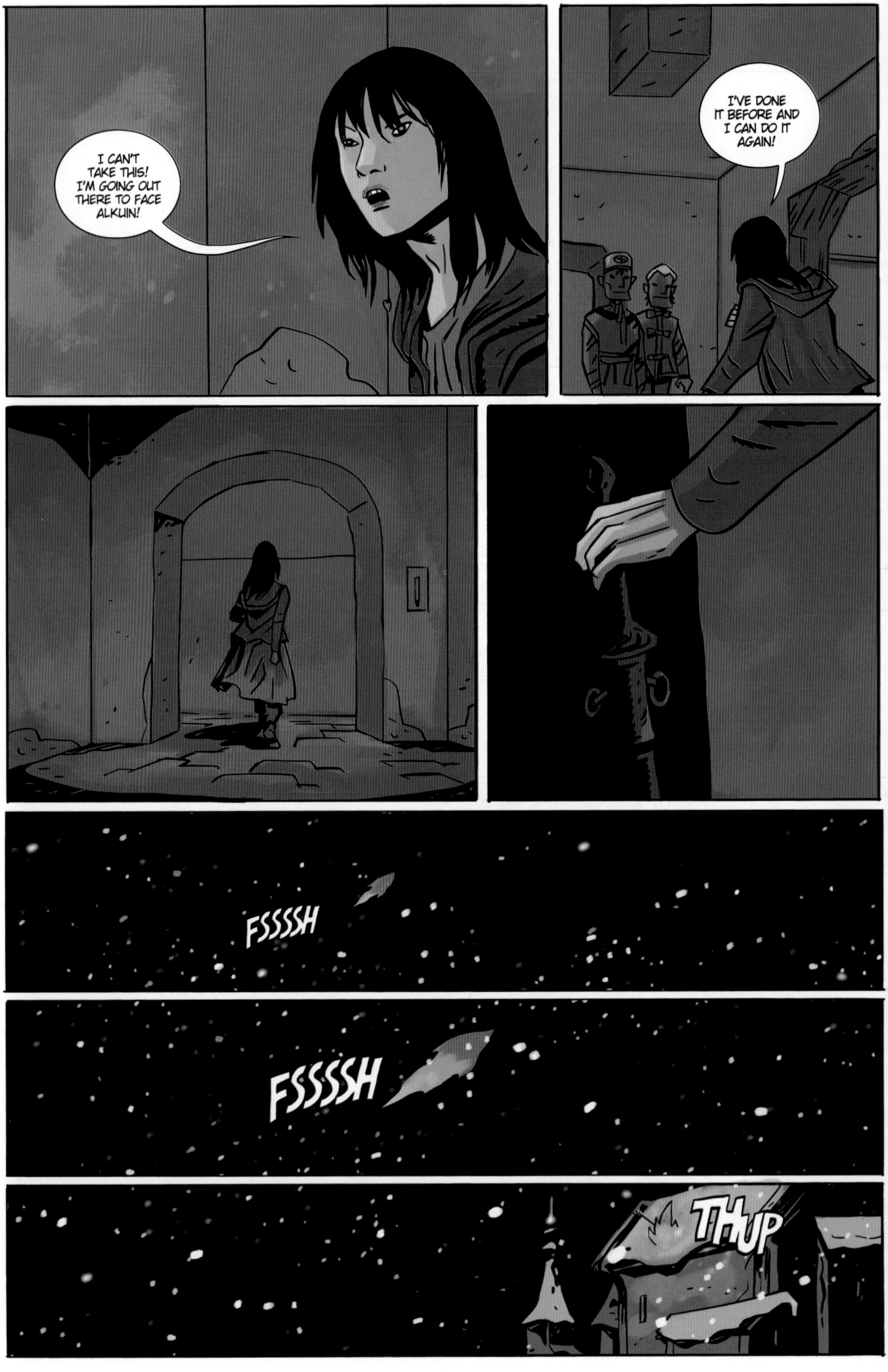
I CAN'T TAKE THIS! I'M GOING OUT THERE TO FACE ALKUIN!
I'VE DONE IT BEFORE AND I CAN DO IT AGAIN!
FSSSSH
FSSSSH
THUP

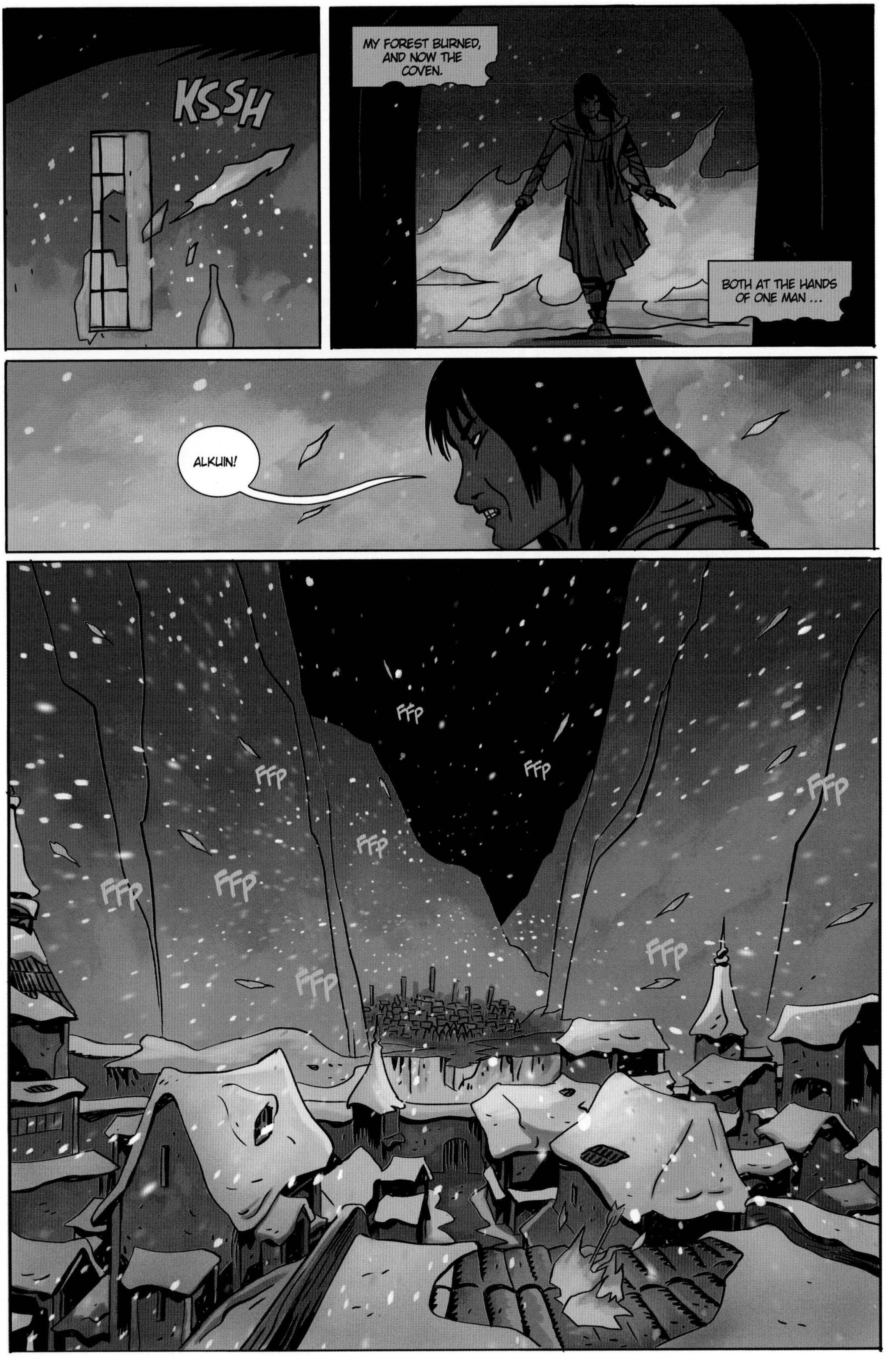
KSSH
MY FOREST BURNED, AND NOW THE COVEN.
BOTH AT THE HANDS OF ONE MAN ...
ALKUIN!
FFP
FFP
FFP
FFP
FFP
FFP
FFP
FFP
FFP

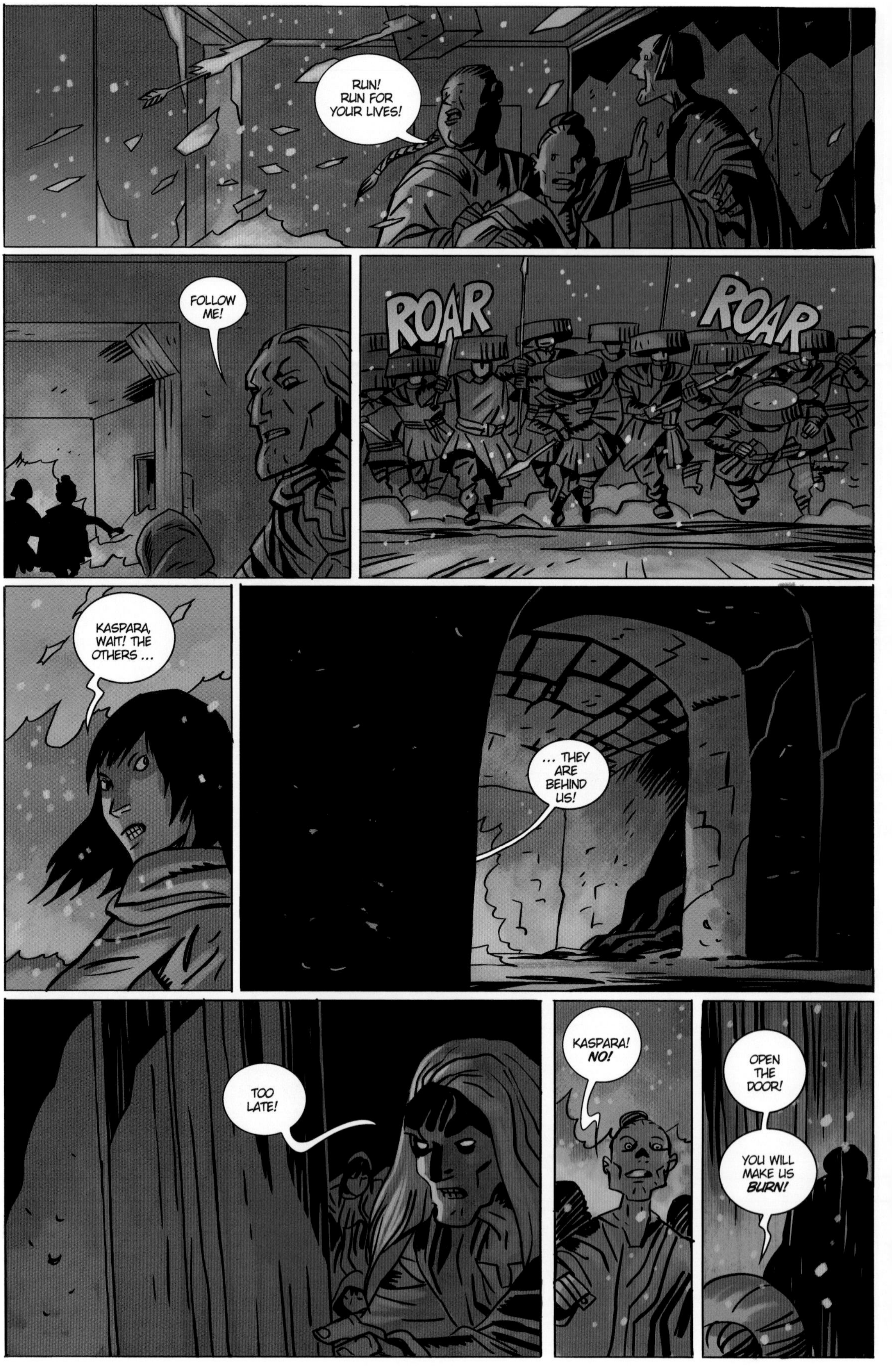
RUN! RUN FOR YOUR LIVES!
FOLLOW ME!
ROAR
ROAR
KASPARA, WAIT! THE OTHERS ...
... THEY ARE BEHIND US!
TOO LATE!
KASPARA! NO!
OPEN THE DOOR!
YOU WILL MAKE US BURN!

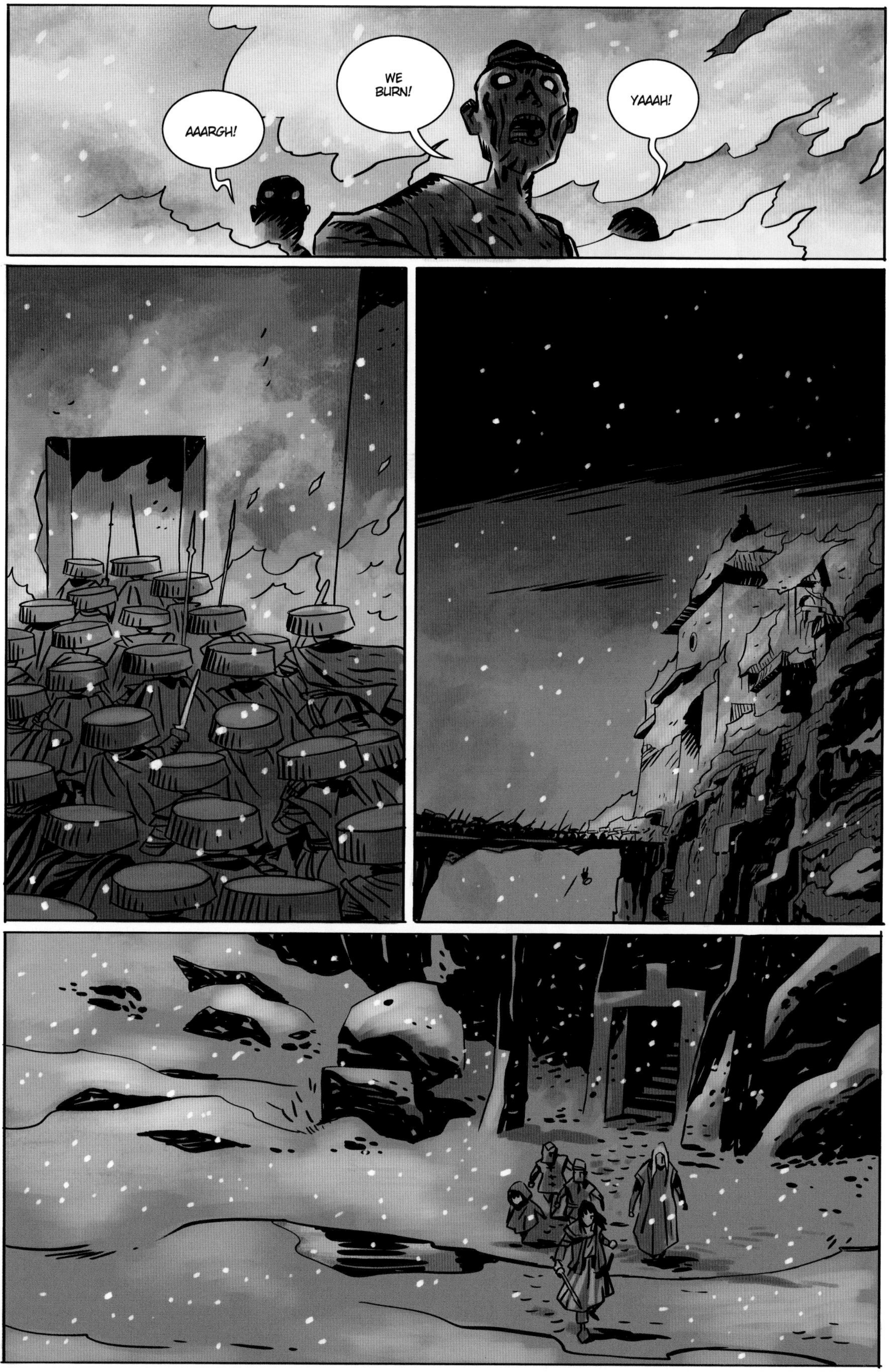
AAARGH!
WE BURN!
YAAAH!

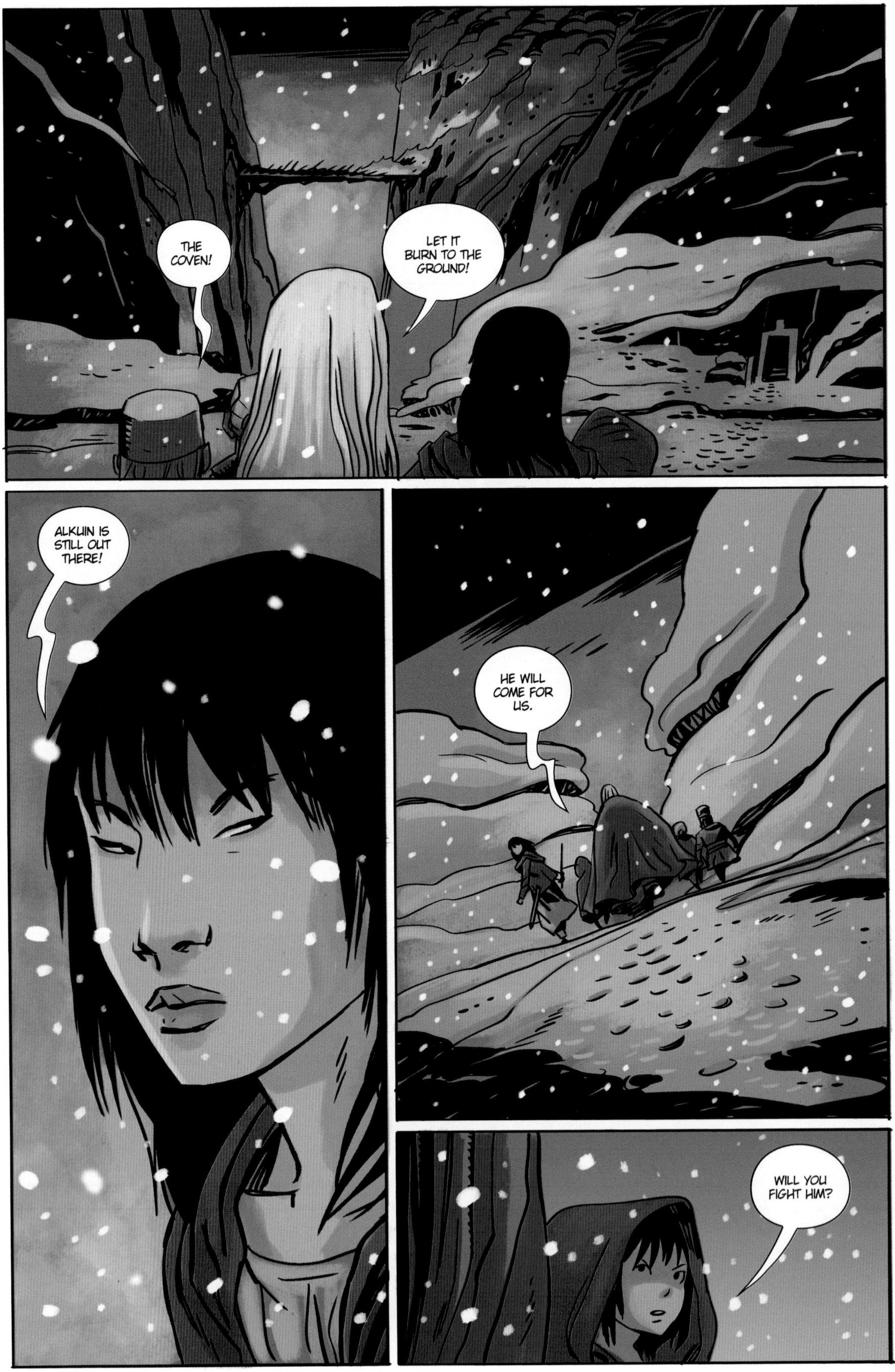
THE COVEN!
LET IT BURN TO THE GROUND!
ALKUIN IS STILL OUT THERE!
HE WILL COME FOR US.
WILL YOU FIGHT HIM?

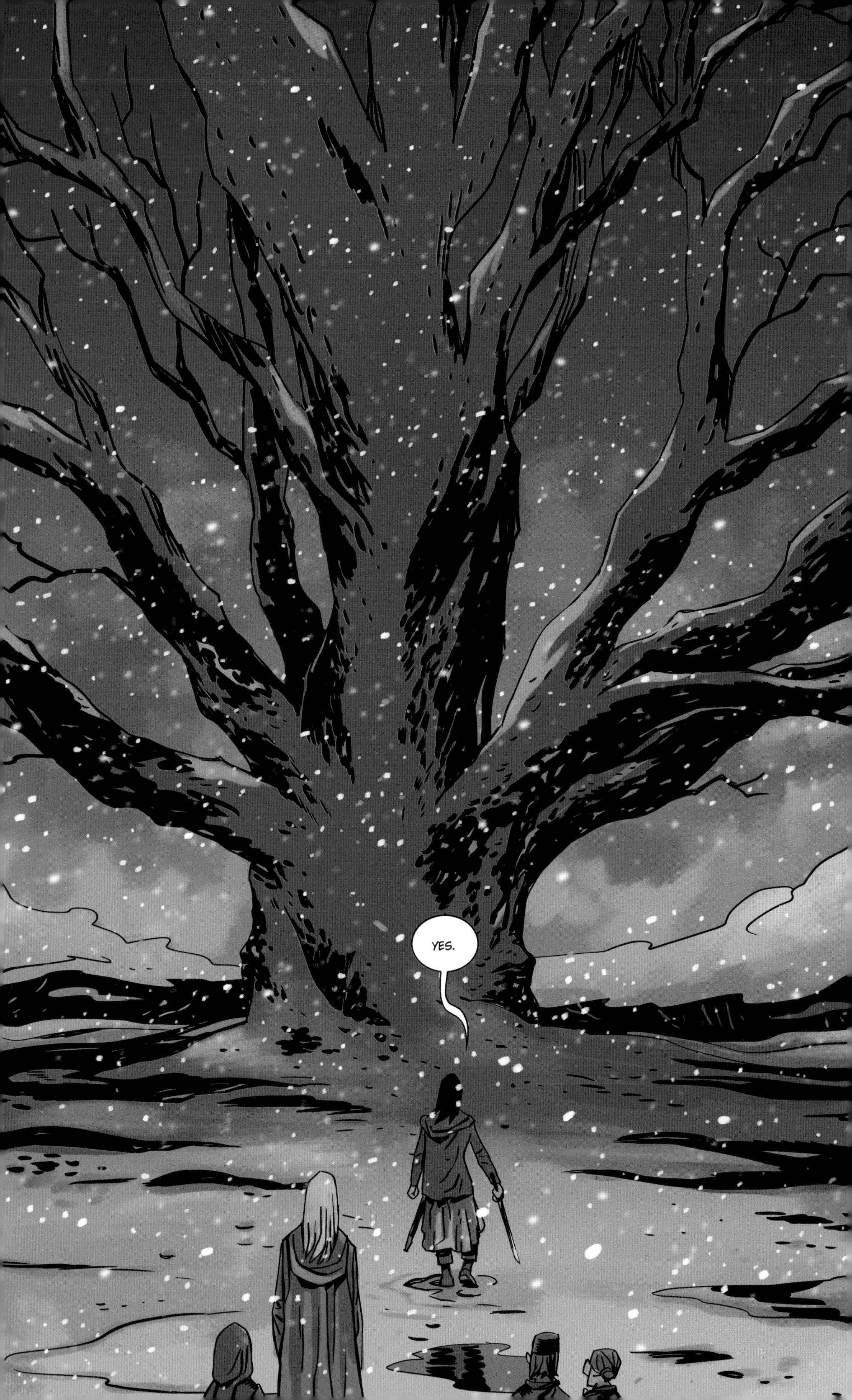
YES.

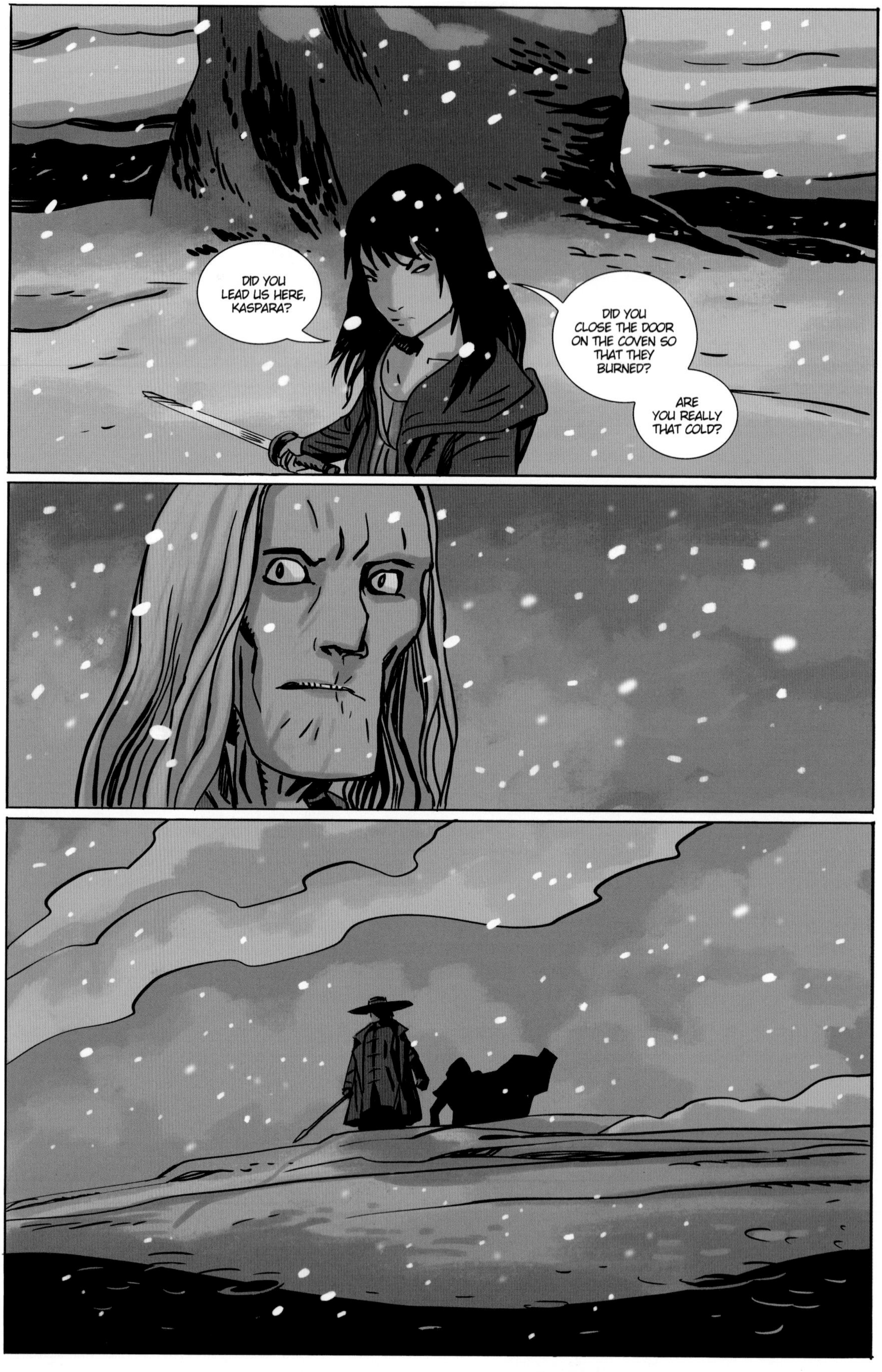
DID YOU LEAD US HERE, KASPARA?
DID YOU CLOSE THE DOOR ON THE COVEN SO THAT THEY BURNED?
ARE YOU REALLY THAT COLD?

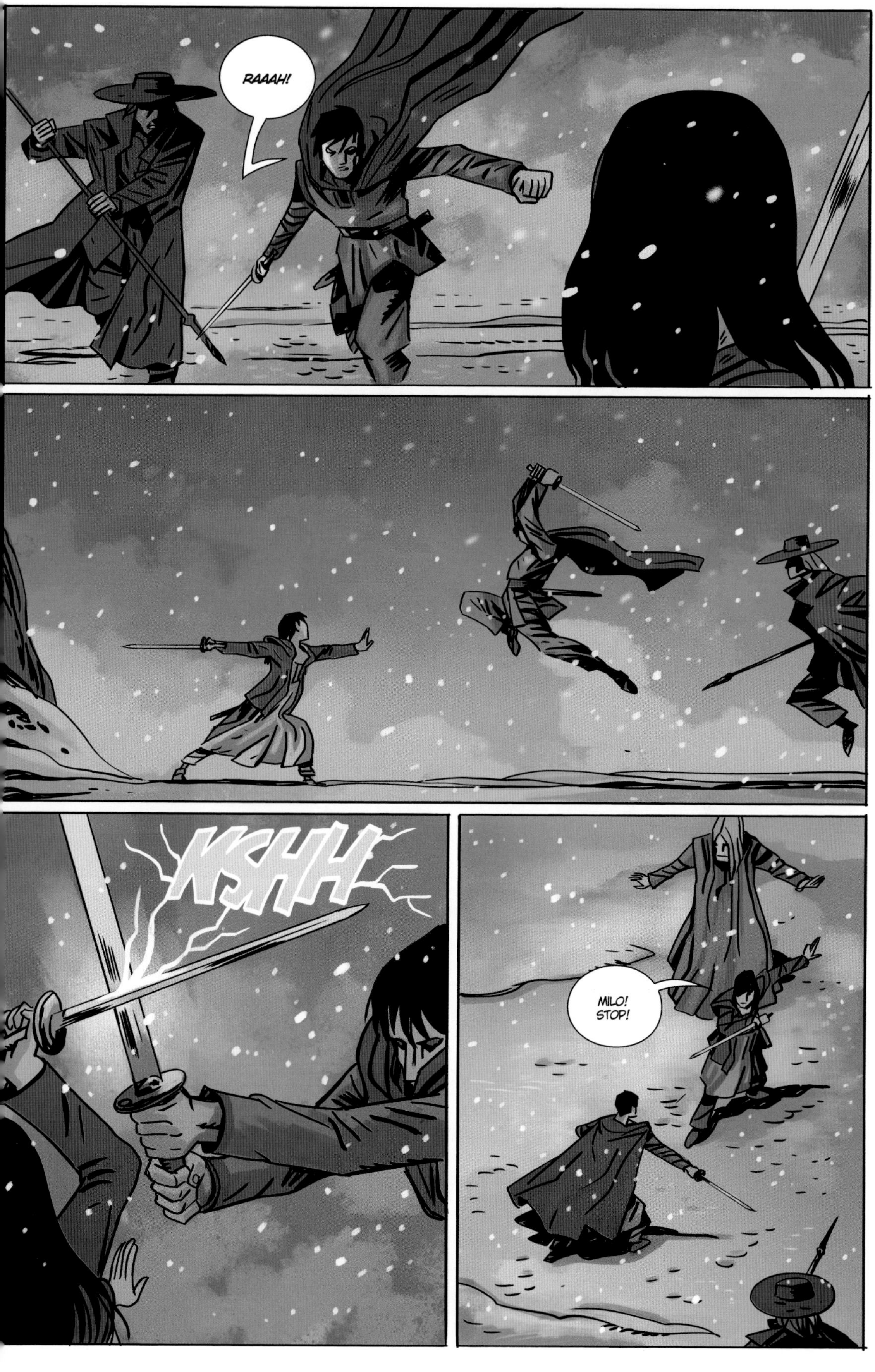
RAAAH!
KSHH
MILO! STOP!

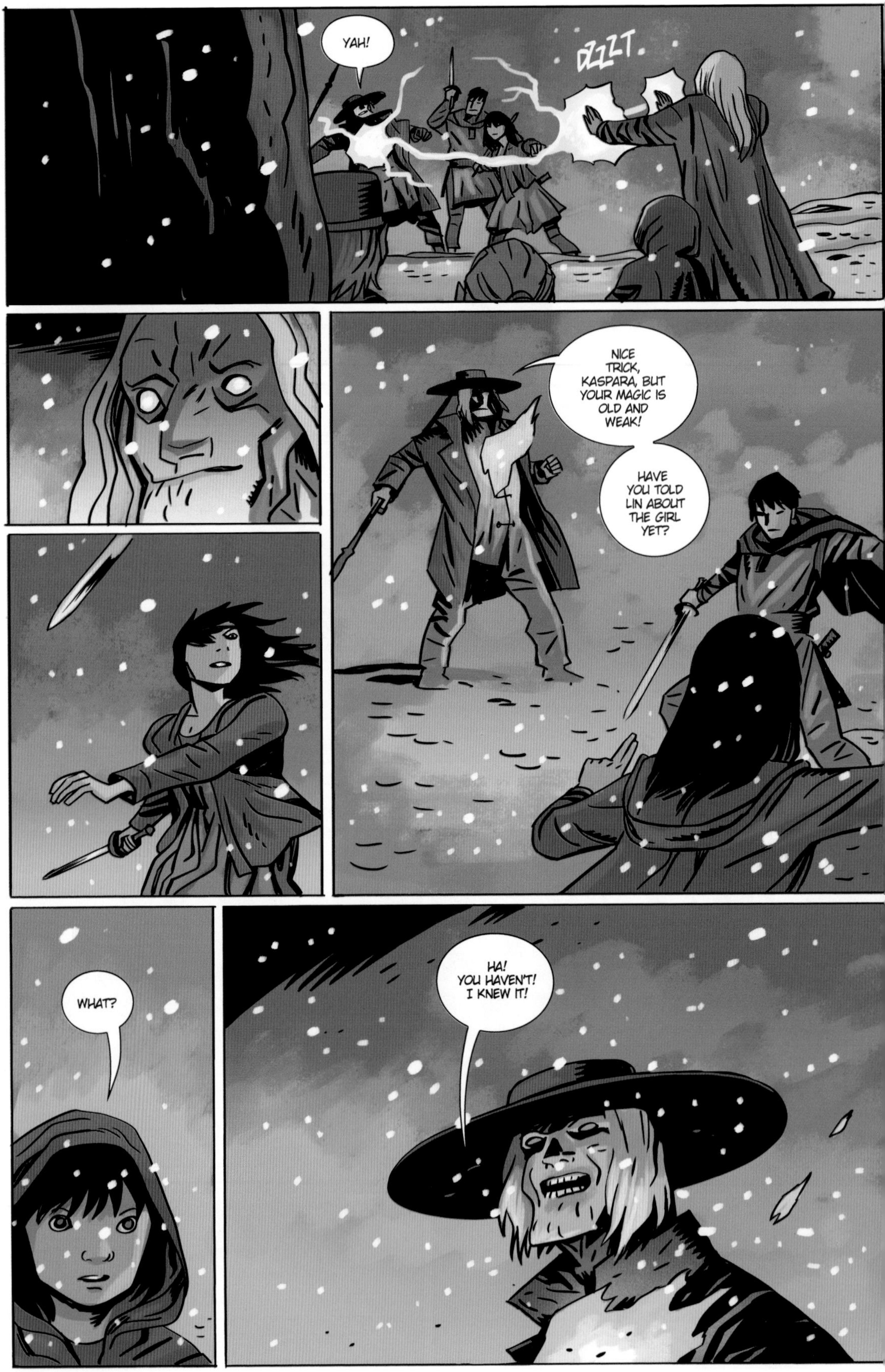
YAH!
DZZZT
NICE TRICK, KASPARA, BUT YOUR MAGIC IS OLD AND WEAK!
HAVE YOU TOLD LIN ABOUT THE GIRL YET?
WHAT?
HA! YOU HAVEN'T! I KNEW IT!

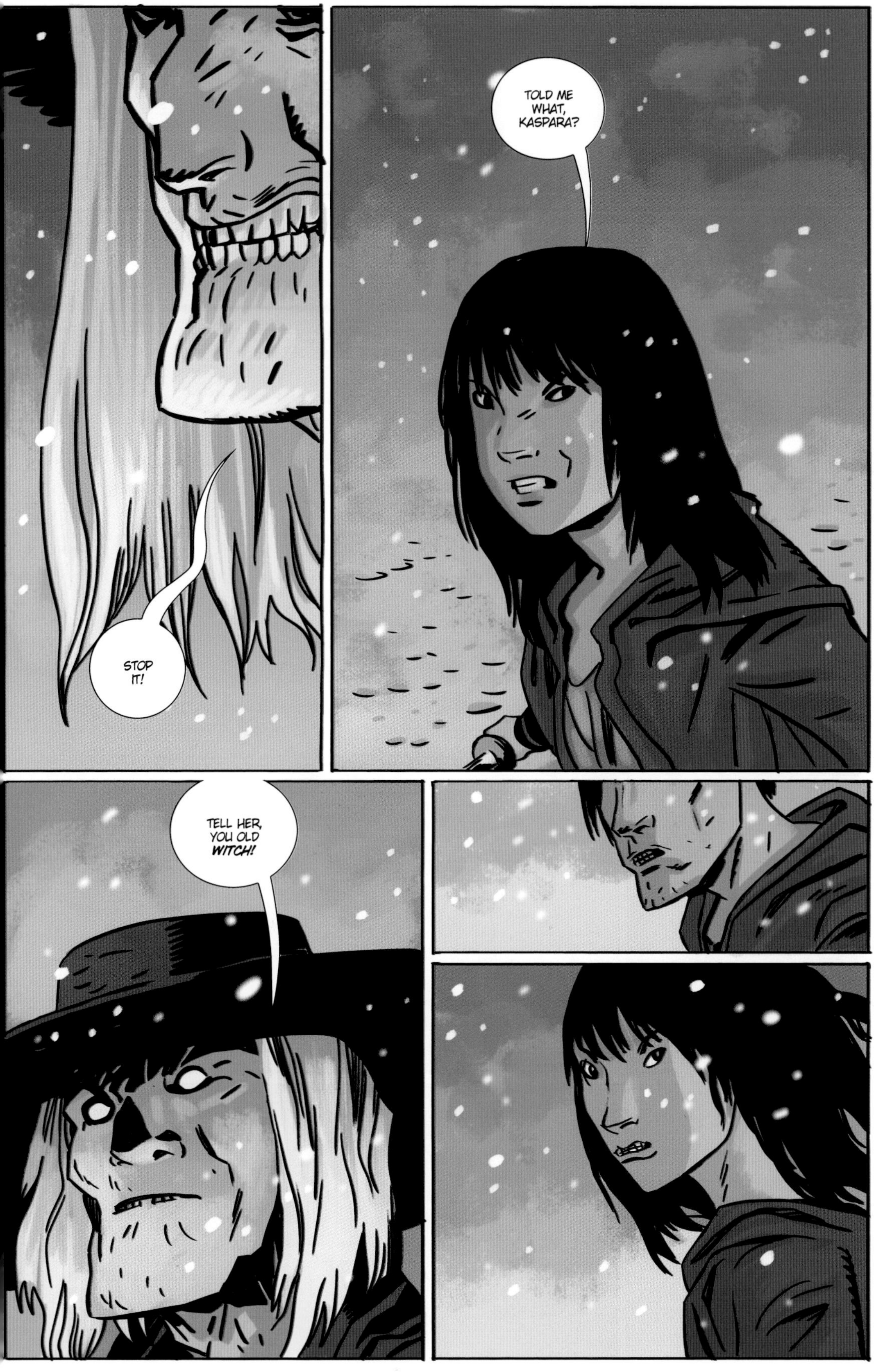
STOP IT!
TOLD ME WHAT, KASPARA?
TELL HER, YOU OLD WITCH!

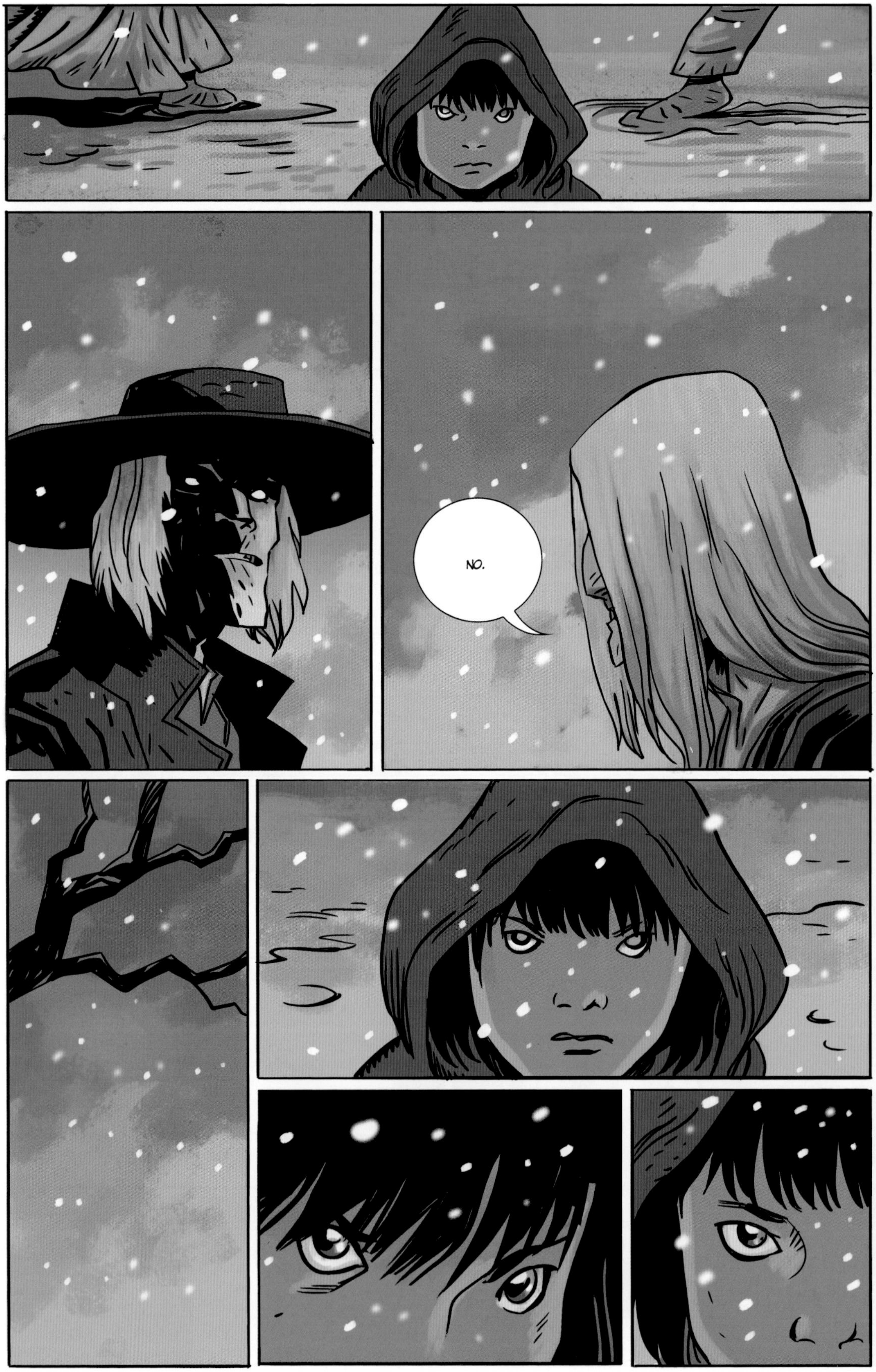
NO.

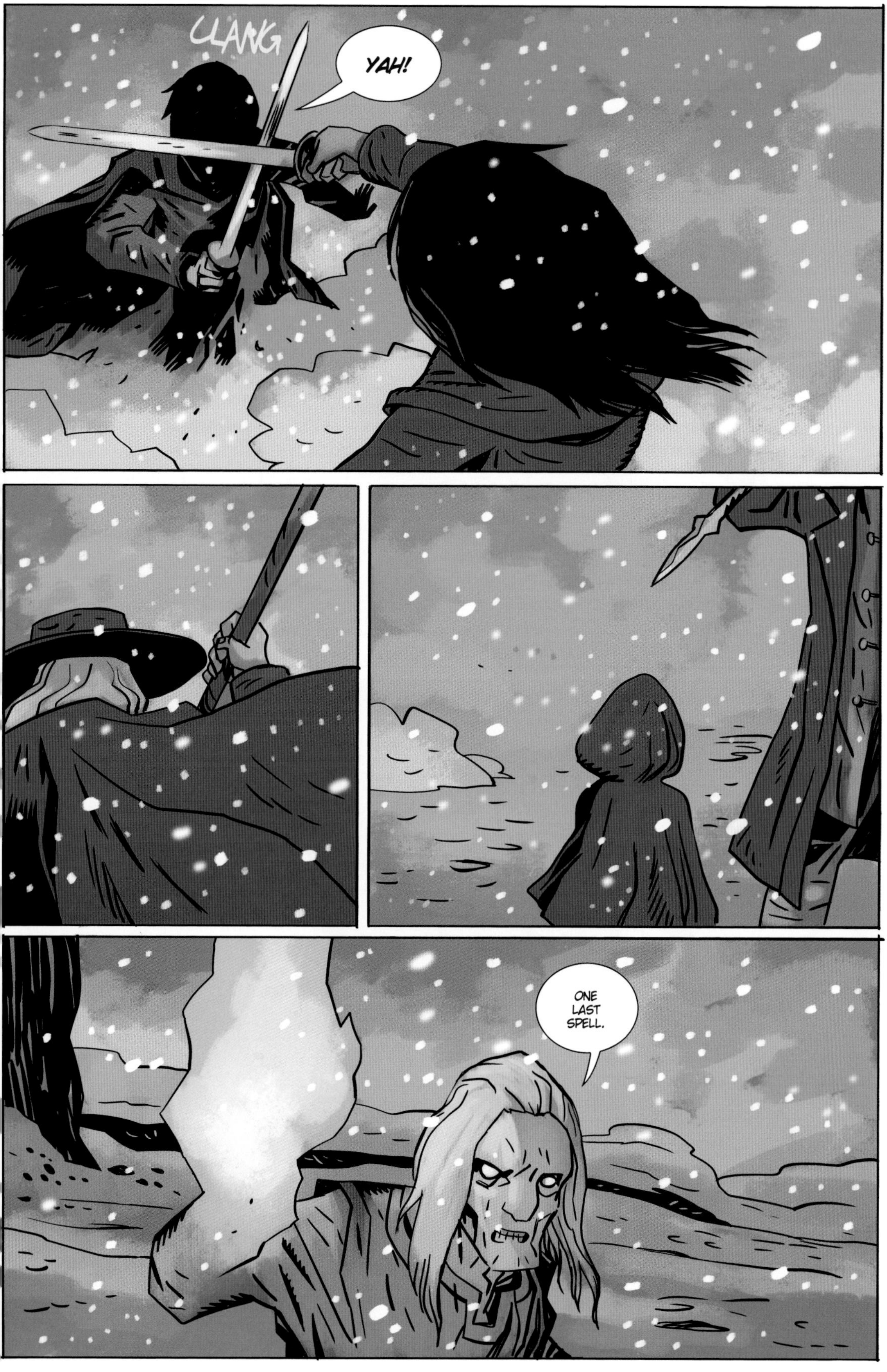
CLANG
YAH!
ONE LAST SPELL.

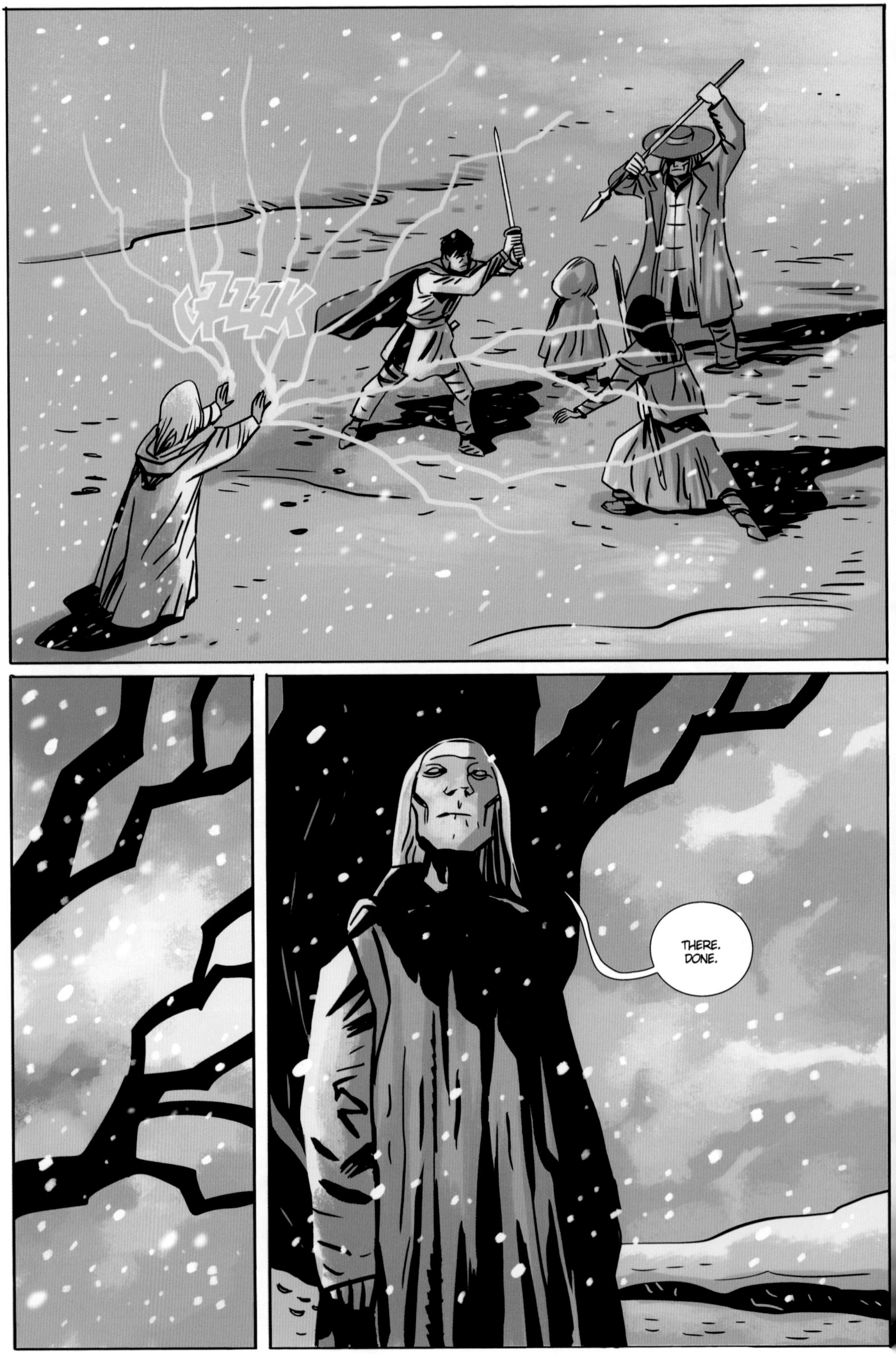

CHHK
THERE. DONE.

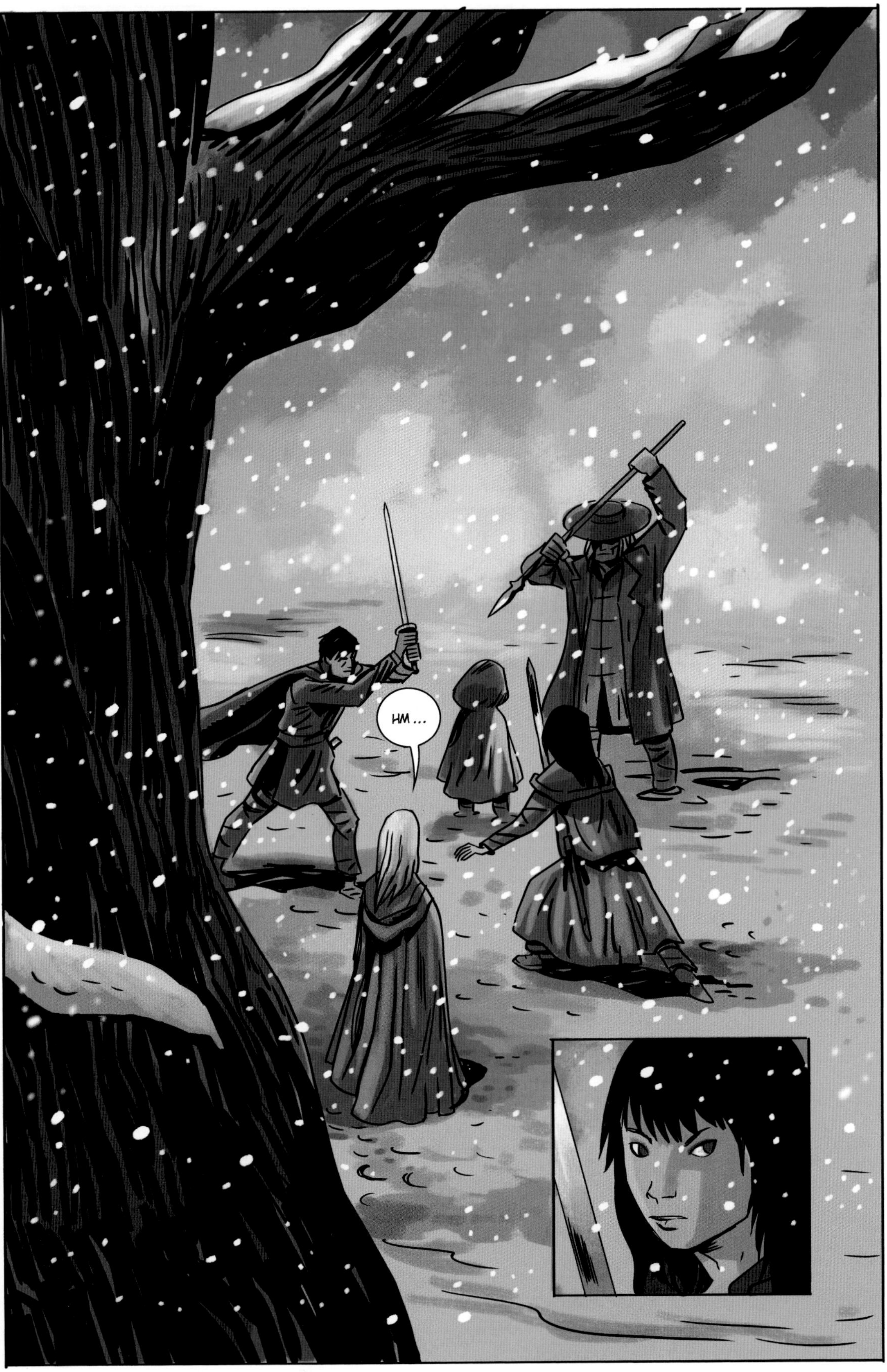
HM...

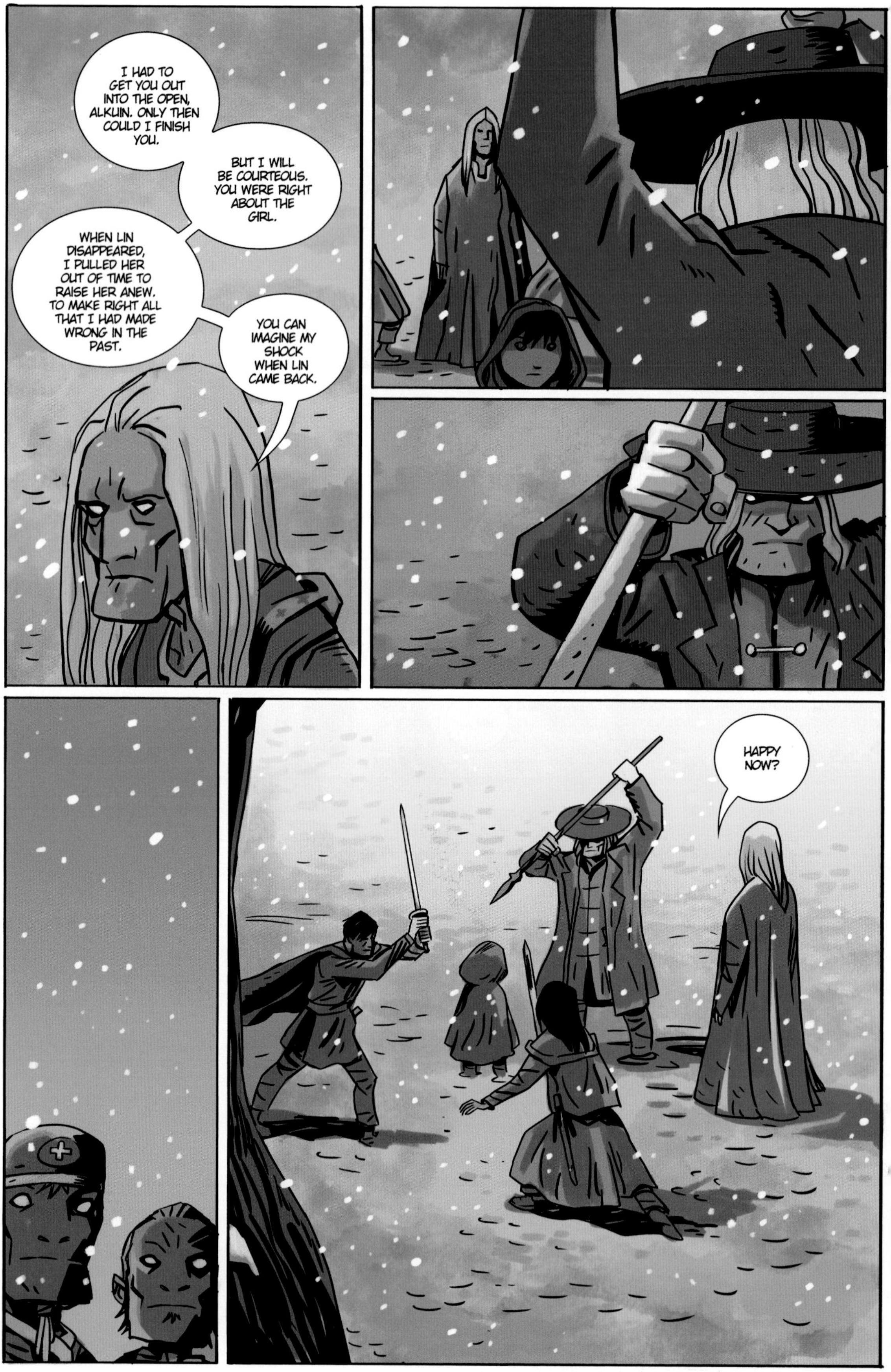
I HAD TO GET YOU OUT INTO THE OPEN, ALKUIN. ONLY THEN COULD I FINISH YOU.
BUT I WILL BE COURTEOUS. YOU WERE RIGHT ABOUT THE GIRL.
WHEN LIN DISAPPEARED, I PULLED HER OUT OF TIME TO RAISE HER ANEW. TO MAKE RIGHT ALL THAT I HAD MADE WRONG IN THE PAST.
YOU CAN IMAGINE MY SHOCK WHEN LIN CAME BACK.
HAPPY NOW?

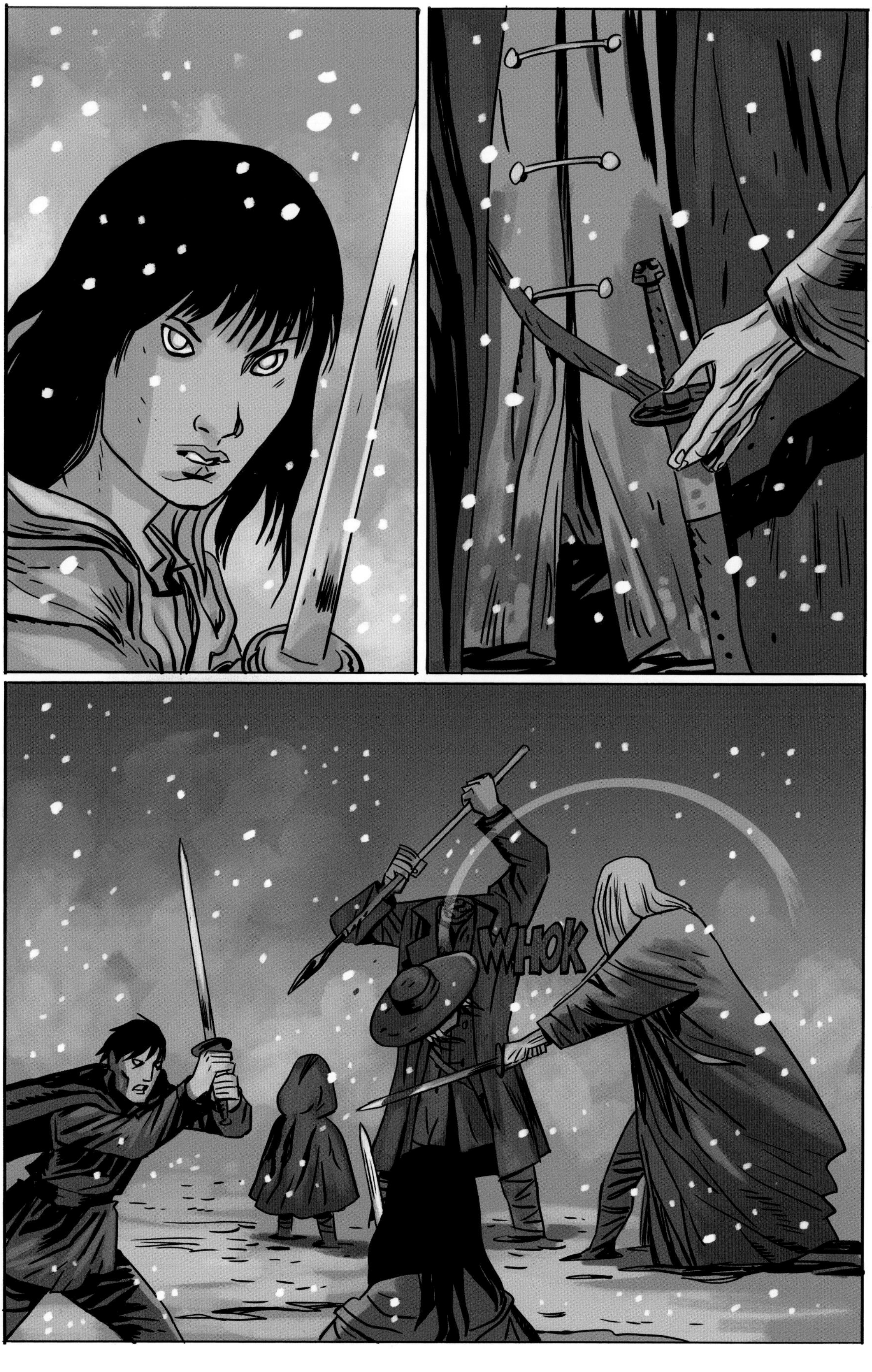
WHOK

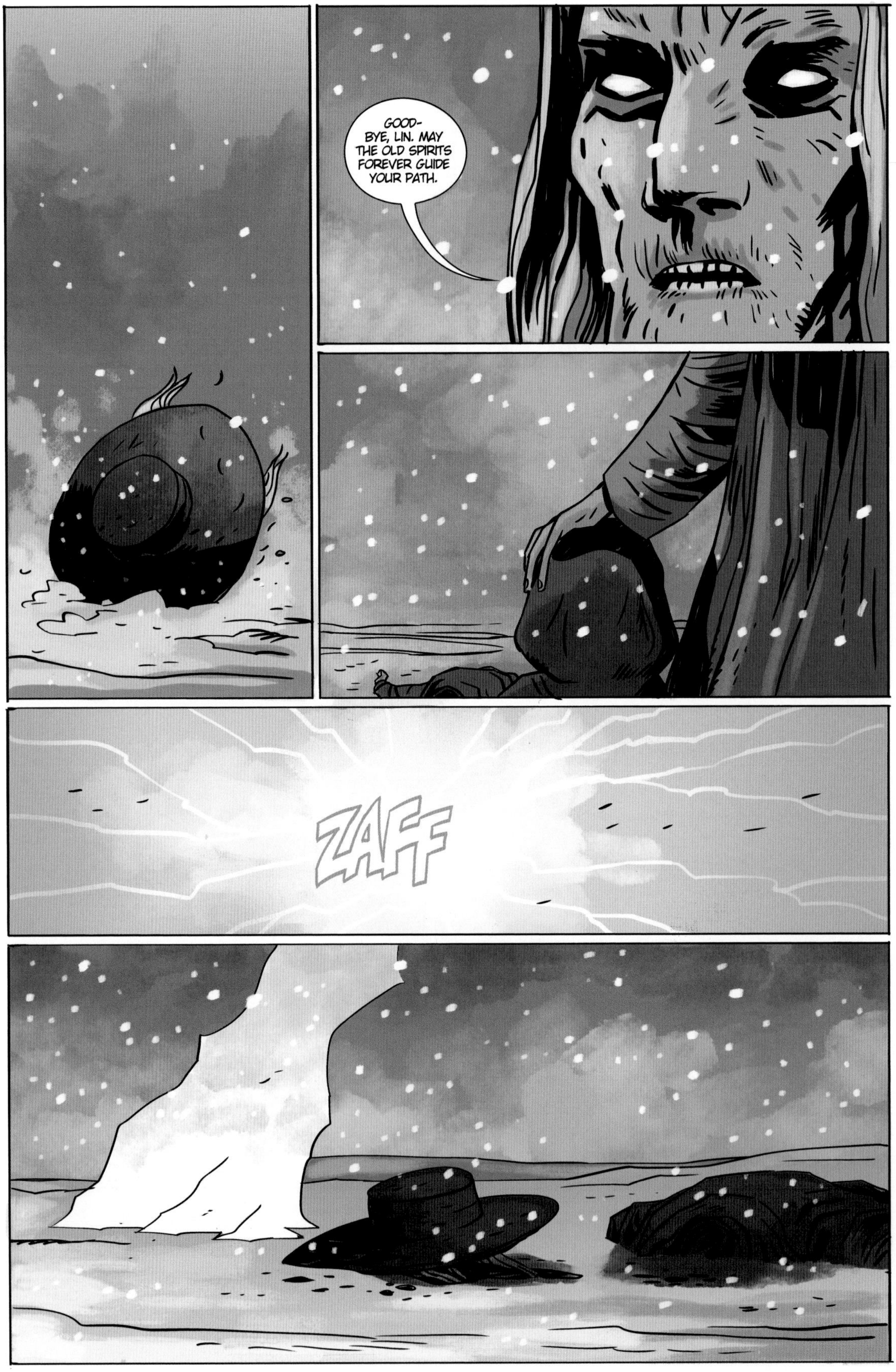
GOOD-BYE, LIN. MAY THE OLD SPIRITS FOREVER GUIDE YOUR PATH.
ZAFF

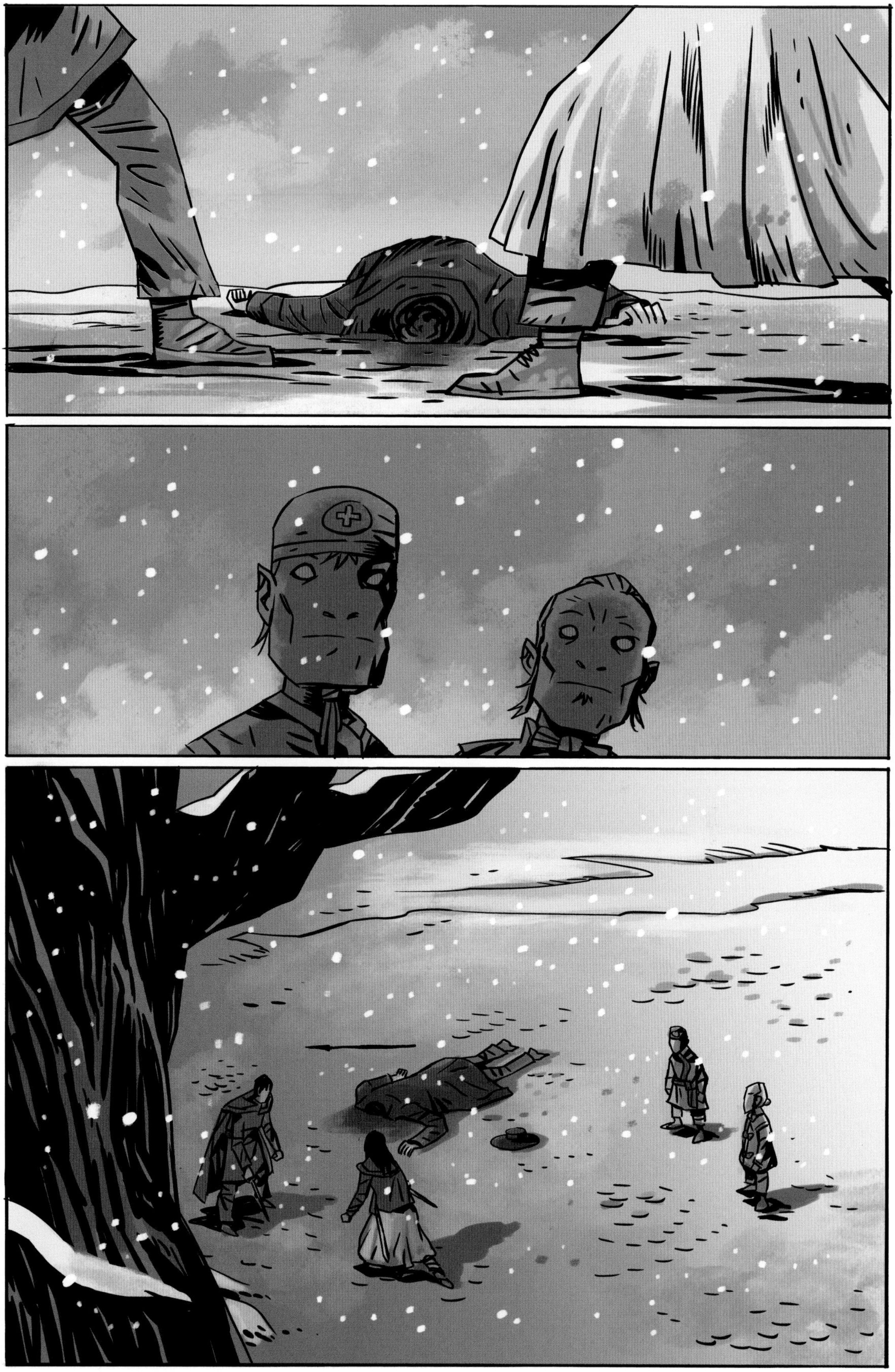

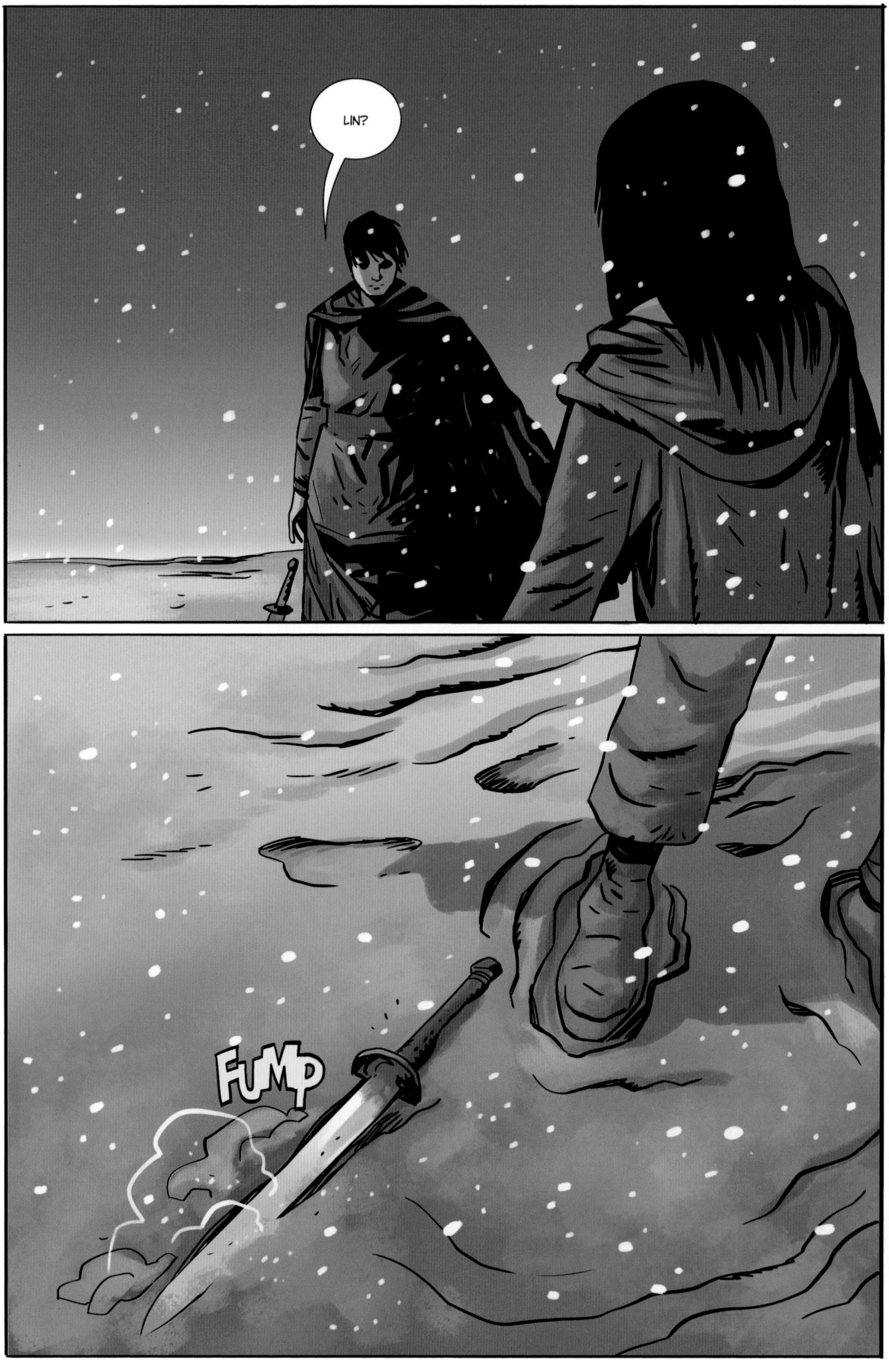
LIN?
FUMP

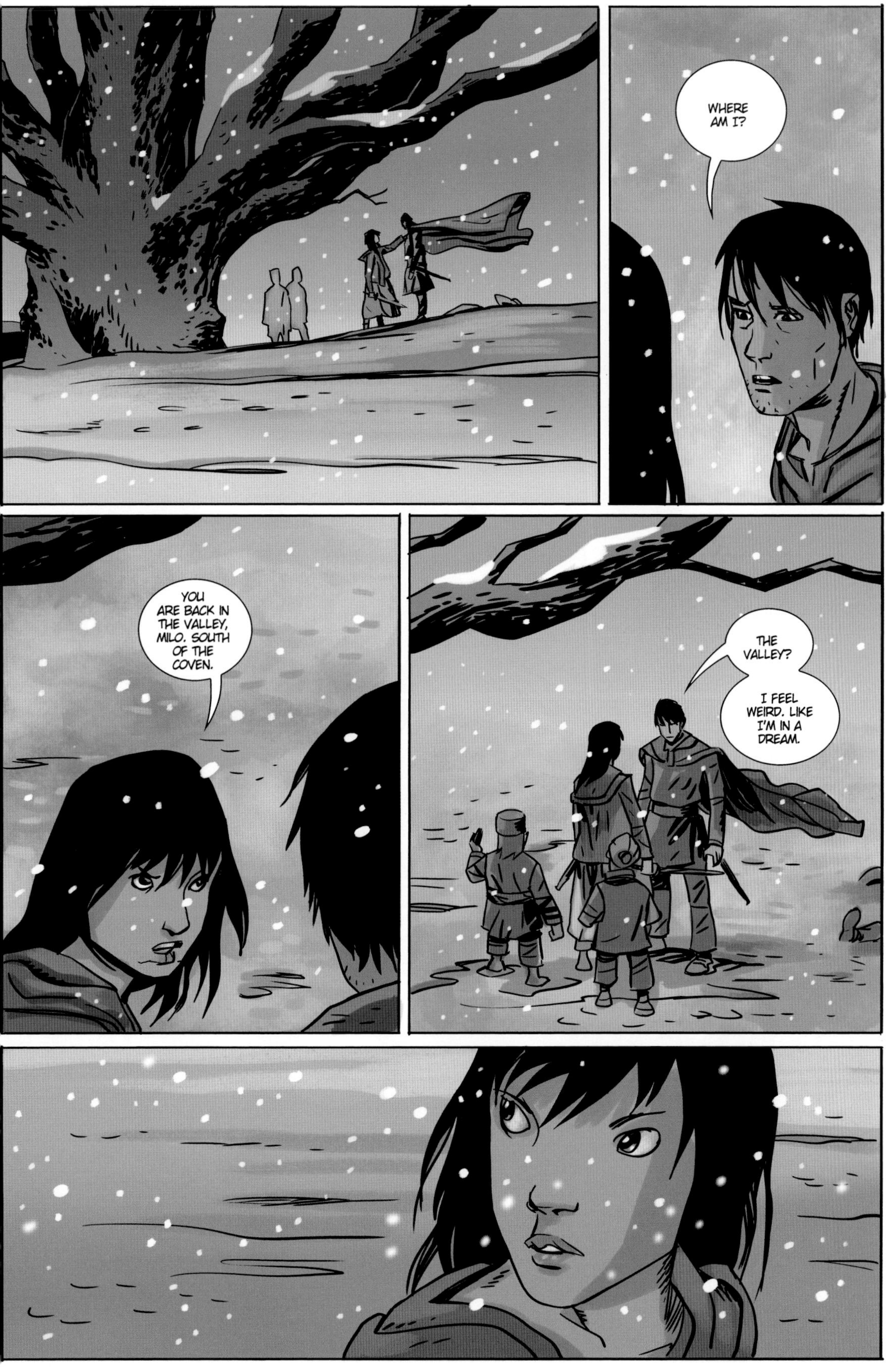
WHERE AM I?
YOU ARE BACK IN THE VALLEY, MILO. SOUTH OF THE COVEN.
THE VALLEY?
I FEEL WEIRD. LIKE I'M IN A DREAM.

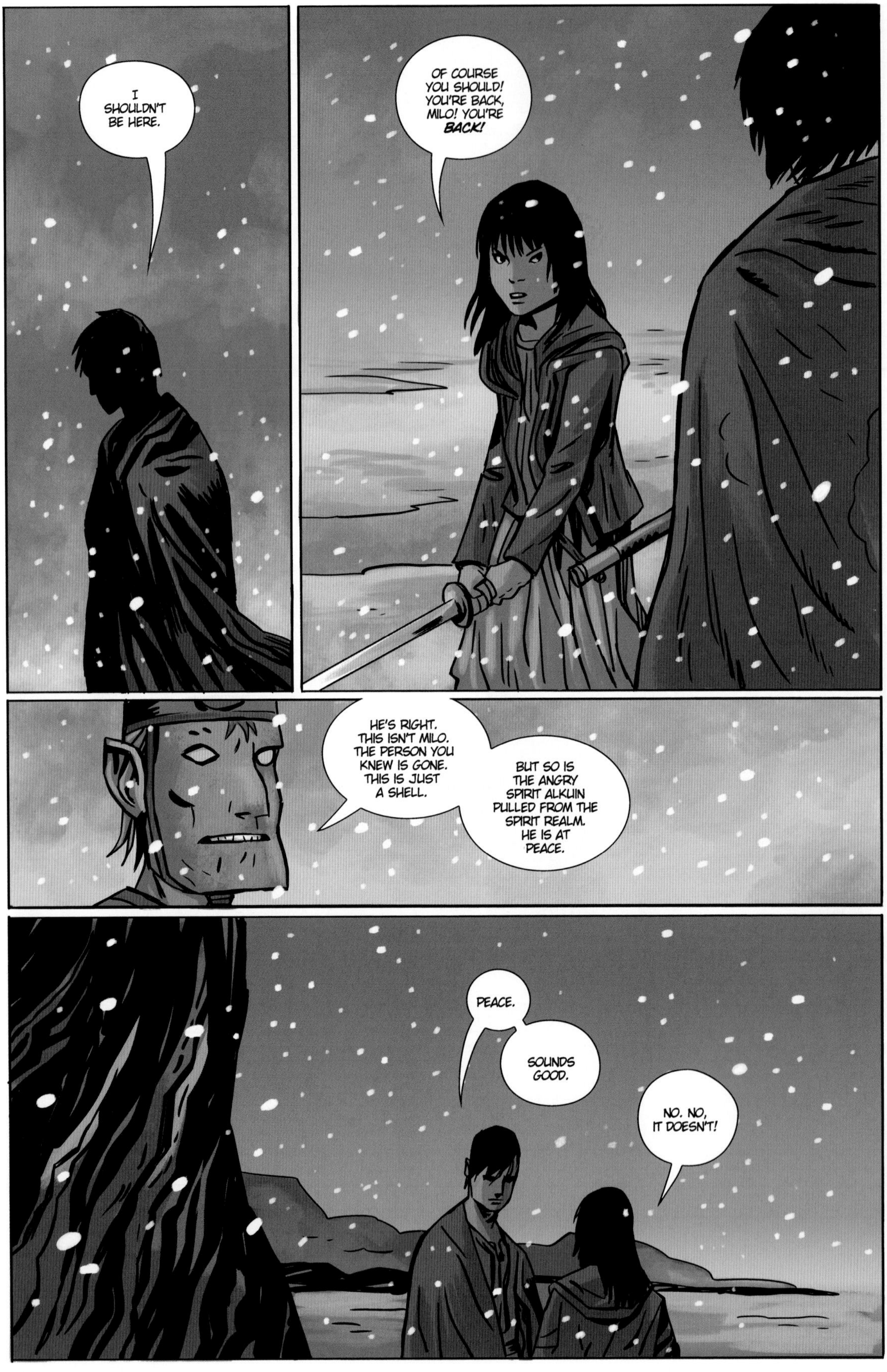
I SHOULDN'T BE HERE.
OF COURSE YOU SHOULD! YOU'RE BACK, MILO! YOU'RE **BACK!**
HE'S RIGHT. THIS ISN'T MILO. THE PERSON YOU KNEW IS GONE. THIS IS JUST A SHELL.
BUT SO IS THE ANGRY SPIRIT ALKUIN PULLED FROM THE SPIRIT REALM. HE IS AT PEACE.
PEACE.
SOUNDS GOOD.
NO. NO, IT DOESN'T!

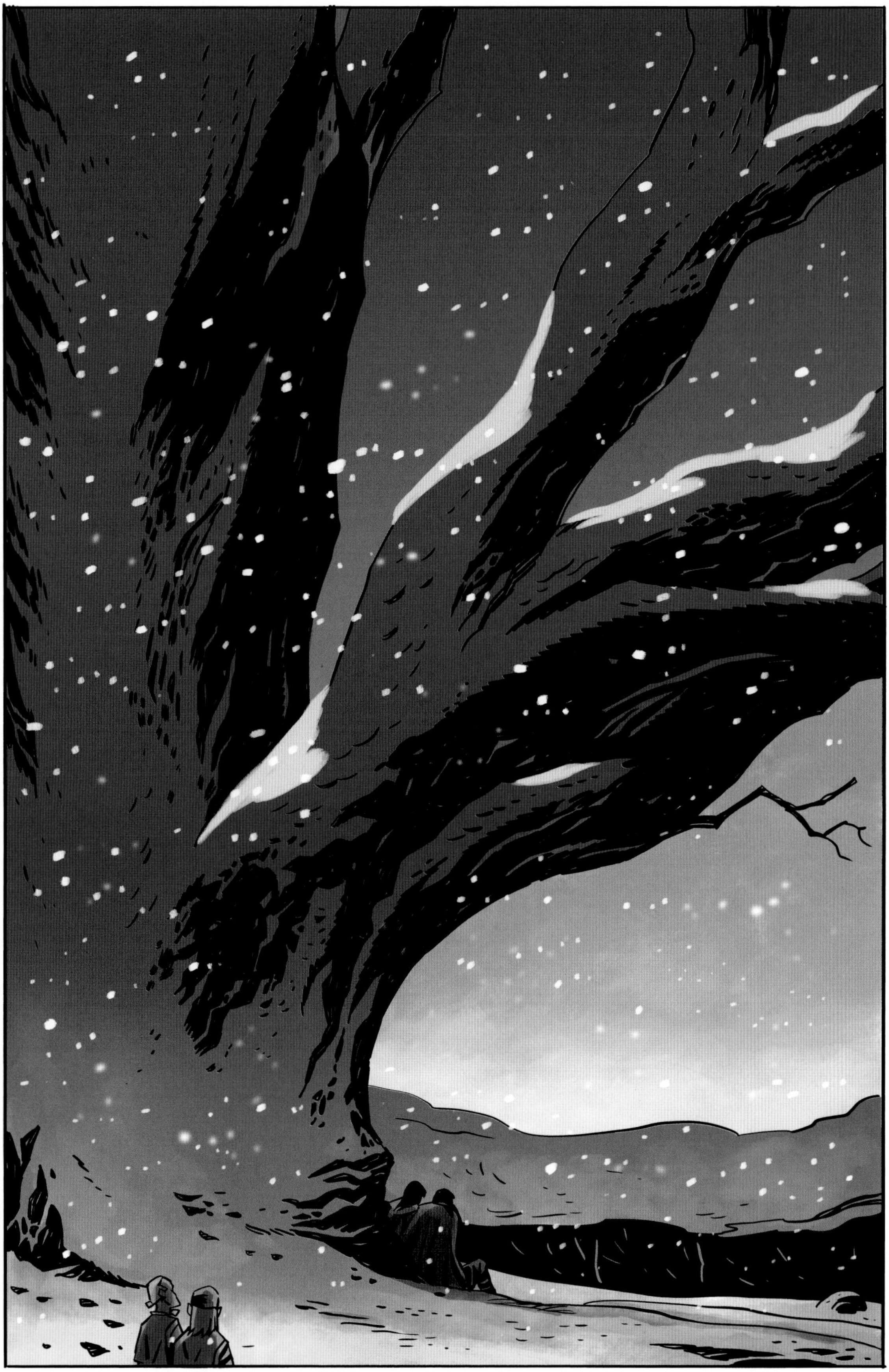

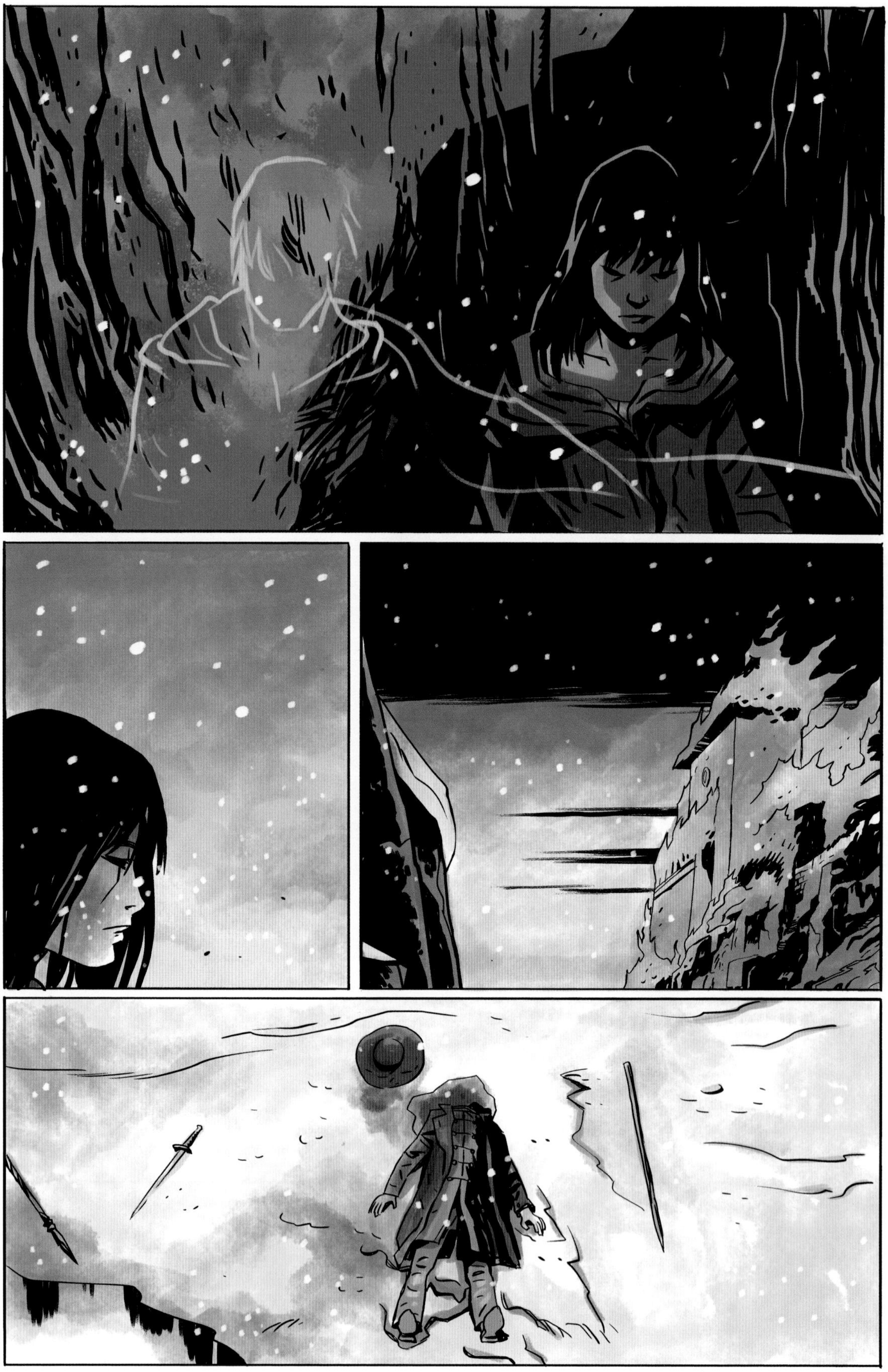

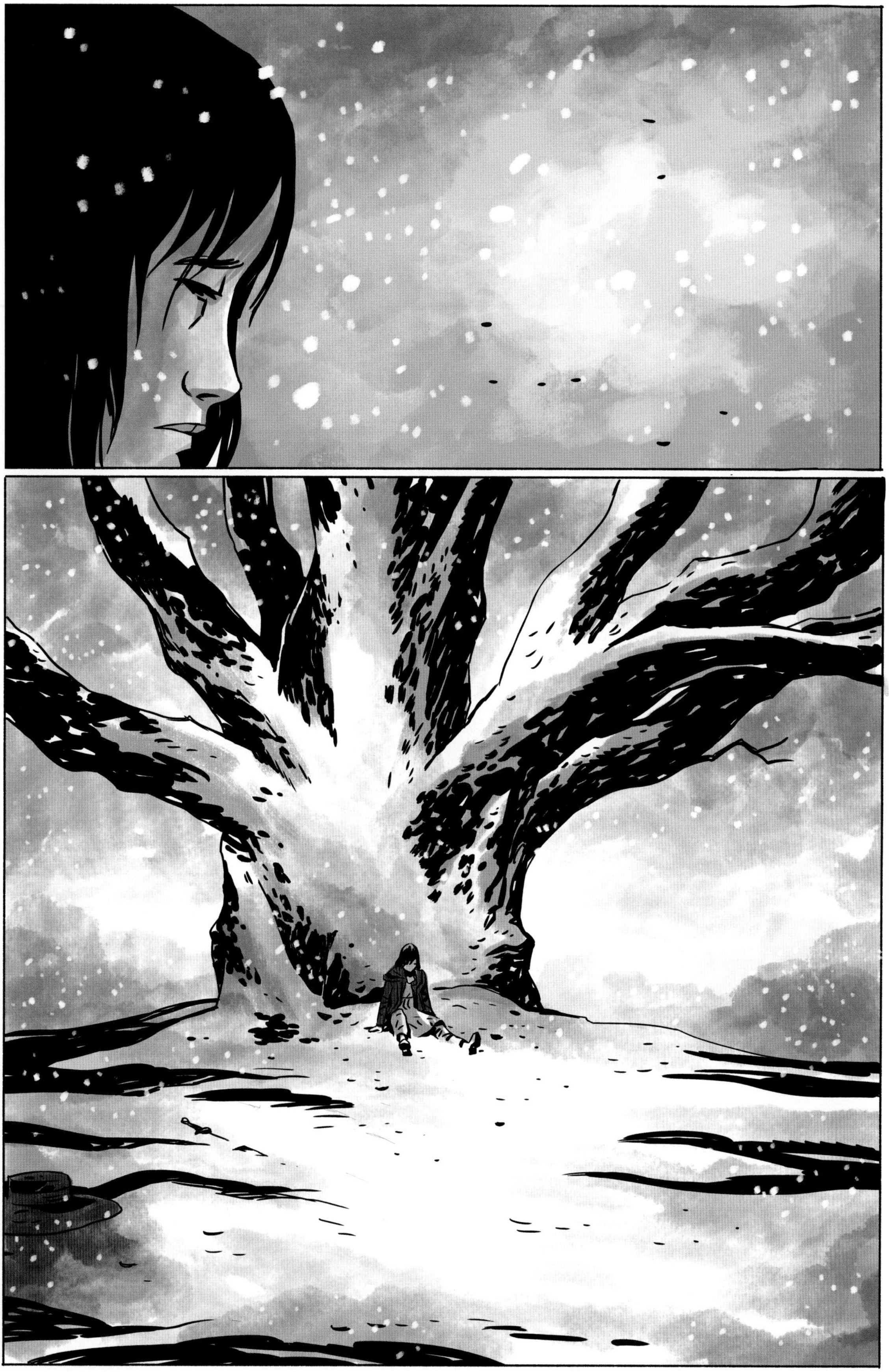

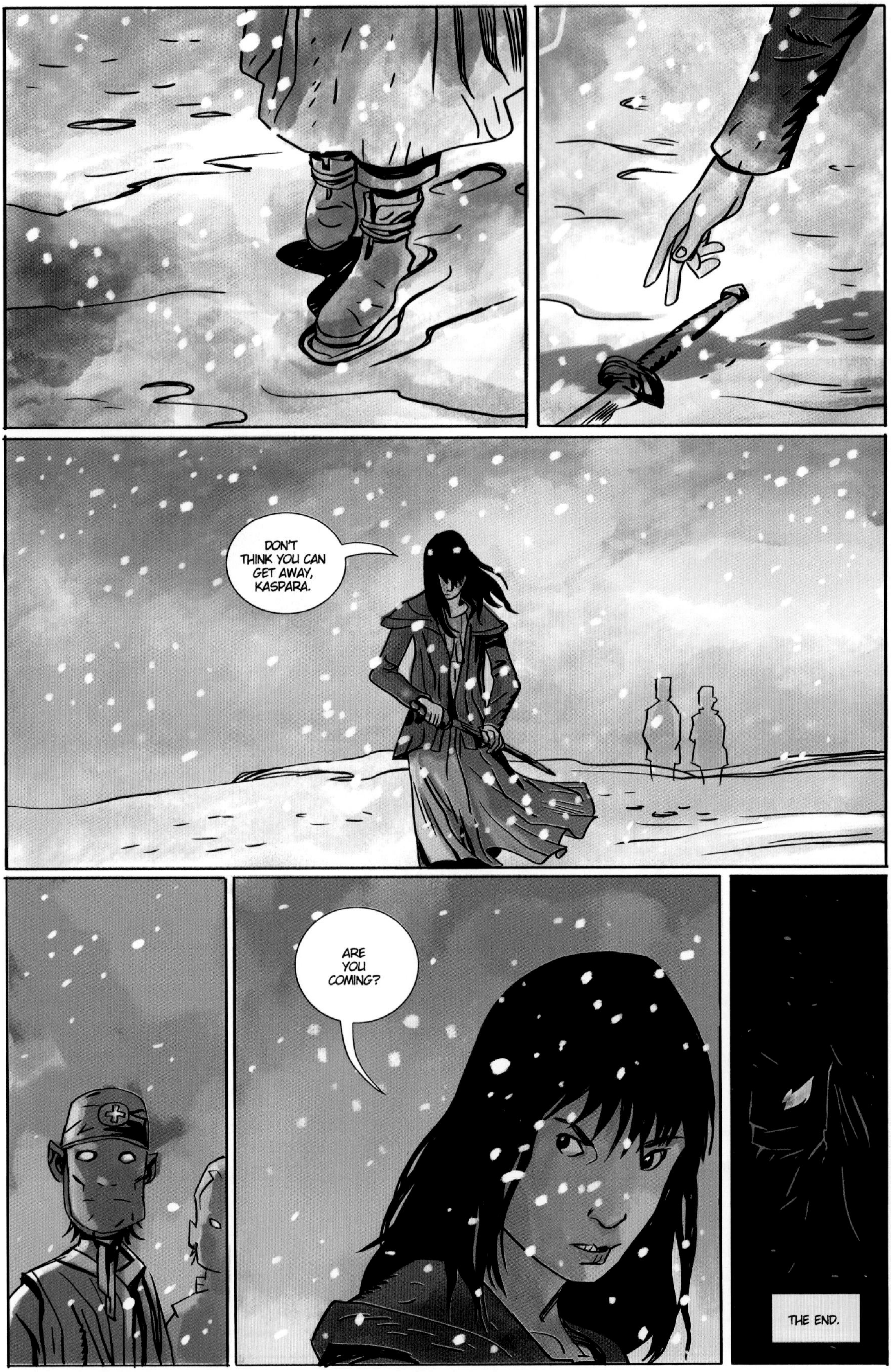
DON'T THINK YOU CAN GET AWAY, KASPARA.
ARE YOU COMING?
THE END.

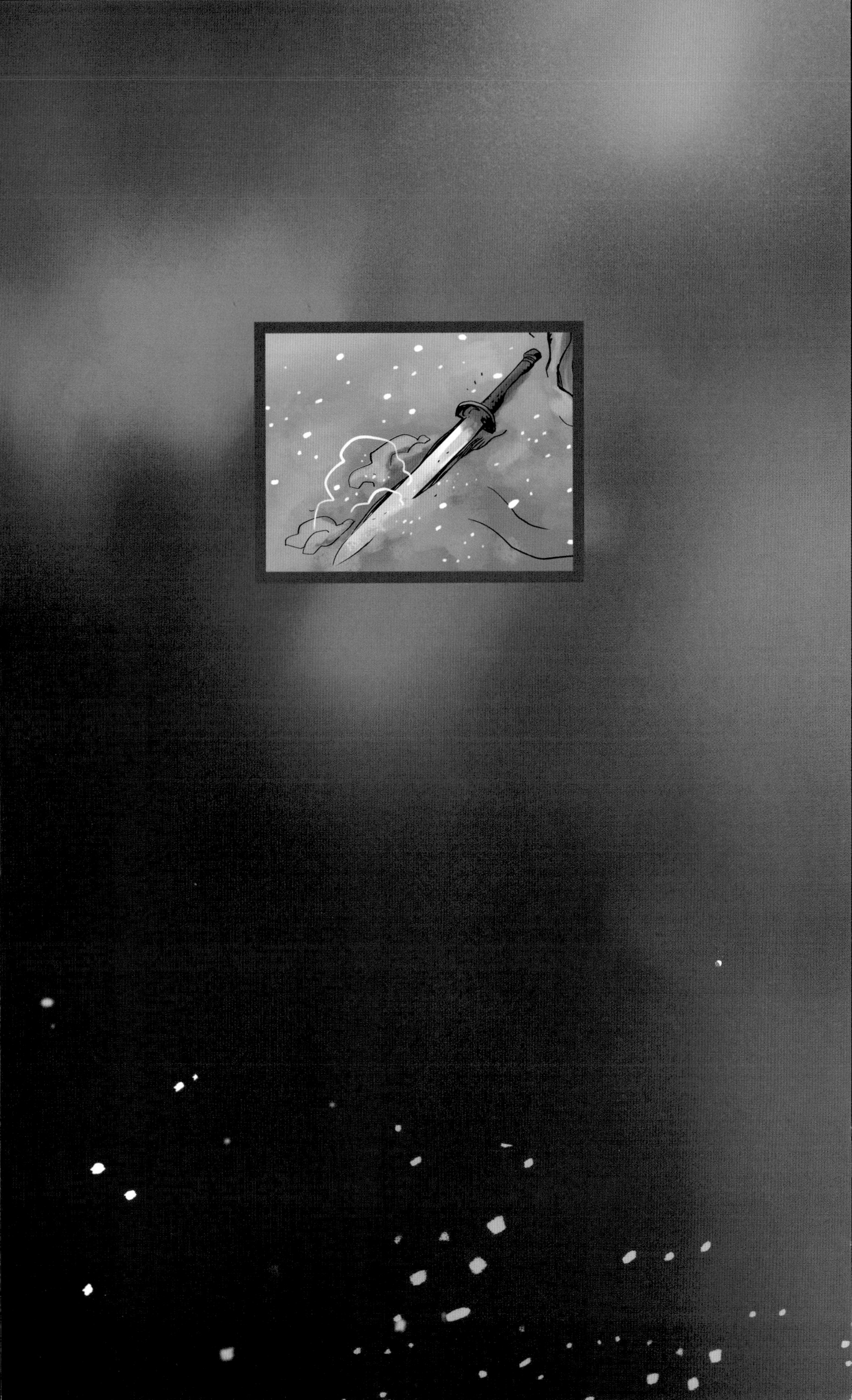

THE PORTENT: ASHES
Sketchbook
BY PETER BERGTING

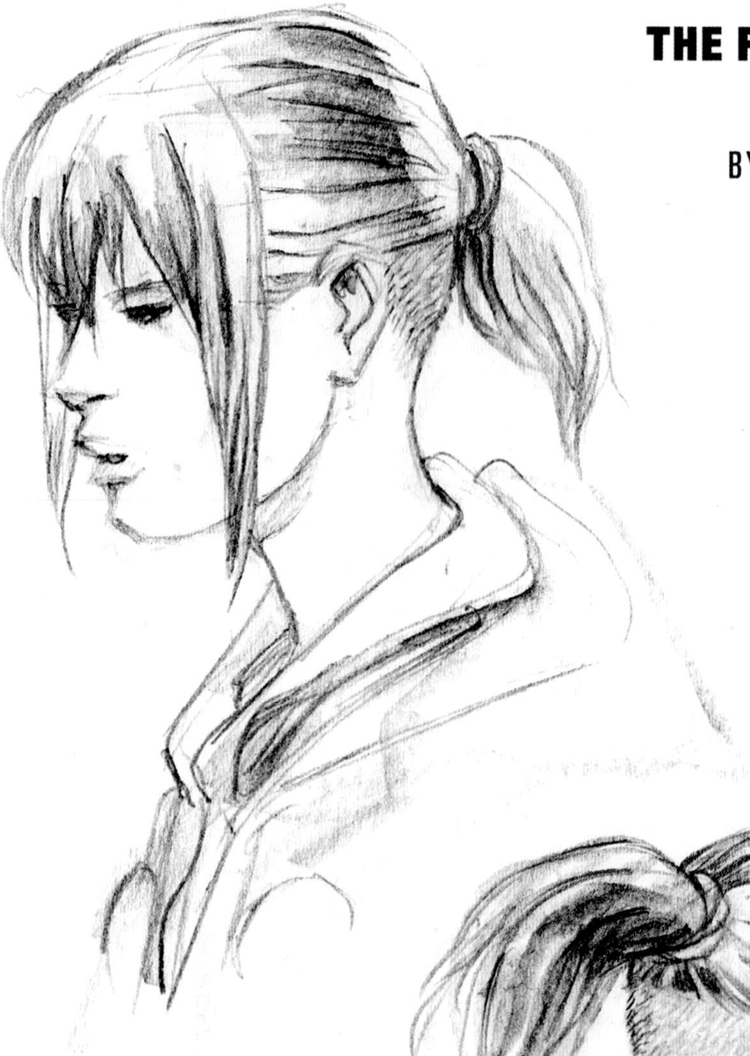

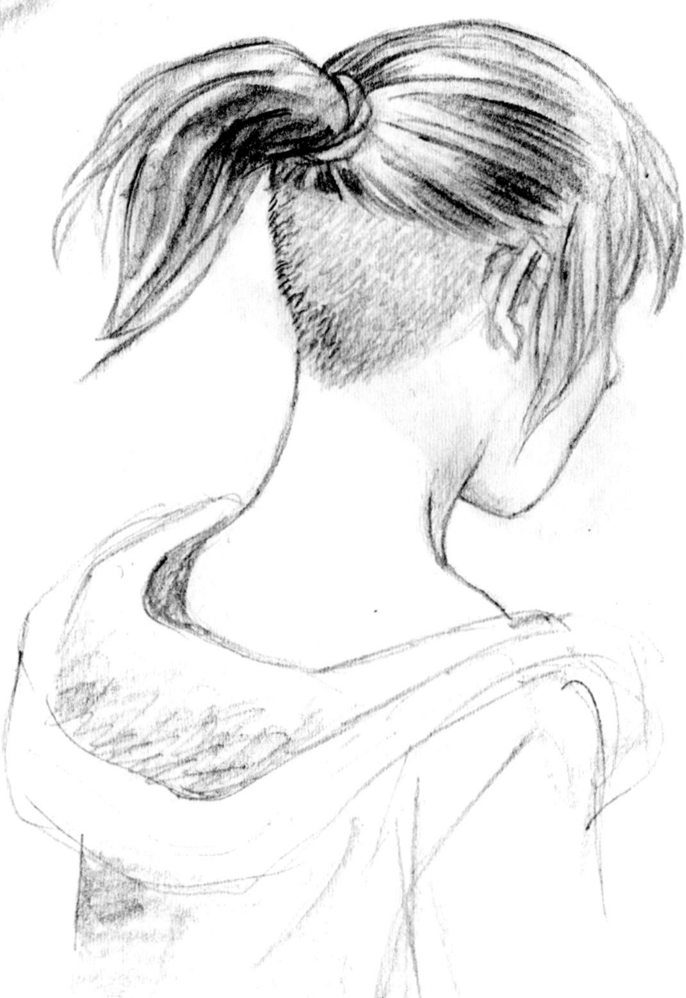

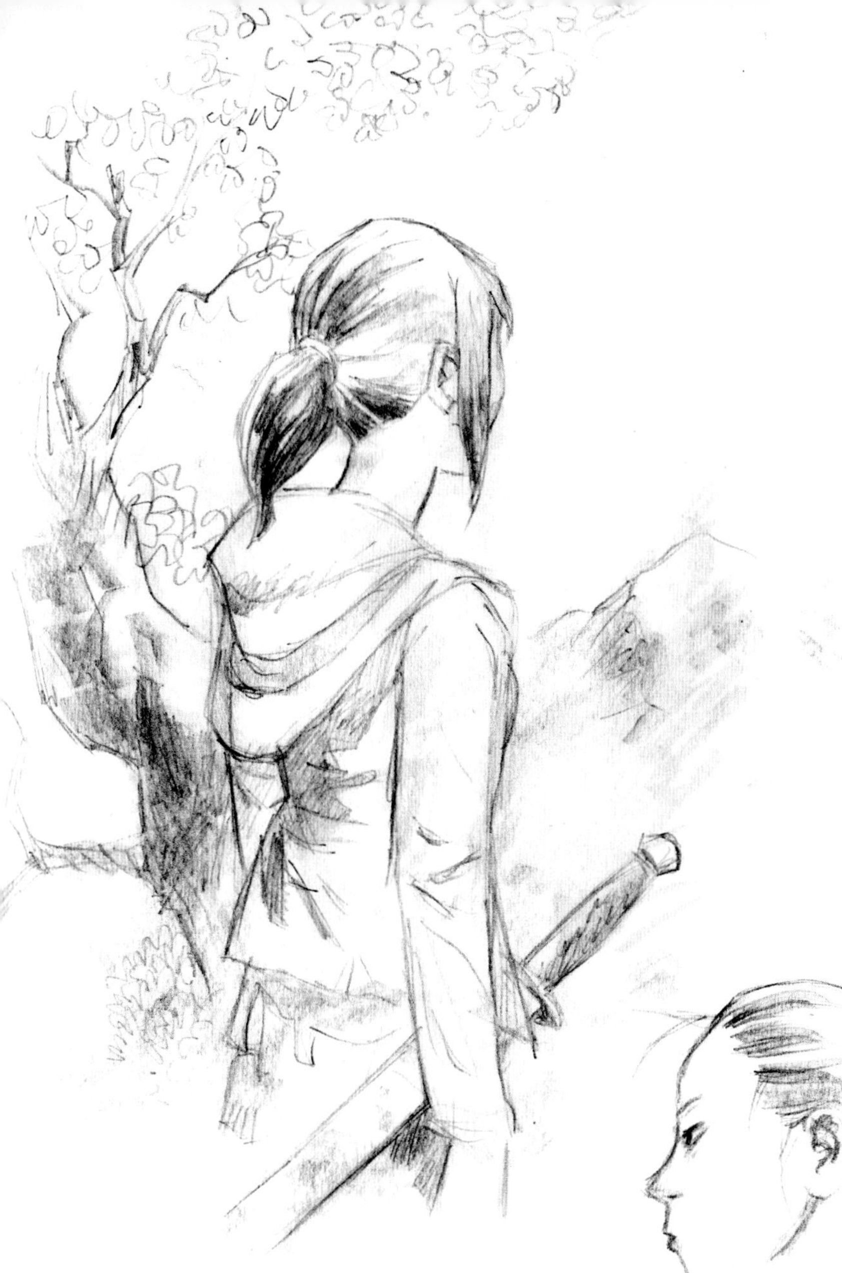

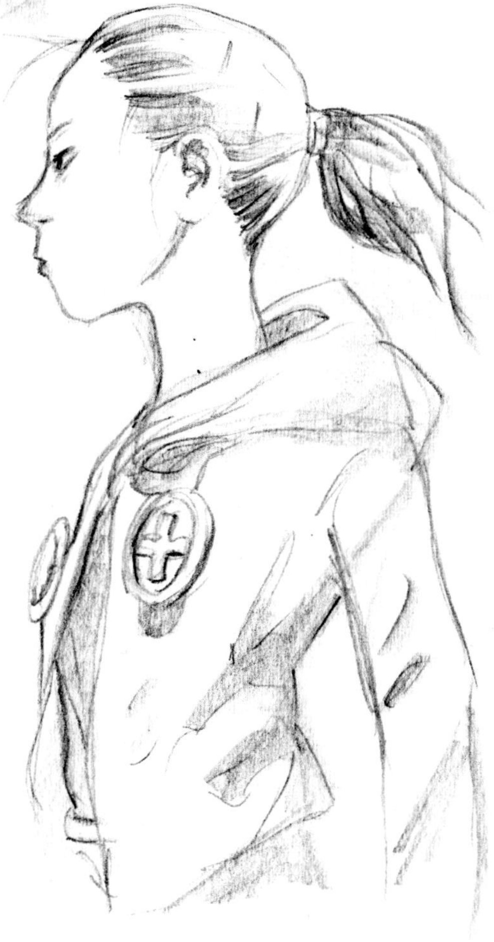

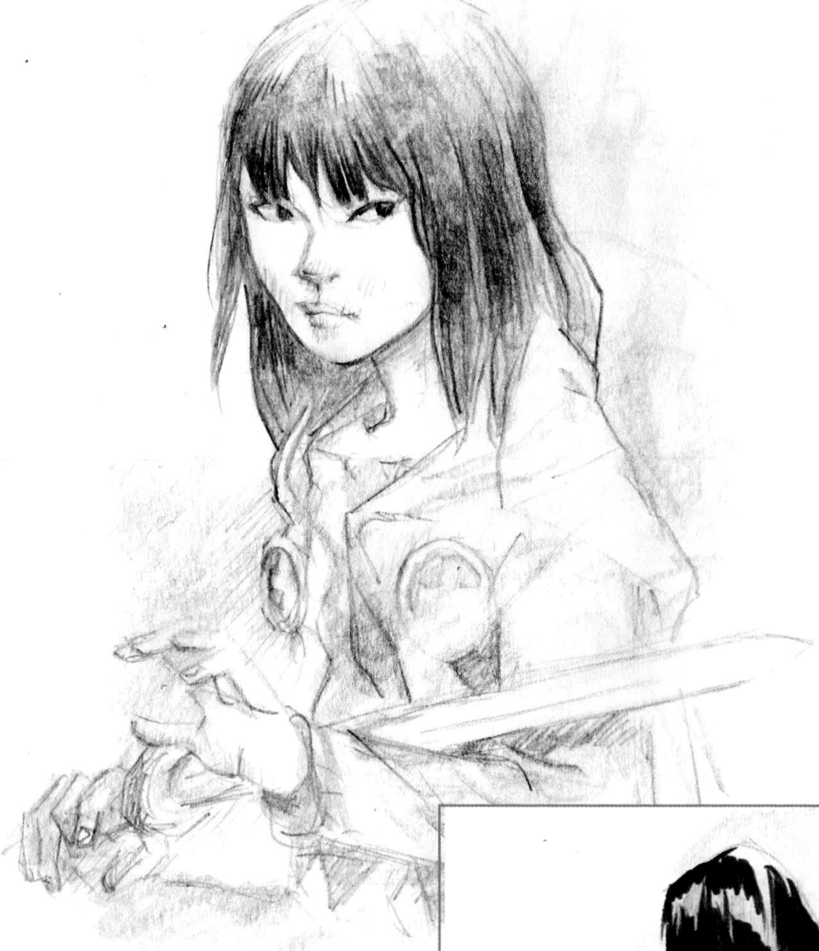

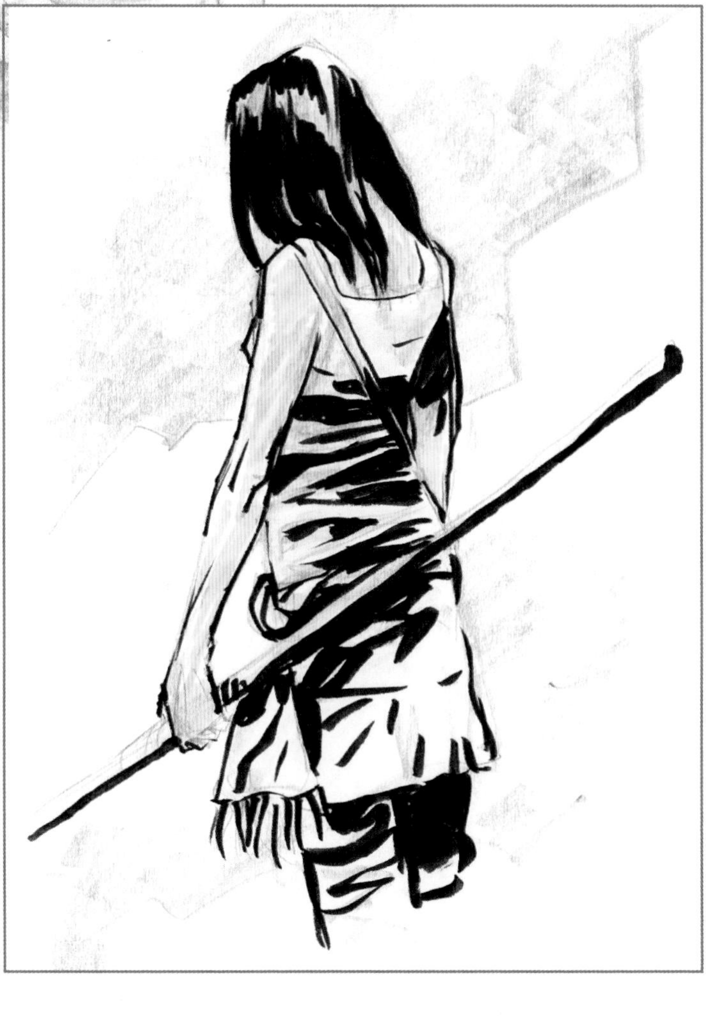

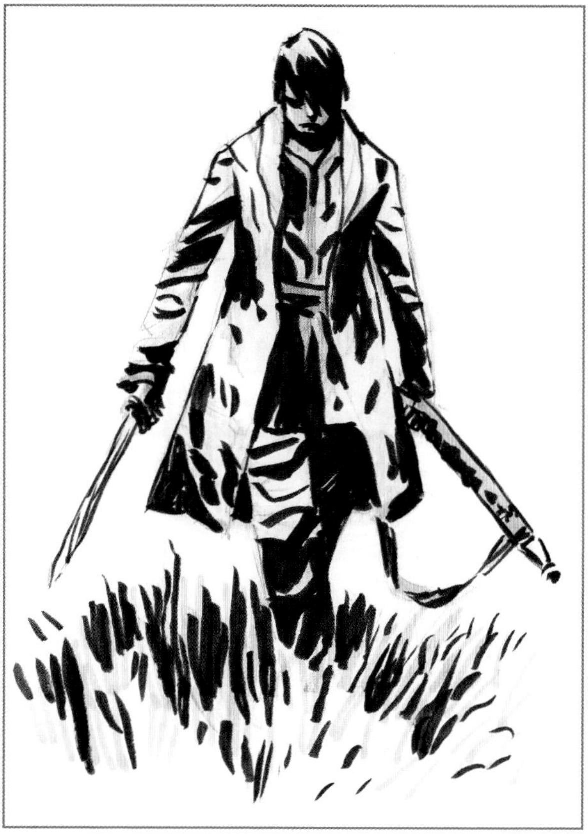

21/5/2013
GBG–ÅMÅL

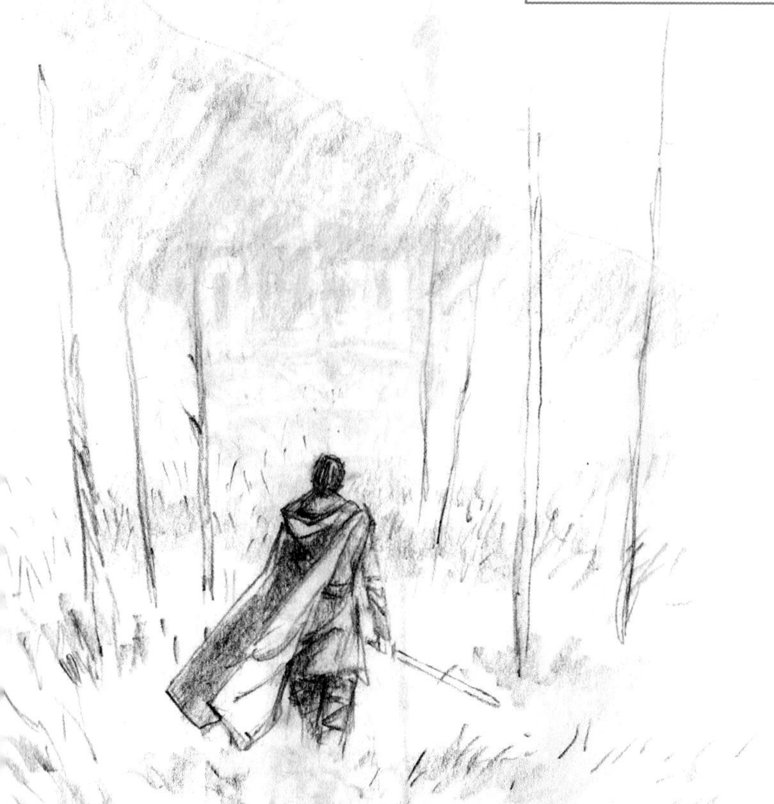

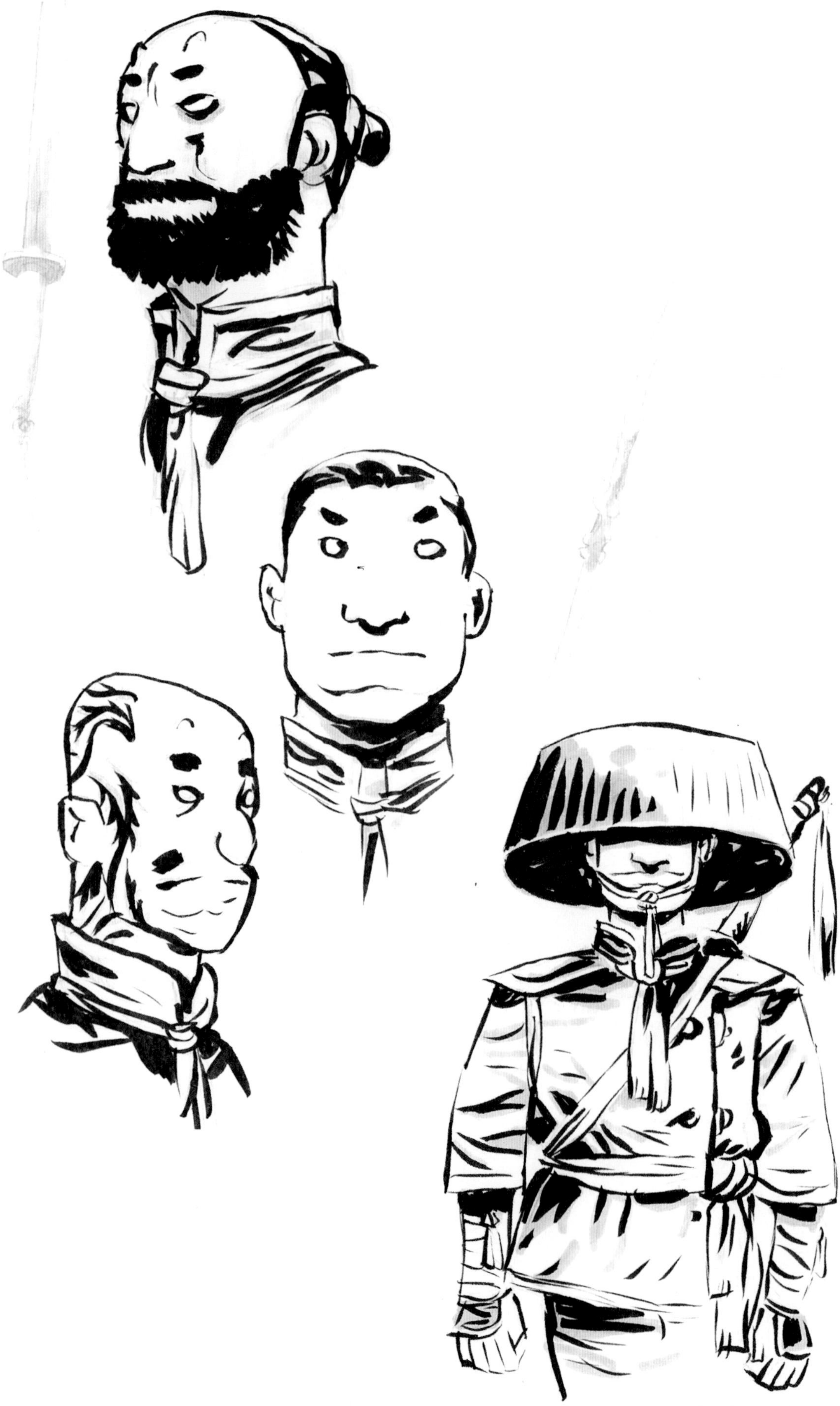

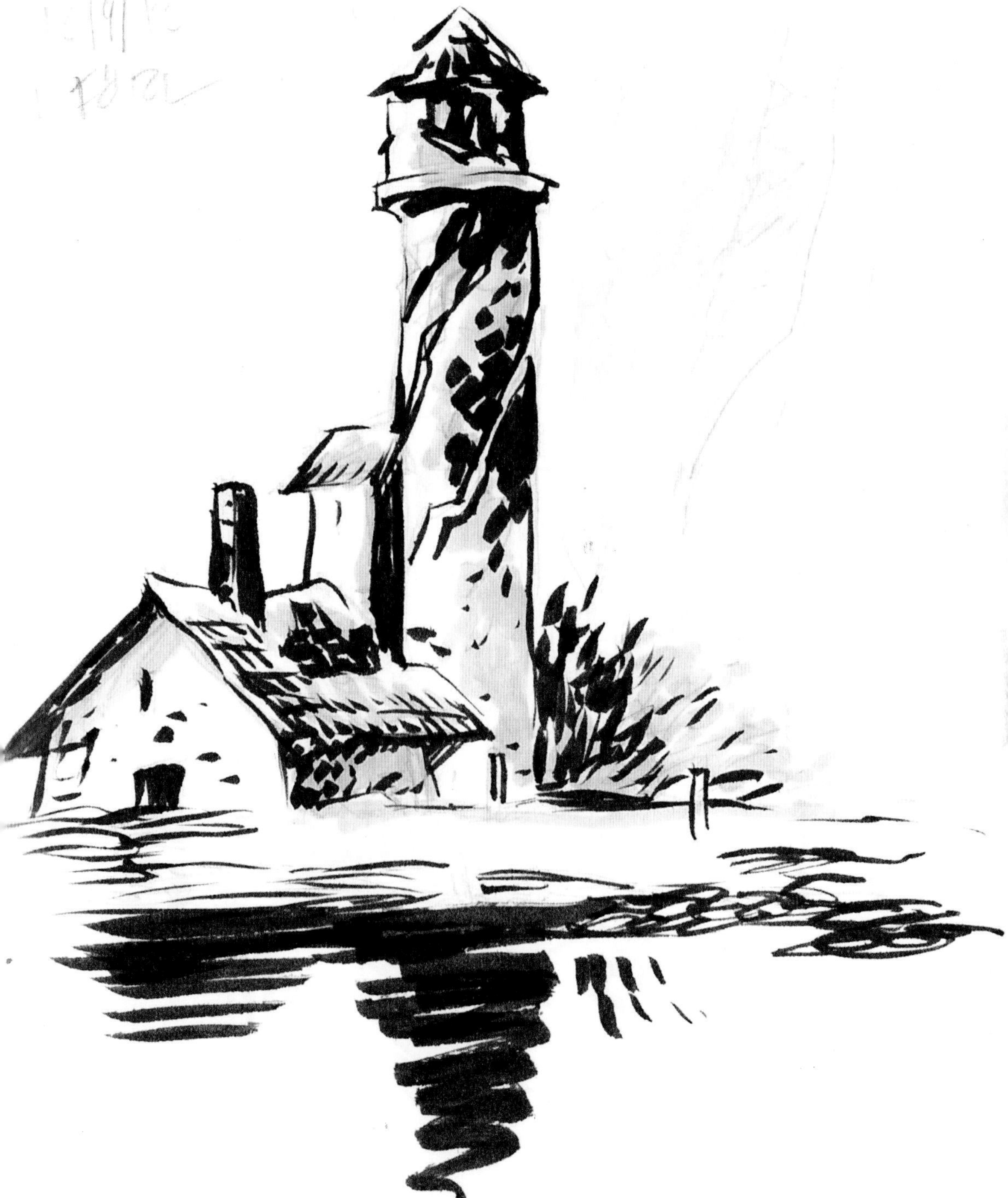

13/9/13 STHLM - ÅMÅL

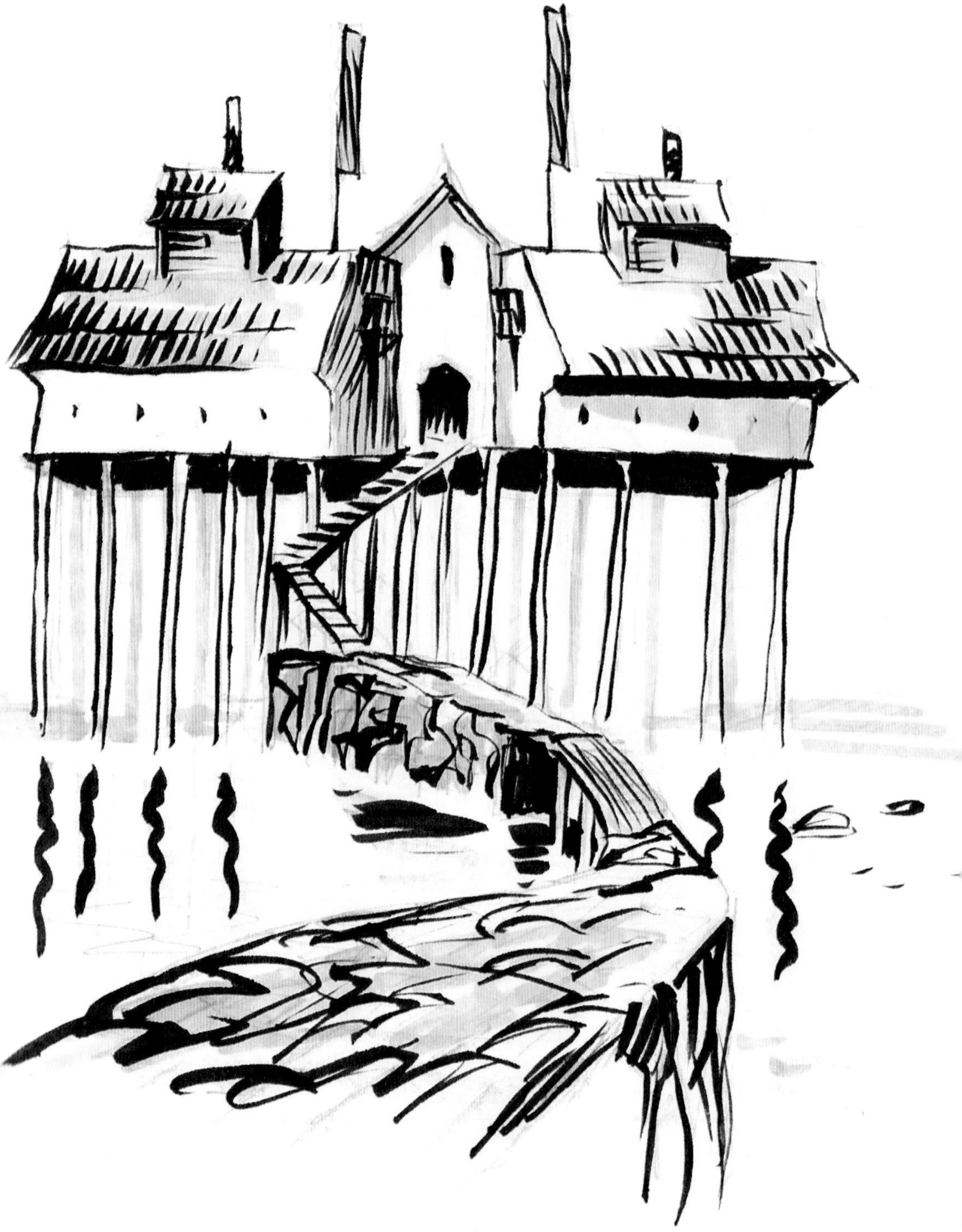

URÖ 23-24/7 /13

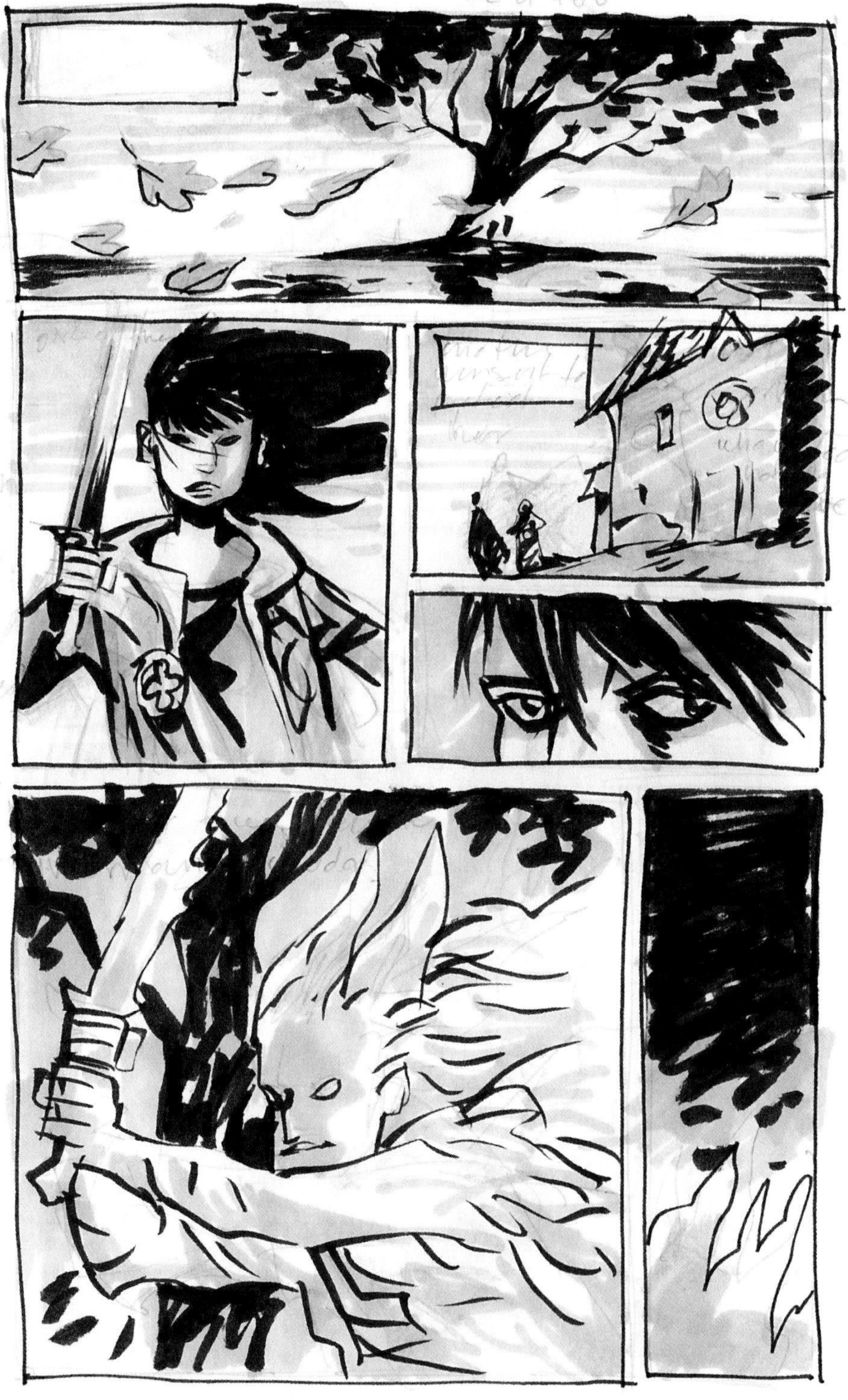

23-24/7/13 URÖ, NORRTÄLJE

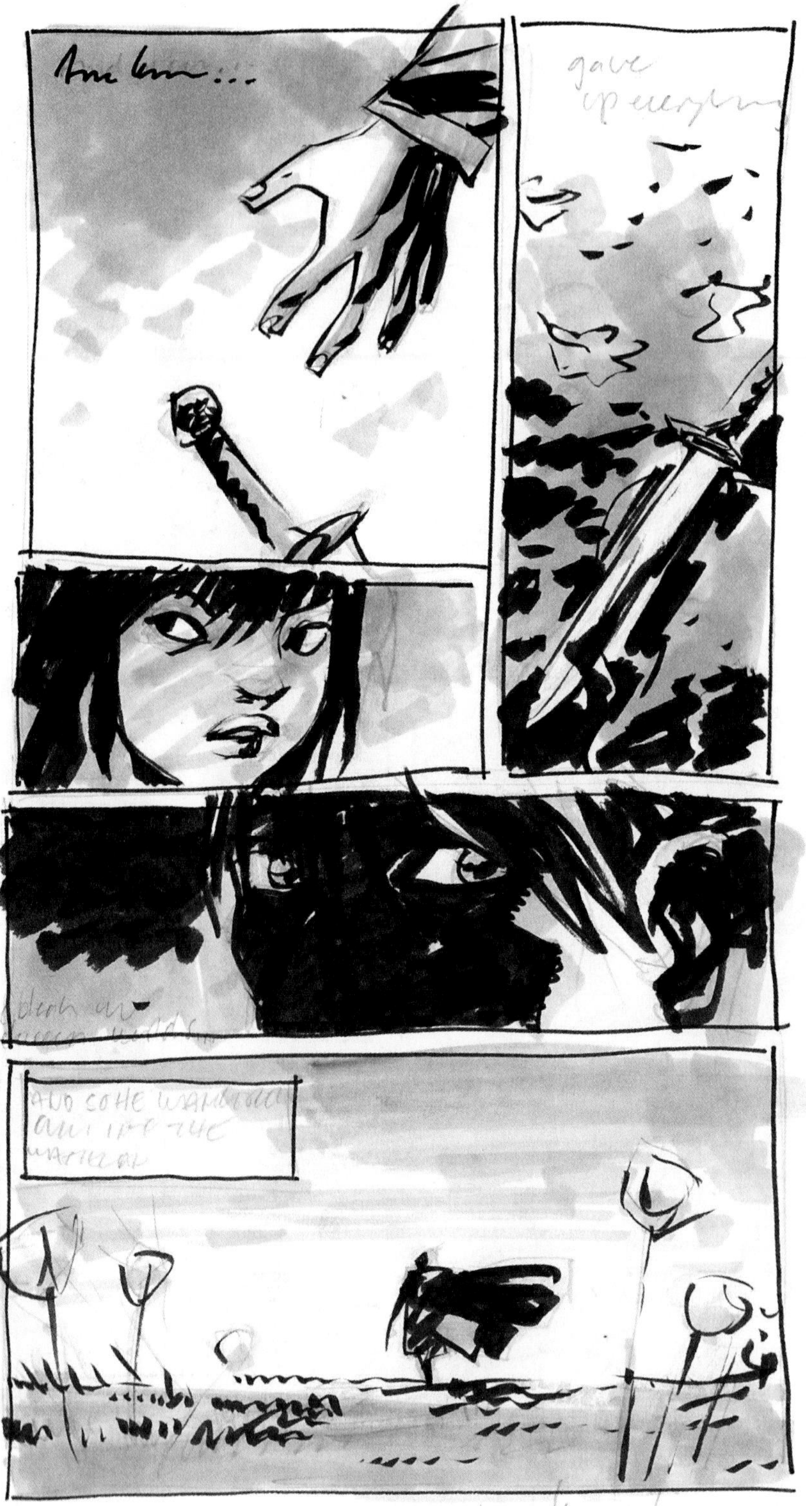
gave

and the girl was
alone again

24/11 15 UKO, NORRTÄLJE

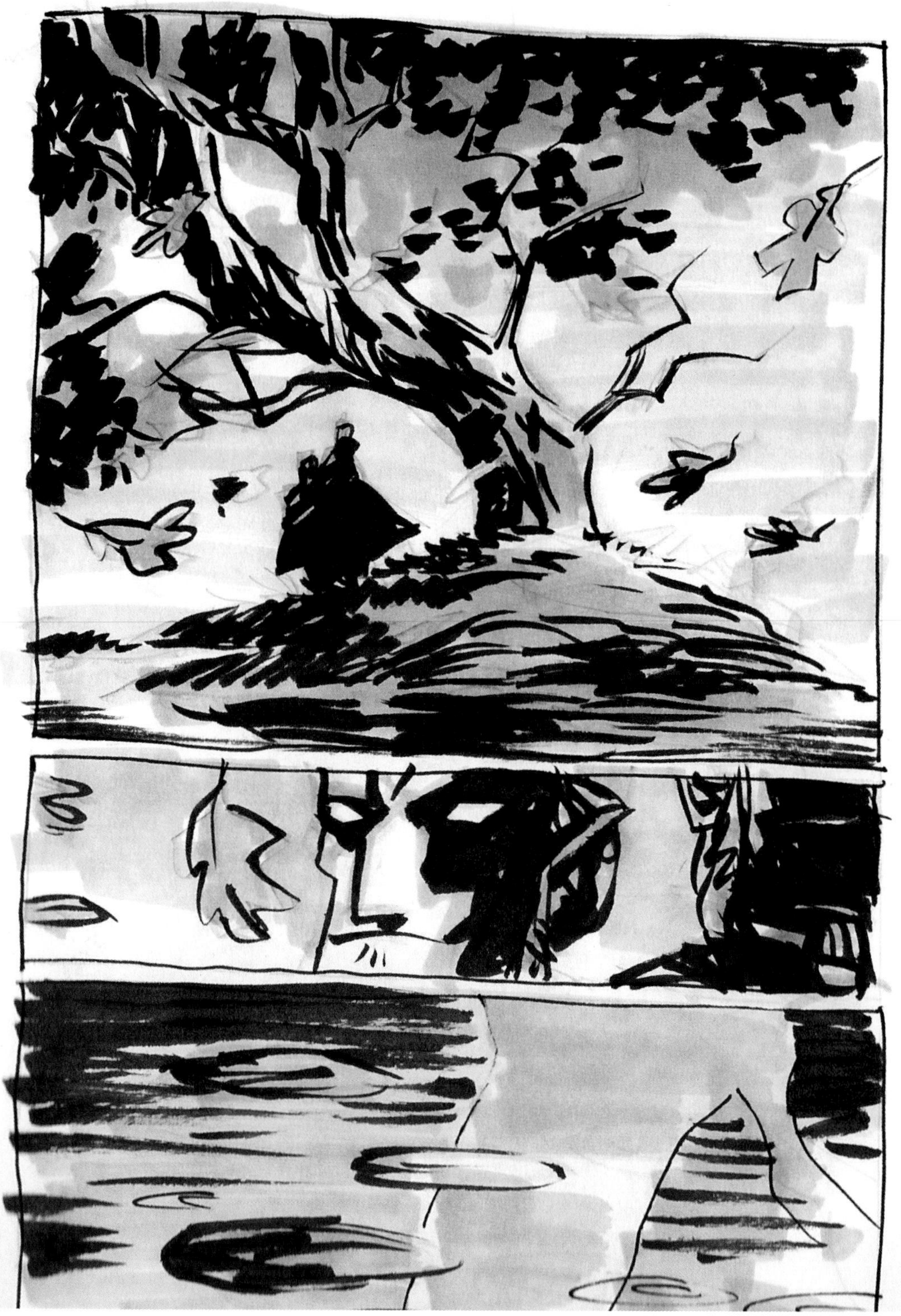

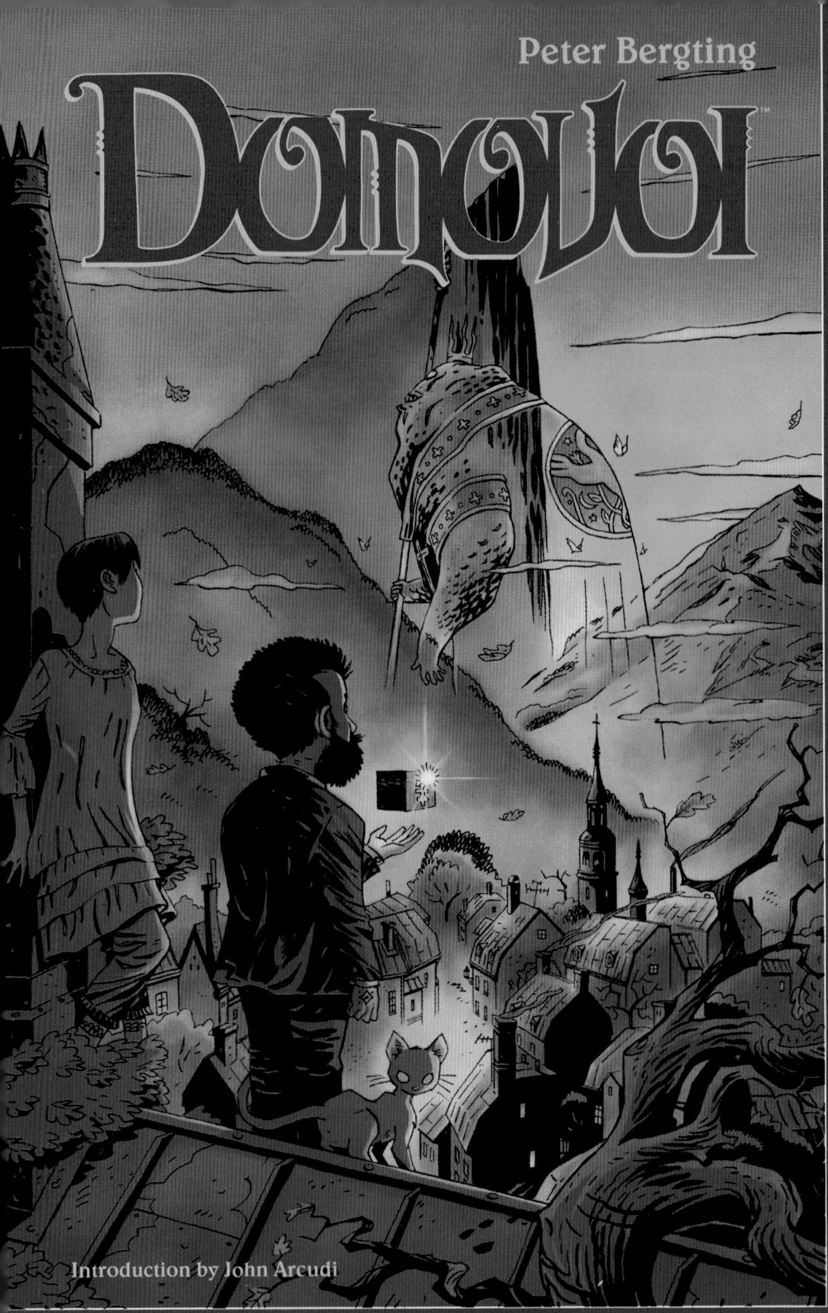
Peter Bergting
Domovoi
Introduction by John Arcudi

IN THE OLD TOWN OF STOCKHOLM, where myths are alive and creatures of folklore haunt the night, an extraordinary young woman named Jennie is caught in the scheme of a cadre of villains who control the means to free the Domovoi—a lethally dangerous, poltergeist-like spirit!

Acclaimed artist and writer Peter Bergting brings deft storytelling and his